GOLD'S GYM™

MASS BUILDING
TRAINING AND NUTRITION SYSTEM

GOLD'S GYM™

MASS BUILDING
TRAINING AND NUTRITION SYSTEM

ED CONNORS, PETER GRYMKOWSKI, TIM KIMBER, AND BILL REYNOLDS

CB
CONTEMPORARY BOOKS

Library of Congress Cataloging-in-Publication Data

Gold's Gym mass building, training, and nutrition system / Ed Connors
. . . [et al.].
    p.   cm.
  ISBN 0-8092-3947-7 (pbk.)
  1. Bodybuilding.   2. Bodybuilders—Nutrition.   I. Connors,
Ed.
GV546.5.G64   1992
646.7'5—dc20   91-44740
                                                  CIP
                                                  Rev.

All suggestions and recommendations in this book are made without warranty or guarantee, express or implied, and the author and publisher disclaim all liability in connection with the use of this information. The material presented herein is not a substitute for the advice of a personal health-care professional. Always consult a physician before taking or administering any drug, including steroids, or undertaking any exercise program.

Cover photo of Milos Sarcev by Jim Amentler
All interior photos by Jim Amentler at Gold's Gym in Venice, San Diego, and Orange County, California
All black-and-white prints made by Isgo Lepejian, Burbank, California
Models: Rich Gaspari, Boyer Coe, Sue Gafner, Frank Hillebrand, Dave Fisher, Joe Lozma, Chris Cormier, Peter Chapman, Joe Dawson, Francis Benfatto, Flex Wheeler, Vicki Sims, Bob Cicherillo, Mike Torchiacia, Bev Francis, Sandy Riddell, and Paul Dillett. *Locations:* Gold's Gym in Venice, Fullerton, San Diego, and Pacific Beach, California.

Published by Contemporary Books
A division of NTC/Contemporary Publishing Group, Inc.
4255 West Touhy Avenue, Lincolnwood (Chicago), Illinois 60646-1975 U.S.A.
Printed in the United States of America
International Standard Book Number: 0-8092-3947-7

25   24   23   22   21   20   19   18   17   16   15   14   13   12   11

Contents

GOLD'S GYM™

MASS BUILDING
TRAINING AND NUTRITION SYSTEM

1
Mass and Power

The desire to be bigger and stronger is fundamental to bodybuilding as well as to many other sports. Football players, for example, train very heavily with weights in the off-season and try to maintain their strength and added muscle mass throughout the season with less frequent power workouts than they are able to take during the spring and early summer.

But whether you're a football player, competitive swimmer, or weight lifter, "simply put, you have to lift big to get big," says Lee Haney, eight-time Mr. Olympia champion. "The more weight you move for a set number of reps on a particular basic exercise, the larger will be the muscles that are brought into play to move that poundage. It just makes good sense that your chest, shoulder, and triceps muscles will be larger if you can bench press 300 pounds for six reps than if you can accomplish the same six counts in

Frontispiece: Richard Gaspari—many time IFBB Pro Grand Prix Champion—shows the current degree of both mass and cuts needed to be competitive in both pro and amateur shows nationally and internationally.

strict form with only 250 on the bar."

In this book we'll cover six distinct approaches to training for added muscle mass and physical strength. Nutritionally speaking, you will learn how the champions at Gold's Gym use computer-generated dietary programs—supplemented with plenty of aerobic training even during an off-season mass-building cycle—to increase lean body mass. You'll find no voodoo secrets for gaining muscle mass and strength, because the process is simple, basic, and straightforward. However, the topic of gaining lean body mass and strength has never been treated in such great detail in one training manual prior to this book.

You don't necessarily have to train at Gold's Gym in Venice, California, or at any of the other nearly 200 Gold's franchises, but we urge you to make use of Gold's if there is one in your area. This is particularly important in terms of your dietary program, because Gold's has exclusive access to the revolutionary Nutritionalysis, a nutrition program computer-tailored to your exact, uniquely personal specifications. This program is explained in greater detail in Chapter 11.

Most of the training programs included herein

will seem simplistic to many veteran muscle-magazine readers. If you are in this group, you're used to reading how Joe Superstar trains his back with a complex program totaling more than 30 sets over six to eight exercises. The truth is that the vast majority of magazine articles present precontest routines of elite bodybuilders who have spent a major portion of their lives building up the recovery ability necessary to benefit from such extensive routines. When they were less advanced—particularly in the off-season—the greatest bodybuilders in the sport trained with basic exercises, relatively heavy weights, and low reps, and for brief periods of time in the gym. Even at the most advanced level, intelligent champions still train this way in the off-season. Sometimes their aerobic workouts for one week will total more training time than they spend in the gym lifting heavy iron.

The training programs we will suggest are uncomplicated, basic, hard, and heavy, because that's what builds up lean muscle mass. With Nutritionalysis the guesswork is taken out of your dietary program as well. We've even included a chapter on the mental approach most appropriate for a bodybuilder dedicated to developing the ultimate degree of muscle mass possible, as well as the physical strength that goes with that mass.

Gold's Gym takes the guesswork out of gaining muscle mass. After reading this training/nutrition/mental-approach manual, you'll know exactly how to go about acquiring the added size and strength that has eluded you up to this point. *You* are the final link in the chain to building mass and power. Read, absorb, pick what's right for your body, and then get into the gym and do something about it!

2
Overview of Mass- and Power-Building Methods

In their quest for huge, powerful muscles, bodybuilders have resorted to scores of methods for gaining weight. Many of these methods are, to say the least, arcane, while others are logical and effective. Of those effective mass-building methods available to us, no single technique works well for every bodybuilder.

We'll discuss six effective methods of mass- and power-building in this chapter. These discussions will be brief and serve as previews for more detailed treatments of each individual method in subsequent chapters. For now, these brief summaries will serve as a framework to which you can attach each method as you master it.

The Classic Approach

Bulk up and cut down—that was the classic approach to gaining muscular body weight at an accelerated rate of speed. The object was to consume huge quantities of food while training more heavily than usual; the combination would pack

California Champion Flex Wheeler shows where mass comes from—really heavy iron, pumped liberally, with a dash of great diet.

on pounds of muscle and fat at a very fast clip. Then, when a predetermined peak body weight had been reached or a predetermined point prior to a competition had arrived, a bodybuilder would reverse the process by eating less and training with lighter weights and higher reps. Weight was lost almost as rapidly as it was gained, and in the end a bodybuilder had hopefully increased his muscular body weight by 5–10 pounds.

Almost every leading bodybuilder prior to the middle 1960s was a proponent of the bulk-up/cut-down school of thought. It seemed to work well for some, while for others it was just an excuse to eat like pigs trying to put the stock of various junk-food companies into fiscal orbit. Many young men—there simply weren't women bodybuilders in those days—went up in body weight and stayed up year after year, talking vaguely about some future contest they were going to enter as soon as they felt they were big enough for it.

Even at the present time many bodybuilders bulk up and try cutting down for competitions with varying degrees of success. It's not unusual to see a bodybuilder hold 30–40 pounds of extra weight on his frame between competitions. Some of the people who adhere to these tactics are very good bodybuilders; most aren't.

The Current Best Approach

Today's bodybuilder has learned from his forebears who really didn't gain much muscle mass over six- to eight-month cycles of bulking up and cutting down. Today the best men and women keep their body-fat percentages under strict control during off-season cycles while training heavily, briefly, quickly, and infrequently. This approach has resulted in some real mass monsters, but mass monsters with the deepest muscularity imaginable.

Champion male bodybuilders attempt to keep their body weights below 10 pounds over competitive weight when in mass-building cycles. Women try to keep their body weights no more than 5–6 pounds above competition level. When a bodybuilder stays this close to competitive shape, it's very easy to knock off the excess stored body fat to reveal an ultimate degree of muscularity.

Olympic-style weight lifting was at the core of the classic approach to gaining mass and power. Flex Wheeler demonstrates his form in a 330-pound jerk from the shoulders.

While bulk-and-cut advocates are forced to come down in weight very quickly since they allow themselves to get so heavy in the first place, modern bodybuilders can follow 12-week diets that are much less strict and allow them to strip off body fat much more slowly. The secret here is that you lose a great deal of muscle mass along with the fat when you crash diet, but you maintain most of that hard-earned mass as the fat is slowly peeled off.

There are still a few advocates of the bulk-and-cut system, but they are usually individuals who have difficulty controlling their appetites. Faced with a chance to follow the see-food diet ("if you can see it, eat it"), they let their weight get totally out of control and seldom make it back to hard contest shape a second time.

Milos Sarcev illustrates the current approach—keeping highly muscular while adding mass slowly and permanently.

In comparison to the classic method the current mass-building approach is very scientific. It is soundly based on a wide range of exercise physiology experiments—plus plenty of practical experience—and it works well. If you follow it, chances are good that you'll make well over 120 percent of the gains in pure muscle mass over the same period as a bulk-and-cutter.

The Power-Lifting Approach

Power lifters, by the nature of their sport, lift very heavy weights in their training. If you happened to glance through a copy of *Powerlifting USA*, the official journal of the sport, you'd see men and women with muscle mass that would defy belief. The heavier-class lifters are absolutely huge; every muscle of their bodies looks like it was transplanted from a gorilla, rhino, elephant, or some other type of huge animal.

In the lighter weight classes you'd really be surprised at how great the lifters look. They diet and strip away all excess fat in an effort to make a particular weight level for their class, and even though they train almost exclusively on squats, bench presses, deadlifts, and similar assistance lifts, they have every muscle group developed to the max. They end up looking like bodybuilders, and many of them have successfully competed in bodybuilding shows without specialized training.

Germany's Frank Hillebrand power lifts—in this case he squats with half of the gym—to add mass to his legs and hip-girdle muscles.

If you're not familiar with power lifting, you'd think power lifters spend a lot of time in their workouts doing max single reps, or at most doubles or triples. In reality they don't go below five reps in an exercise, and usually they hover around 8–10 repetitions per set. The only time they go below five counts in a lift is a couple of weeks out from a competition, so they can gauge their strength in order to choose appropriate starting lifts for the day of their competition.

They don't eat much like bodybuilders either. In power lifting there is an emphasis on massive amounts of protein intake, particularly in the manner of protein shakes, but there's little emphasis on taking scientifically formulated freeform or branched-chain amino acids. Intake of vitamin and mineral supplements is haphazard for the most part; few power lifters make any systematic effort to take in the nutrients a superathlete requires to build the type of muscle mass they have.

The Heavy-Duty Approach

During the late 1960s and early 1970s when he was promoting his new Nautilus machines, Arthur Jones wrote a series of articles in *Iron Man* magazine, as well as two *Nautilus Bulletins*, that outlined his personal notion of how bodybuilders should train for maximum muscle mass and maximum strength levels. Bodybuilders by the thousands flocked to Jones's corner and tried his methods, which worked for a few genetically gifted individuals and didn't work for the rest of the bodybuilders who tried his workouts.

One successful convert of Jones's approach was Mike Mentzer, who went on to win Mr. America, Mr. Universe, and Heavyweight Mr. Olympia titles, as well as a couple of International Federation of Bodybuilders (IFBB) Pro Grand Prix titles. Mentzer was also a writer for Joe Weider's *Muscle Builder & Power*, the forerunner of both *Flex* and *Muscle & Fitness*; he wrote article after article and even issued a series of very popular mail-order courses espousing what he called his own Heavy Duty System, a slight adaptation of Jones's methods.

Heavy Duty required a bodybuilder to do very limited sets—as low as 1–2 for small body parts and certainly no more than 4–5 for larger and more complex muscle groups. But each set had to be taken to the absolute limit of human mus-

Heavy Duty? Not for IFBB pro champ Renel Janvier! He does low sets, but high reps with maximum weights at all times.

cular endurance. First it was taken to the point of momentary muscular failure in strict form, then it was pushed even farther with 3–5 forced reps, and finally it was totally nuked with 4–6 additional forced negative reps, all done in a series without rest between changes of method.

Heavy Duty required few workouts per week, usually three full-body sessions for beginners and intermediates and four for advanced body-

Aussie Sonny Schmidt has it all, although he trains body parts only once per week!

builders: one session for half of the body on Mondays and Thursdays and one session for the second half on Tuesdays and Fridays. In between a bodybuilder was encouraged to rest as completely as possible to restore his energy levels for the next workout.

In terms of diet a calorie was considered a calorie, regardless of the food it came from. A calorie of a cheese Danish was the same as a calorie of chicken breast: prior to a competition Mike Mentzer was famous for eating a cheese Danish now and then.

For gifted bodybuilders like Mike Mentzer, his brother Ray, and a handful of others, this Heavy Duty method worked wonders. For most others it didn't result in the degree of muscle mass it was touted to provide, and it did lead to chronically sore joints in many bodybuilders.

The Newest Rage

Taking full notice of the importance of recovery in building large, powerful muscles, many bodybuilders now train each muscle group only once per week although they still work out 5–6 days weekly. This system is not particularly new, but it gained great popularity recently when Andreas Cahling wrote about it in *Flex* magazine.

Weaker body parts are trained early in the week when energy levels are higher, but no workout lasts more than about an hour. Some sessions are almost laughably short, as few as 15–20 minutes. Bodybuilders are careful not to fully exhaust their muscle-liver glycogen supplies in a workout. In other words, they don't push so far that they couldn't actually train for 20 minutes longer, because it seems the body recovers more quickly when it isn't pushed to glycogen depletion.

Both strength and muscle-mass gains come relatively quickly on this system. Since a muscle group is trained only once every seven days, it's rare to do a workout for the chest or some other body part without noticing that you've grown stronger since the last session for the same muscle complex. If you've grown stronger, your muscles have gotten a little larger as well.

It doesn't seem to matter what type of diet is followed with this method. Cahling is a vegetarian, and others who follow his lead embrace virtually every aspect of bodybuilding nutritional practices.

The Hard-Gainer Approach

Inevitably there are hard-gainers in bodybuilding, individuals who overtrain very easily and don't make gains in muscle mass at any notable pace. The harder they try to build up, the fewer results they see from their efforts. To achieve desired results a hard-gainer has to cut back on his workouts and pay special attention to his nutritional program.

Hard-gainers can attain acceptable muscle growth if they are willing to stick to basic exercises in their routines, to work each muscle group only once per week while splitting their body parts into three sections trained on nonconsecutive days each week, and to keep their reps within 5–8 while using maximum weights in perfect form in all sets.

In terms of diet they have to be careful to consume a high-protein/high-calorie regimen with no missed meals. Plenty of protein-rich shakes are recommended, as is a full spectrum of vitamins, minerals, enzymes, and amino acids. Combine this type of diet with the described training program and any hard-gainer can put on 3–5 pounds per year of pure muscle. That might not sound like much, but if you saw a lean five-pound roast, you'd know that it's a lot of beef!

In the following six chapters we'll go into greater depth on each of these mass-building methods. The classic approach is treated in Chapter 3, the current best approach in Chapter 4, the power-lifting approach in Chapter 5, the heavy-duty approach in Chapter 6, the newest rage in Chapter 7, and the hard-gainer approach in Chapter 8.

Three distinct physical types—J. J. Marsh, Shawn Ray, and Gary Strydom—with remarkably similar approaches to gaining mass and power. Train heavy and eat until you drop!

3
The Classic Approach

Bodybuilding has progressed in clearly defined eras. During the 1940s, 1950s, and 1960s, Bill Pearl personified the ideal bodybuilder. A four-time National Amateur Bodybuilding Association (NABBA) Mr. Universe winner, Pearl was very massive and perfectly proportioned, with a small waistline for his high body weight (240 pounds at 5′11″) and broad shoulders. But he was not particularly muscular by today's standards. He had great muscular separation but lacked the striations and cross-striations common in top competitive bodybuilders these days.

While Pearl remained the ideal into the early 1970s, Frank Zane probably set the trend for the era of hypermuscularity during the middle and late 1970s, particularly from 1977–79 when he won three consecutive Mr. Olympia titles. Zane, too, was ideally proportioned and had excellent symmetry, but he did not have the extreme muscle mass of a Bill Pearl or an Arnold Schwarzenegger. Zane made up for his lack of huge muscles by developing one of the most highly detailed physiques of all time. Even his striations had striations, and in a back double-biceps shot, his muscles were not merely separated but were subdivided into scores of striations along the lengths of the muscle bellies.

Arnold Schwarzenegger was a special case because he embraced both the big-and-proportionate era and the hypermuscular era. When he first began winning NABBA Mr. Universe titles at only 20 years of age, he resembled Pearl—hugely muscled, well-proportioned, but lacking any fine details of muscularity. The last man to defeat Schwarzenegger was Frank Zane at the 1968 IFBB Mr. Universe, and the Austrian Oak learned a great lesson at that competition when he was defeated by a man who weighed almost 60 pounds less than he did. Within a couple of years Schwarzenegger had discovered how to diet and train to combine hypermuscularity with his huge muscle mass and became the greatest bodybuilder of all time.

The present era is personified by Schwarzenegger's condition during the early 1970s as he was winning six consecutive Mr. Olympia titles. Every top contest winner at present is hugely proportioned, very well-balanced from one muscle group to the next, symmetrical, *and* extremely hard looking. If a man doesn't have the striated glutes that Rich Gaspari unveiled at the Arnold Schwarzenegger IFBB Pro Muscle Classic in 1987, he isn't considered to be in contest condition. And if he doesn't have Tom Platz's cross-striated quadriceps, he's similarly out of condition regardless of how muscular-appearing he might be over the rest of his physique.

Special types of mass training have been standard during each of the aforementioned eras. During the Bill Pearl era, the ideal method of gaining muscle mass and power was to bulk up and cut down, compete, then bulk up again. Although a few bodybuilders these days still eat themselves nearly to death in the off-season, this bulk-and-cut regimen is long out of style.

While Pearl would weigh in the 240–42 range for a competition, his off-season weight might go up 25–30 pounds above competitive levels. This weight gain was deliberate, because Pearl followed the theory that a bodybuilder would gain a lot more muscle mass much more quickly if he would gain as much weight as possible—even though much of it was fat and excess water—during an off-season cycle.

The men who bulked and cut during the Pearl era (there was no women's bodybuilding until 1980) reads like a who's who of world bodybuilding during the 1950s and 1960s. Just a few of these individuals were Dick Dubois (Mr. America), Lynn Lyman (Mr. California and a consistent Mr. America runner-up), Doug Strohl (a Mr. Universe class winner), Red Lerille (Mr. America), Ray Routledge (a Mr. America personally trained by Pearl), Joe Abbenda (Mr. America and both Pro and Amateur NABBA Mr. Universe), Freddy Ortiz (Mr. America, Mr. World), Rock Stonewall (Mr. America and Mr. World class winner), and even Lou Ferrigno (Mr. America, twice Mr. Universe, and Mr. International) in his early years.

Lou Ferrigno's case is interesting, so let's read it in his own words: "I'm just a hair under 6′5″ in height, and when I was 18 I weighed 221 for the competition I entered that year. I decided that I'd bulk up to at least 300 pounds, then train down and enter every competition in sight weighing something in the 240–50 range.

"I ate everything that wasn't nailed down and almost put my family in the poorhouse doing it. I drank up to two gallons of milk per day because I had been told that milk was a great weight-gaining food. I trained as heavily as I could in all of my basic exercises, and within 6–7 months I'd cracked the 300-pound barrier, ultimately topping out at a massive 305. The earth

shook when I walked, and I was sure I'd weigh at least 250 pounds once I'd trained down and lost my excess body fat.

"I reversed the process, beginning to diet and train lighter and faster. The weight came off, but it was a real battle, particularly to remove the last 15 or so pounds of fat that I'd put on. It took me about 20 weeks to reach contest condition. Do you know what I weighed once I got into shape, after putting all of that effort into getting huge and then training down? Only 225 pounds, or four pounds more than I'd weighed a year before.

"Since that abortive experiment with bulking up and training down, I've never done it again," Ferrigno says. "Nowadays I just train hard, eat right, and gradually add weight that is primarily

Mental approach before each heavy set ensures maximum muscle fiber recruitment.

Constant monitoring in gym mirrors has nothing to do with Narcissus. The object is to be sure no vestige of fat slips in as the muscle mass increases. The athlete is Bob Cicherillo.

National NPC Middleweight Champion Vicki Sims takes a between-sets break for a sip of a carb drink. Note the difference between bulked-up off-season shape and her normal supersharp contest condition.

pure muscle mass. I wouldn't recommend bulking up and cutting down to anyone, except perhaps for someone against whom I knew I'd be competing in a year!"

The Method of Bulking and Cutting Down

The diet when bulking up was pretty simple. It consisted of the "see food" diet—if you see it, eat it! Milk and milk products were a high priority because they helped to pack on weight very quickly, even though a lot of it was water retention from milk allergies that most people have. High-fat foods like steaks, whole eggs, and even pork chops were encouraged.

The idea was more or less to eat all day, consuming at least six full meals and probably a minimum of 7,000 calories per day. Even when you weren't hungry, you were supposed to eat. I know one old-timer who confessed to setting his alarm clock so he could get up in the middle of the night and eat once or twice more. He didn't want us to use his name, but he did mention that he made his best gains in body weight (not necessarily in muscle mass) when he'd eat at least twice in the middle of the night.

There weren't a lot of food supplements in common use during the bulking era, but concentrated protein powder was available. If a bodybuilder couldn't eat food, he could make a protein- and calorie-rich shake by mixing protein powder with ice cream in a blender to keep the calories rolling into the old system.

Training programs changed in that they were concentrated around basic exercises for lots of sets of relatively low reps with monstrous poundages. It wasn't unusual to see a 260-pound bodybuilder do 20 sets of bench presses with weights ranging from 375 to over 400 pounds. Even though he might only get one or two reps on his own, he could always have a training partner help him with a couple of forced reps to make it look like a real set. Strict form was avoided at all costs because it kept bodybuilders from lifting really heavy weights.

The main cutback diet in the bulking days was low carbohydrate. Low-calorie diets didn't come into vogue until the late 1970s or early 1980s. A bulked-up bodybuilder with a show 12–15 weeks off would start on a low-carbohydrate diet, and the weight would come rolling off. First the excess water retention would go, and a bodybuilder would experience a very sharp drop in weight, since it takes carbs in the system to retain extra water. The fat would gradually wear off as well, but at great cost, because a considerable amount of muscle mass would also be lost on this type of diet.

Very few bodybuilders on a low-carb diet can do much of a workout, particularly when it comes to handling respectable poundages in any type of exercise. A low-carb diet simply doesn't allow enough glycogen in the muscles and liver to fuel a hard, heavy workout. Our intrepid bulk-and-cutter would train as hard as possible nonetheless, even though his workouts would be laughably easy by today's standards. Because he couldn't handle heavy poundages in any of his basic movements, he'd be unable to retain some of the muscle mass that he might have had if he'd been able to train heavier.

In the end a bulk-and-cutter would reach the degree of contest condition acceptable for the era. He'd win a trophy, be mentally stoked to try it all over again, and be off on a bulking binge. We've known some bodybuilders who have gained up to 30 pounds in one week after competitions, although about half of that is excess retained water. Even so, it's a tremendous amount of weight to add to your system and can have an adverse effect on blood pressure, to say nothing of the overworked digestive system.

The Pros and Cons of Bulking and Cutting

The main pro of bulking up is that you can eat anything you want, and many bodybuilders use this as an excuse to completely pig out. Certainly you will gain weight very quickly, but you'll end up looking like a lump of *caca* by the time you're through packing on the pounds.

Another pro of bulking up is the ego trip you'll be on when you see how much you can lift when you're that heavy, but that's illusory. You're lifting more weight primarily because you have thicker joints and muscles, not because your muscles are necessarily stronger. And hoisting all of that heavy iron is murder on your skeletal system. A lot of old-timers confess that they have sore joints all over their bodies from bulking up.

Flex Wheeler can still do full splits when he weighs 250 pounds in the off-season, 30 over his contest level. Full-body flexibility actually improves muscle mass.

On the con side of the ledger, it's very unhealthy to be overweight. Your blood pressure can be totally off the normal scale, particularly if you're indulging in anabolic steroid use at the same time you're adding body weight. You will be fatigued beyond description throughout the day and will probably need 9–10 hours of sleep per day just to stay approximately even with your recovery requirements.

Being extremely, unnaturally heavy is very hard on the skeletal system even if you don't compound the problem by lifting monstrous weights. You'll risk permanent injury to the arches of your feet; your knees, hips, elbows, and shoulders will be overtaxed to the point where you may permanently injure them. Your spinal column just isn't made to support all of that extra weight in a standing position, so unless you lie on your back in bed 20 hours per day, you'll end up with back problems sooner or later if you bulk up excessively.

The main disadvantage of bulking up and cutting down is that it simply doesn't work well for more than a minority of individuals. Lou Ferrigno's experience is very common in competitive bodybuilding. Many potentially superb bodybuilders decide at one point to bulk up and then never seem to find the time to come back down. They are never seen on the contest stage again, at least not in anything approaching true competition condition.

We've called bulking up and cutting down the classic method of building extra muscle mass and strength, and it should probably remain a part of the history of bodybuilding back in the 1950s and 1960s. I'm sure readers will want to give it a try anyway—everyone wants to exist on fast foods after 10–12 weeks on a strict contest diet—but don't do it unless you simply can't control yourself. And if you do bulk up, take careful note of the harm you're doing to your body. Then think seriously about following the current best approach to mass- and strength-building as outlined in Chapter 4.

4
The Current Best Approach

"If you listen to people in the gym, you'll find two opinions: you can try to gain muscle mass either very quickly or relatively slowly," notes Ron Love, National Physique Committee, Inc. (NPC), Heavyweight National Champion, IFBB Pro World Champion, and IFBB San Jose Pro Grand Prix Champion. "By training heavily and cramming a lot of high-fat food down your throat, it is possible to gain weight quickly. But in most cases this weight gain has an excessive proportion of fat in it. Once you've packed on a large amount of fat, you have an extremely difficult time losing it prior to a competition. Most guys who go on crash weight-gain programs generally burn off a lot of their hard-earned muscle mass in the process of honing down fat.

"During the beginning stages of your involvement in bodybuilding it's possible to gain 20 or more pounds of muscle the first year. Beyond that point it's highly unlikely that you'll gain even 1 pound of quality muscle per month.

Plenty of midsection work keeps you sharp as you add muscle mass to your frame. Just look at the abdominals—ridge by ridge—on Yugoslavia's Milos Sarcev.

Though you should shoot for 1 good pound per month, don't be too depressed if you gain only half or less than that. Remember, 6 pounds of prime muscle tissue—the amount you'd gain in a year at a half pound per month—makes a tremendous difference in the way you look.

"Be consistent and patient and stay highly motivated at all times," Love concludes. "Rome wasn't built in a day—neither has any great physique been developed in less than five or six years. Anything worth having takes time and plenty of work to achieve, particularly in bodybuilding."

Samir Bannout, 1983 IFBB Mr. Olympia, also advises bodybuilders to take the slow approach, primarily to avoid creating proportional imbalance: "It's possible to make great gains in mass by working only on those muscle groups that respond most quickly for you. However, this practice will result in grossly out-of-balance physical proportions, which leads nowhere competitively. As a rule of thumb, it's a good idea to make gains in muscle mass only as quickly as the improvement rate of your most stubborn body part. Think mass, but also think proportional balance, and you'll eventually win a big title or two."

Most of today's superstar bodybuilders follow the modern method of adding muscle mass to their physiques. They stay lean throughout the year; men attempt to keep their body weights within 10–12 pounds of contest level, and women maintain weights within 5–6 pounds of what they would carry onstage.

Staying lean like this allows bodybuilders to train much harder than if they allowed their diets to get out of hand and added anything between 20–50 pounds of excess body weight, part of it muscle mass but most of it useless fat and excess water retention. A leaner, meaner bodybuilder trains harder than an overweight athlete because he or she doesn't have to lift all that extra weight in many of the basic exercises (e.g., squats, dead-

Guess who? Any bodybuilding aficionado can tell you at a glance that "the glutes from Mars" belong to pro star Renel Janvier, born in Haiti, but now living in southern California where he works out at Gold's in Venice.

lifts, chins) that make up a standard mass-building program. Being lean and mean also makes it easier to walk around and perform daily tasks simply because you're not doing it with a 50-pound weight strapped around your waist and butt.

One minor advantage to gaining excessive amounts of body weight in the off-season is summarized by Fred Hatfield, Ph.D. One of the first and lightest competitive power lifters to squat with more than 1,000 pounds, Dr. Hatfield is the author of *Bodybuilding: A Scientific Approach*, a popular scholarly treatise on bodybuilding also published by Contemporary Books. "Being thicker does give a bodybuilder or power lifter increased tissue leverage, and he will be able to lift heavier weights in most basic exercises as a result," Hatfield wrote. "Sergio Oliva won three consecutive Mr. Olympia titles during the late 1960s with one of the smallest waistlines imaginable. Such a small waistline gives little support through the middle of the torso, and Oliva was not able to squat very heavy when he was in contest shape. Only when he was heavier and his waist was thicker during an off-season mass-building cycle could he really squat with some impressive weights, which in turn made his legs even larger and more impressive than they already were once he'd trained down for his next show."

We can argue that tissue leverage isn't all it's cracked up to be in bodybuilders because what is made big in the off-season tends to be very difficult to make small again for a competition. The object of bodybuilding is to make the muscles, not thick joints or the supersuits and heavy wraps that power lifters use, do the work.

Listen to Tom Platz, IFBB Mr. Universe and the man with the greatest upper-leg development of all time, who is currently the talent director for the World Bodybuilding Federation (WBF): "I've tried squatting with heavy knee wraps and can use much heavier poundages when I do, but it's the extra leverage of the wraps that is lifting the weight, not my quads. I've always made it a point to do squats without using wraps at all, so my quadriceps and buttocks do all of the lifting. I'm very sure my legs would never have reached their ultimate degree of development if I'd consistently used heavy knee wraps. I think you do need to wear a lifting belt when you squat, but avoid the wraps unless you actually have to protect an injury, and then use them as lightly as possible."

Case Histories

Lee Haney

It's difficult to think of a more accomplished competitive bodybuilder than 6'0", 255-pound Lee Haney, who owns a burgeoning gym empire in Atlanta, Georgia, and has his own television show on ESPN. Haney started training after he broke his leg in high-school football. "They sent me into the weight room to rehabilitate my atrophied leg muscles," he recalls, "and I never came out again. Once I had experienced the thrill of being able to add muscle mass to my frame, I was an ex-footballer and lifetime bodybuilder."

Lee Haney won the first two competitions he entered, and he's rarely been defeated since. The

The big guy's gotta be used to it by now! Lee Haney has his hand raised in victory by IFBB president Ben Weider after being announced as winner of the 1991 IFBB Mr. Olympia. This was a record eighth-straight win for Lee.

Lee Haney receives the adulation of a handful of his thousands of fans after winning the 1991 IFBB Mr. Olympia, his record-setting eighth consecutive victory in this prestigious event.

Coastal USA is held annually in Atlanta, and Haney traveled down from his home in Spartanburg, South Carolina, to compete in the teen division. He won not only that but also the open division, which someone talked him into entering after seeing how he devastated the kids his own age.

Haney went on to win the Teenage Mr. America that year, scaling 210 pounds at his present height. Later he won the NPC Junior Nationals (Overall), and in 1982 he won the Heavyweight and Overall NPC Nationals and Heavyweight World Championship in IFBB competition in Brugge, Belgium. The following year he won the prestigious IFBB Pro Night of the Champions plus a made-for-film event called the Caesar's Palace Pro Invitational, held as a men's event to complement the women's show which was filmed for *Pumping Iron II: The Women.*

In 1983 Haney journeyed to Munich, Germany, where he placed third in Mr. Olympia, behind Samir Bannout and Mohamed Makkawy but ahead of three-time winner Frank Zane. This was the last time Haney lost a competition. Since 1984 he's won eight consecutive Mr. Olympia titles and the occasional IFBB Pro Grand Prix event if it was held close enough to an Olympia and the prize money was good.

"In 1991 I won my record-setting eighth-straight Mr. Olympia title weighing 256 pounds of rock-hard muscle," Haney states. "During the off-season between the 1990 and 1991 Olympias my normal training weight was 265–68 pounds, which kept me within my goal of remaining no more than 10–12 pounds above my projected competitive body weight. The only time I strayed a bit higher was over the holidays at the end of the year, and that extra 5–6 pounds was almost exclusively from excess water retention. Once I was back on my off-season maintenance diet I was back down to 266 in less than a week. At Thanksgiving and Christmas it's virtually impossible to control my diet, and in that respect I don't think I'm any different from most other top bodybuilders.

"I won my first Olympia in 1984 weighing 238 pounds, up 6 pounds from the previous year. Seven years later I weighed 256 pounds onstage, a net gain of 18 pounds, or about 2 pounds of solid muscle mass per year. I'm a patient man, and this is a very acceptable degree of progress for me, because I'm well aware that mass gaining

is a matter of gradually diminishing returns. The first year you train steadily, you might be fortunate enough to put on 20 pounds of muscle, but the second year it may be only 10, the third only 6, and the fourth only 4–5. Since it gets harder and harder to make gains in lean body mass, I'm happy with an average of 2–3 new pounds yearly.

"The secret to my success has always been to keep my body weight down within striking distance of my competitive level by constantly monitoring my diet during the off-season," Haney explains. "My off-season diet is pretty much the same as what I eat prior to a competition, but the quantities of food are larger. I train heavier and use a higher proportion of basic exercises during the off-season than I would prior to an Olympia. This gets me in great shape every year, with no sweat losing the extra weight.

"Early in my bodybuilding involvement I did try bulking up and training down, but it didn't work for me. I put on 30 pounds over a six-month period and then tried to train down for a competition. After four months of sweating away and starving myself, I'd made a net gain of only two pounds, just about what I'd have expected if I'd followed my normal method of keeping my body fat percentage under control during the off-season and simply training harder and heavier, particularly on a muscle group that I thought was weak the previous year."

Rich Gaspari

Talented Rich Gaspari won the NPC National and IFBB World Light-Heavyweight Championships as an amateur. As a pro he has placed second three straight years in Mr. Olympia and won a host of IFBB Pro Grand Prix events, including the highly prestigious Arnold Schwarzenegger Pro Classic the first time it was held in Columbus, Ohio, in 1989.

"I'd competed as a heavyweight in the 1983 Nationals and placed sixth in my class as Bob Paris won that class and the overall title," Gaspari says. "I was thinking of myself as a heavyweight all during the off-season following that show. I ate like a pig and was squatting over 700 pounds for reps at least once per week. I went up from about 210, which I'd weighed at Nationals, to almost 260 before I decided to move out to California for six months to take Lee Haney up on his offer to be my training partner.

"You wouldn't believe how strictly I had to diet to get into contest shape for the 1984 season. I was on such low calories that I was weak in the gym and Lee was kicking my tail from one end of Gold's Gym in Reseda, California, to the other. But in six months I did lose nearly 70 pounds, which put me in terrific shape for a 21-year-old with six years of training under his belt. That was actually an artificially low body weight for me—I was about 188 for Nationals and 192 for the World Championships, both of which I won.

"Because my weight was artificially low I entered the Night of the Champions the following year at 207 and shocked everyone with my apparent improvement. I was huge and ripped, but about 10 pounds of that improvement was just muscle mass that I'd worn away getting ready for the 1984 show and then gained back over the winter.

"I've always made fast improvement—save for one Olympia—by keeping my body weight under control, always remaining 10 pounds or less above my contest-level body weight. I had trained at a much higher weight and felt lethargic all of the time. I was strong, of course, but I couldn't train very fast and I didn't make many real gains in muscle mass. Most of the weight I had put on was due to water retention and excess fat," Gaspari recalls.

"The only mistake I made was leaving my usual competitive weight of 215 to get up to 228 in an effort to defeat Haney at an Olympia one year. I was huge looking but lacked my usual diamond-hard cuts. It was a case of making the mistake of listening to too many of my friends, who kept telling me I had to be bigger to defeat Lee. Well, it didn't work, and the following year I was back down to my normal competitive weight, with all of my usual cuts and vascularity.

"The secret of making fast gains is definitely to keep my body weight relatively low in the off-season so I can train both hard and fast. If you use heavy weights and rest no more than 60 seconds on an average between sets, you're going to pack on muscle mass very quickly. This all means that I have to watch what I eat even in the off-season—I never let myself lose control for a single day year-round—but it works wonders for me. I'm sure it'll work the same for anyone else who has the self-discipline to try this method."

Debby McKnight

Debby McKnight is 5'5½" and started body-building in 1984 after watching Nationals that year in New Orleans. She was a self-confessed pencilneck, weighing only 105 pounds when she started. Within five years she had won the Heavyweight and Overall titles at both the NPC Junior USA and Open USA. She now weighs 143 pounds at contest time and competes professionally. She also manages the Nutritionalysis program at Gold's Gym in North Hollywood, California.

The most startling thing about McKnight is that she looks in contest shape year-round. "I always watch my diet," she says, "even in the off-season. Fats are my enemy, because they yield nine calories per gram when metabolized versus only four calories per gram for either protein or carbohydrate. If I eat fat and gain a few pounds, I just don't feel right in the gym. I'm not any stronger, and I'm definitely more lethargic. With any extra weight I'm breathing so hard after a heavy set that I actually have to pause longer before I start the next one than I would if I keep my weight down."

Keeping her weight down for McKnight means maintaining it in the range of 145-48 pounds, which is only 2-5 pounds over the level at which she competes. She's extremely powerful at that low body weight, as evidenced by full sets of 8-10 reps with 80-pound dumbbells on incline presses and a 40-pounder on one-arm preacher curls.

"Comparitively speaking, I think it's harder for a woman to get into contest shape," McKnight says, "so why not stay as close as possible all year? Sure, it requires discipline, but with some thought you can make the blandest meal taste good. I use 25-30 packets of aspartame daily in the off-season, even putting it on my salads. And I use Molly McButter on everything from egg whites in the morning to steamed vegetables at night.

"If you're heavy when you start bodybuilding, I'd suggest dieting hard and doing plenty of aerobics until you have your body-fat percentage under control. You should be able to see your abdominal muscles in sharp relief at all times, or you aren't even in contest shape. This will take some effort and dietary reeducation, but it's worth the trouble it takes.

With the currently most popular mass-building method, this is about as far out of shape as you'll ever want to be. We won't embarrass the owner of these abs by giving readers his name.

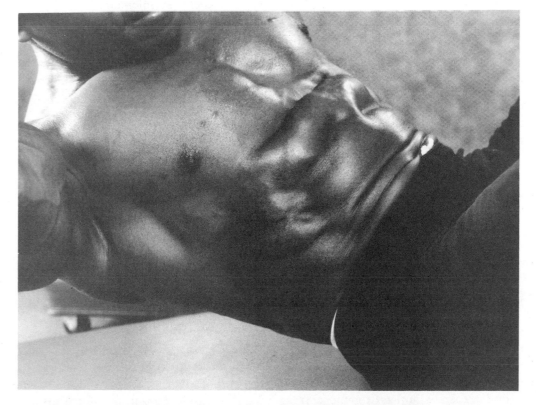

By comparison, this is a touch too smooth. We had monetary offers *not* to publish this pic, but deemed it too instructive to leave out of the book.

"Once you're down in body-fat weight, start training as heavily as possible each workout while maintaining good form. I'll do forced reps and drop sets on the last set of two of each basic exercise I perform in a workout, but otherwise it's just me and the weights. The heavier you train, the larger your muscles will become in the long run," she reminds. "And if you retain proportional balance as you build up, you'll be tough to beat in any competition."

Robby Robinson

Robby Robinson, who won the first two Night of the Champions competitions, is another bodybuilder who tries to stay lean all year. Let's listen to his advice on off-season dieting for building muscle mass while keeping fat weight down.

"No question about it, protein is essential if you intend to increase muscle mass," Robinson says. "Your object when attempting to gain muscular body weight, then, should be to ingest sufficient amounts of high-quality protein along with enough complex carbohydrates to fuel heavy workouts, while at the same time keeping dietary fat intake at a bare minimum.

"Animal-source proteins are the best for most bodybuilders. Several vegetarian bodybuilders have become high-level competitors, although even they relied heavily on eggs and milk products for protein. To a significant extent your diet may also utilize supplemental sources of protein in the form of concentrated protein powders and free-form and branched-chain amino acids.

"I personally don't eat much red meat during the off-season or precontest phases—perhaps only once a month in the off-season—because it's much too high in fat and it's difficult to digest. I also don't rely too much on milk products, only consuming a nonfat yogurt now and then in the off-season. My chief sources of protein are chicken and turkey with the fatty skin removed before the poultry is broiled, fish, egg whites, and amino acids.

"Classic weight-gain nutritional practice always involves eating more than three meals per day; usually 6–8 is the norm. The reasoning is simple: it's possible to force a lot more amino acids—the end products of protein digestion—into your bloodstream when eating more fre-

quently. The human digestive tract is capable of processing between 20–25 grams of protein from any given meal, so it's obvious that six meals per day will allow you to digest twice as much protein each day as three daily meals.

"Each of your six meals should include animal-source protein—at least 20 grams of it per meal—as well as sufficient complex carbohydrates to blast through every workout. My own preference is complex carbs from potatoes, rice, yams, and pasta, because they yield a more sustained type of energy flow. Simple sugars from fruit and any type of junk food tend to give everyone an energy peak followed by a low-energy valley, something that is not conducive to successful bodybuilding."

Robby Robinson contributed the following weight-gain meal plan. Meals are at intervals of 2–3 hours. Note how low in fat content the meals are.

Meal 1: egg whites, oatmeal with a bit of nonfat milk, aminos, vitamin-mineral supplements

Meal 2: broiled fish, baked potato, green salad (lemon juice for dressing), iced tea (with aspartame sweetener), vitamin-mineral supplements

Meal 3: broiled chicken breast (no skin), rice, steamed green vegetables, herbal tea, vitamin-mineral supplements

Meal 4: repeat Meal 2

Meal 5: repeat Meal 1 or 3

Meal 6: repeat Meal 1

Gary Strydom

"Food supplements are vitally important when attempting to gain muscle mass in an off-season cycle," notes Gary Strydom, a Night of the Champions victor in the IFBB before he turned to the WBF and won its first competition in June 1991. "Because of my high metabolism I have experienced difficulty in gaining mass over the years. Now I routinely consume 7,000 calories per day in the off-season, and I firmly believe that heavy use of supplements has helped me greatly in packing on the mass.

"Obviously, free-form and branched-chain aminos are essential, free-form taken 30 minutes prior to each meal and branched-chain consumed after each workout. I will go through bottle after bottle of these supplements both in the off-season and prior to a show. They are relatively expensive, but my philosophy is to always rely on the best supplements available. Amino capsules are almost directly assimilated into muscle tissue, requiring little or no digestion. They prevent any unnecessary burden on the digestive system.

"I'm also careful to consume a couple of multipacks of vitamins and minerals per day, always with meals," Strydom continues. "They provide nutritional insurance against any dietary deficiencies that might be holding you back from awesome gains in muscle mass. And I take additional amounts of the water-soluble vitamins B complex and C, which can't be stored in the body like oil-soluble vitamins. The water-solubles must, therefore, be ingested frequently throughout the day.

"B-complex vitamins are fundamental to weight gain; several of them stimulate appetite and help increase muscle mass following a hard workout. I don't think it would be excessive to take one or two high-potency B-complex vitamin capsules every couple of hours throughout the day when in a mass-building phase."

Weight-Gain Training

Keeping in mind the training frequency and total-sets thresholds appropriate to your level of bodybuilding experience, listen to Mike Quinn, who won the Heavyweight/Overall U.S. Championships as an amateur and is now a WBF superstar: "Most of your program should be formulated around basic exercises in which you can use big weights for relatively low repetitions. Basic exercises work the large muscle groups of the body synergistically with other large and/or small body parts. Good examples of basic movements are squats, bench presses, seated low-pulley rows, and overhead presses with a barbell, two dumbbells, or on a machine."

A list of the best basic exercises for each body part follows:

Legs: squats, leg presses (angled, seated, vertical), stiff-legged deadlifts

Back: chins, pulldowns (front and back),

Austrian Andreas Munzer won his IFBB pro card by taking first in the World Games in 1989. His striations have cross-striations!

barbell/dumbbell/pulley rows, deadlifts, shrugs, upright rows

Chest: bench presses, incline presses, decline presses, parallel bar dips

Shoulders: overhead presses, upright rows

Arms: close-grip bench presses, standing barbell curls, all types of presses and rows

Forearms: barbell reverse curls, barbell wrist curls

Calves: seated/standing calf raises, donkey calf raises

Abdominals: hanging leg raises, crunches

France's Francis Benfatto, in early season shape for the Iron Man Classic in February 1991, looks about this good year-round. It's one of his secrets of appearing in super shape at each Mr. Olympia.

"It's best to perform relatively low reps when in a mass-building cycle," Quinn continues. "Scientific research and plenty of personal experience by hundreds of thousands of bodybuilders have conclusively demonstrated that the best repetition range for mass building is between five and eight, always done in ultrastrict form.

"There's danger in doing low reps without a proper warm-up, since handling heavy poundages cold raises the risk factor of injuries. Therefore, you should combine both high reps with light weights and low reps with heavy poundages for each basic movement in your routine. The best way to do this is to either pyramid or half pyramid your sets, reps, and training weights."

Following are examples for the bench press of the full and half pyramids Quinn is talking about.

SAMPLE BENCH-PRESS ROUTINES

Full Pyramid

Set Number	Reps	Poundage*
1	12	135
2	10	175
3	8	205
4	7	225
5	6	245
6	5	260
7	6	245
8	7	225
9	8	205
10	10	175
11	12	135

Half Pyramid

Set Number	Reps	Poundage*
1	12	135
2	10	175
3	8	205
4	7	225
5	6	245
6	5	260
7	15–20	185**

*Poundages are chosen arbitrarily merely for the sake of illustration.
**A pump set is optional.

"Forced reps are applicable on the last set or two of each basic movement," says Lee Haney. "But be sure to use strict form when performing forced reps, in order to avoid injuries. It's possible to use cheating reps to extend a set past failure, but there's too much risk of injury when you abandon good biomechanics while using heavy poundages."

Combining Haney's and Quinn's training suggestions, here is a suggested mass-building program.

SAMPLE EXERCISE PROGRAM

Monday/Thursday

Exercise	Sets	Reps
Hanging Leg Raises	2–3	10–15
Leg Extensions (warm-up)	2–3	15–20
Squats	7	15–5*
Stiff-Legged Deadlifts	5	15–8
Seated Low-Pulley Rows	7	12–5*
Barbell Shrugs	5	15–8*
Standing Barbell Curls	5	12–8*
Seated Calf Raises	5	15–8*

Benfatto is actually a bit smaller than he looks, due to his emphasis on perfect proportions and his naturally small joints, both of which conspire to make him look bigger than he is.

Tuesday/Friday		
Exercise	Sets	Reps
Incline Sit-Ups	2-3	20-25
Barbell Incline Presses	7	12-5*
Parallel Bar Dips	5	12-8*
Seated Machine Presses	5	10-5*
Barbell Upright Rows	5	12-6*
Close-Grip Bench Presses	5	10-6*
Barbell Wrist Curls	5	15-8*
Standing Calf Raises	5	15-8*

*Pyramid exercises.

It's clear that any bodybuilder can gain muscular body weight at an acceptable rate *if* he or she carefully follows the suggestions outlined in this chapter and stays highly motivated. Moreover, this can be done naturally without the use of tissue-building drugs. Be consistent, train hard, maintain an optimum bodybuilding diet, and you'll soon have the high degree of muscle mass you desire. The experiences of thousands of bodybuilders prove it!

The Final Edge

The newest wrinkle in high-level bodybuilding is to first deplete carbohydrates and then load them, while at the same time load sodium and then deplete. This strategy is supposed to get the water in your body where you want it, out from under your skin and into the muscles and vascular system. Many top bodybuilders have had mixed results with this method, but we will describe it nonetheless.

Carbohydrate depletion generally begins seven days prior to the competition with four days of strictly limited carbohydrate intake. Less than 30 grams per day are taken in for the four days, and aerobic intensity and posing practice are elevated in duration during the depletion phase. Then, for three days leading up to the show, a bodybuilder loads 200–250 grams of complex carbohydrates per day (depending on body size and general need).

When carbohydrates have been completely depleted from the system with the four-day marathon, your body will supercompensate by storing even more glycogen than usual in your muscles, liver, and bloodstream. These carbs draw extra water into the muscles, making them appear fuller than they really are, and draw water into the vascular system, making the veins appear much more prominent than normal.

The sodium loading-depletion cycle also lasts seven days. For the first four days, you take in progressively more sodium each successive day, starting with about 2 grams the first day, 3–4 the second, 4–5 the third, and up to 6–7 on the fourth. This will cause quite a bit of water retention, but if you're mentally prepared to accept your bad appearance, you shouldn't be tempted to drop out of competition.

For the final three days, *no sodium whatsoever* is consumed. This means drinking steam-distilled water to make sure you don't ingest any sodium and paying very strict attention to a table of food values to be sure you don't consume any sodium in the foods you eat. Obviously, you won't want to salt anything when you're depleting sodium.

Sodium loading-depletion fakes out the aldosterone hormone production cycle, which tends to kick in when you're nervous around the time of a show. When it kicks in you'll automatically retain water whether you've had sodium in your system or not, but this way aldosterone is not released. Sodium can't keep water lodged beneath your skin, so it's sucked out of those areas and into the muscles and vascular system like it should be.

The problem with this carb-sodium system is that it seems to work very well for some bodybuilders and not at all for many others. Some of the ones for whom it works have had to make many adjustments during off-season dry runs to get it down right. Some even go so far as to precisely measure their urine output so they know just how much distilled water to put back into their system!

Dan Duchaine, who has earned the sobriquet "the Steroid Guru," wrote in the December 1990 issue of *Modern Bodybuilding* that, "I don't believe in depleting during the last week before a competition. It never seemed to work at all that well with most of the bodybuilders I know that have tried that route. Most of them ended up making themselves ill by restricting their carbs and calories too severely while at the same time increasing their training volume. This whole depleting added to eight or more weeks of dieting is a severe shock to the body, and a shock that the body doesn't respond to in a positive manner. . . . I feel that after several weeks of dieting the body is already sufficiently depleted.

Frank Hillebrand handles a half ton of plates for angled leg presses at Gold's in Venice like they were empty tin cans.

In most cases to further restrict carbohydrate intake beyond that point will not be to your advantage.

"Although the generally accepted time to carb up is three days, the competitors I work with take two weeks to carb up. I feel that to obtain optimum muscle size and fullness is dependent on completely rebuilding the amino acid pools around each muscle cell, along with general whole body rehydration with fluids and minerals."

If you choose to carb load/deplete and sodium load/deplete, do so carefully and with plenty of experimentation during dry runs in the off-season. If you hit it as correctly as some bodybuilders we've seen, you can look up to 20 percent better onstage than if you didn't undergo these two processes!

5
The Power-Lifting Approach

If you follow power lifting with any regularity through its official journal, *Powerlifting USA* (a one-year subscription of monthly issues costs under $30 at the time of writing and can be obtained from Box 467, Camarillo, CA 93011), you'll notice that the best men and women in the sport have the type of muscle mass that every bodybuilder is after. Those who have to make some of the lighter weight classes literally look like competitive bodybuilders at contest time.

Scores of power lifters have also competed extremely well in bodybuilding. One of the best examples is Mary Jeffrey, who has won a multitude of World Championships in power lifting. Just to show how strong this dynamo is, Jeffrey has an official 275-pound bench-press world record in the 123-pound class. With an absolute minimum of specialized bodybuilding training—actually about all she did was diet a bit more than she usually does to make weight—Mary Jeffrey waltzed into the American Athletic

Union (AAU) Ms. America competition a few years ago and won her class and the overall title so easily that she's never bothered to compete in bodybuilding since.

Bev Francis, who owns a Gold's Gym on Long Island, New York, has placed as high as second in the Ms. Olympia and won the IFBB Pro World Bodybuilding Championship. Prior to becoming a bodybuilding specialist, she won five power-lifting World Championships, set scores of world records, and was the first woman to officially bench press more than 300 pounds. Her peak effort of 330 doubled her body weight at the time.

There are scores more men who have been world-class power lifters and also won high-level bodybuilding titles. One name that comes immediately to mind is army communications specialist Joe Dawson, who is a near World Champion in power lifting and has won two NPC Lightweight National Championships.

There are 20 more world-class power lifters competing today (we're still talking about the men) who could make the switch to bodybuilding in a couple of months and win high-level titles. Michael Ashley, the world's premier natu-

Bob Cicherillo has won an overall NPC Junior National title. At certain times of the year, he's a near power lifter.

ral bodybuilder (he has won an IFBB World Light-Heavyweight Championship that was drug tested and won the drug-tested Pro Arnold Schwarzenegger Classic), was a great power lifter until knee problems pushed him more into bodybuilding. But he's squatted nearly 800 pounds in the 198-pound weight division.

A few years back, Phoenix bodybuilder Pat Neve won the overall U.S.A. and his class more than once in Mr. America. He held the light-heavyweight (181 pounds and under) bench-press world record longer than any power-lifting record has stood on the books. I believe it took either seven or eight years for people to catch up with him enough to break his bench-press record, and by then Neve had won every amateur bodybuilding title of any note in the United States and made countless magazine covers.

It used to be de rigueur for serious bodybuilders to spend two, three, or four years as power lifters before really getting serious about bodybuilding. The theory then was that power lifting built the type of base that allowed a bodybuilder to be bigger and more cut than his competitors. A two-time Mr. Olympia victor and member of the initial Gold's Gym in Venice, California, Dr. Franco Columbu is a typical example of this style of thinking. At one point he held either world or European records in every power lift in his 181-pound weight division and was a serious competitive bodybuilder at the time. I've seen him do 10 easy reps in the deadlift with 675 pounds and 6 with 715, just as an ordinary part of his back workout at Gold's during a peaking cycle for an early 1970s Mr. Olympia competition.

Terminator Arnold Schwarzenegger, while not quite as strong as his smaller Sardinian training partner, has also deadlifted more than 700 pounds in strength exhibitions prior to giving his posing exhibition. After a while he stopped lifting because his physique had become so thick and muscular that people were interested only in seeing him guest pose. But Arnold's power-lifting background is well known among individuals who were Gold's habitués in the early 1970s.

I could go on and on with lists of great power lifters who became great bodybuilders and vice versa. Currently emphasis is more on symmetry and intensely deep cuts rather than ultimately huge muscle mass on the competitive stage, so few current bodybuilders bother with heavy training at all, let alone power lifting. But they're making a mistake, because they'll never get the real mass without using the heavy weights, and power-lifting competition is one of the best ways to get very strong—and very massively built—very quickly.

So How Do Power Lifters Train?

If you had to guess, you might think power lifters do a lot of maximum single efforts in the gym, or at most doubles, triples, or sets of five. But this type of training is seldom seen in power-lifting-oriented gyms. Perhaps you'll see it only a couple of weeks out from a competition so an athlete can determine his strength levels and choose appropriate starting poundages for his competition.

Most of the time power lifters are doing sets of 5–8 (a lot go up to 10–12 reps per set), but with much heavier poundages and in somewhat looser form than even the strongest bodybuilders. For example, there are guys like Ken Laine benching over 700 nowadays, and they might typically work up to 6–8 reps with 650 in heavy bench workout.

Power lifters don't do a lot of sets in a workout, perhaps only 15–20 hard sets in one session. They train only 4–5 times per week because they realize that their bodies need recovery time to gain strength and mass. It's not uncommon to see the best bench pressers in the world benching only once per week or once every 10 days and then resting the movement completely—perhaps doing assistance exercises—in the interim.

The first issue of *Powerlifting USA* that I pulled out of my closet had two deadlifting programs in it, and while occasional single reps were interspersed, most of the sets were done with a minimum of five repetitions. Power lifters tend to train the deadlift with significantly lower reps than either bench presses or squats, and particularly squats. A squat routine by a world champion in another issue didn't have a set of less than 8 reps in it, and most of them were 10–12 reps.

One unique thing most power lifters do is cycle their training so they go through 8- to 10-week cycles. They start out light early in the cycle and progressively add weight until they

Hypermuscular and ultrapowerful IFBB pro Debby McKnight lives in Sherman Oaks, California, and runs the Nutritionalysis programs at Gold's in North Hollywood. An overall U.S. Champion, Deb weighs under 150 and reps out with 225 on barbell incline presses.

Bench presses—a key upper-body movement done by all power lifters and power bodybuilders.

peak out the last week. Then they start the cycle over and over, occasionally making a maximum peak for an important competition. Bodybuilders would do well to follow this example because they would have less injuries and would coax gains in mass and strength more quickly than if they were going all out every workout. If you try to go to 100 percent every session, your body is going to tell you it can't cope with that style of workout. Why not listen to your body?

The final feature of power lifters' workouts is that they do very few movements in each training session. Everything is based on the squat, bench press, and deadlift, all of which they do in competition. A typical routine consists of one of these lifts and two or three assistance exercises.

An assistance exercise is one included to build up the same area as the primary lift. Let's say you're working harder than usual on your bench press. Assistance exercises in a bench-press routine might be incline presses in a power rack for partial movements, pulley pushdowns, and perhaps lat machine pulldowns, since the lats help push a bench-press bar upward over the first few inches of its range of motion.

You won't see power lifters doing any type of calf movement—at least I never have—nor anything direct for their deltoids, trapezius muscles, abdominals, hamstrings, or forearms, yet each of these areas is massively developed nonetheless. The secret is that heavy basic movements work so many muscle groups that you can go all out on 10 total sets of bench presses and sit back knowing you've actually worked most of your upper body to the limit along with your pecs, anterior deltoids, and triceps.

I'd be the last person to tell you that training like this is easy, because it isn't. It's grueling to do 10-rep sets of squats at 200 pounds of body weight, which I used to do with 500 pounds minimum during a brief fling with power lifting.

The keys to a power-lifting workout follow, so you don't have to think very hard to make up your own routine:

- 3–5 workouts per week
- frequently only one session per week on each lift
- low numbers of total sets per workout (20–22 at the top end)
- everything heavy, but medium reps nonetheless (sets of 5–8 repetitions are most common)
- virtually no foo-foo isolation movements— everything a power lifter does is a basic movement

It's a simple program, but all serious male and female bodybuilders should put in at least one or two years at it if they are serious about winning national- and international-level titles. Strong men and women are also almost invariably massively developed individuals. You've heard it a hundred times—lift big to get big—but there's nothing more true in bodybuilding.

Power-Lifting Diet

When power lifting became an official sport in the mid-1960s, power lifters were frequently recruited from the bodybuilding ranks. Once relieved of the onus of maintaining a good diet year-round, these men (there were no women power lifters until many years later) eschewed normal diets and many lived on junk foods. This has changed dramatically.

Today's power lifter is just as well informed about quality nutrition as is a top bodybuilder. He or she is equally concerned about what to eat to build strength and the additional muscle mass that leads to even more strength for power-lifting competitions.

We won't bore you with dietary basics in this chapter because Chapter 11 is devoted entirely to bodybuilding mass- and power-building nutrition. This is how serious power lifters eat, too. Anyone with any degree of literacy will learn everything he or she has to know about eating to get big and strong by digesting Chapter 11, even if you have to eat it a couple of times!

Concentrating before a heavy preexhaustion upper-chest superset of incline flyes and incline presses.

6
The Heavy-Duty Approach

From a scientific standpoint the heavy-duty approach to bodybuilding training has more going for it than any other system. Without a doubt the way to achieve maximum mass and strength in a muscle is to train it very heavily, very briefly, and completely to the limit of its strength endurance for a particular workout, then let it rest for several days before repeating the cycle.

The problem with heavy duty is that some have taken it much too literally. These people recommend workouts lasting only a set or two for each muscle group, suggesting maximum weights without sufficient preworkout warm-ups and routines with so little variety of exercises in them that, while mass is achieved, physiques built with these methods are huge but lack muscular detail. One of the biggest problems in the long run has been that most adherents to heavy duty have ended up with more heavy-duty joint injuries than heavy-duty muscles and strength.

Nautilus—the Genesis of Heavy Duty

A very interesting man named Arthur Jones had tinkered in home workshops for years in an attempt to build the perfect exercise machine, one that would vary resistance placed on the working muscle(s) and make it heavier at points where the natural strength curve of the muscle was stronger.

Both a genius and an eccentric, Jones had spent much of his life collecting wild animals for zoos and private reserves. He'd survived plane crashes, political coups in countries where he was hunting for specimens, and many animal and reptile bites. The floors in some offices at his Nautilus headquarters in De Land, Florida, were made of heavy glass, and gators and crocs roamed freely beneath the feet of his executives. One of Jones's experiments was an attempt to breed the largest rattlesnakes in captivity.

During the late 1960s Jones discovered the secret to what would become his Nautilus empire—a cam of variable radii. A cam is a pulley, and when the radius is varied the amount of force required to turn that pulley either increases (if the radius is made smaller) or decreases (if the radius is made larger). The end product looked somewhat like the shell of the nautilus, a common seawater mollusk; hence the name of the end product.

At first Jones had only a pullover machine,

which he touted in magazine articles (mainly in *Ironman*) as the be-all and end-all of torso development. He predicted that only one or two sets to complete failure on this machine three times per week would build upper-back muscles that defy description. Actually this never happened, because most of the people Jones put through workouts on his equipment (Sergio Oliva, Arnold Schwarzenegger, Franco Columbu, and Casey Viator) already *had* back muscles that defied description. But the notion of low sets taken to complete failure persisted.

Jones outlined his system of training in article after article as well as two Nautilus bulletins (thick, self-published books filled with more wisdom). A lot of what Jones said made great sense, and to some bodybuilders the idea of getting through a normal 1½- to 2-hour workout in 20–30 minutes was appealing. Everyone wants something for nothing, or at least something for less than it normally costs. Soon half of the bodybuilding world was beating a trail to Florida to worship at the feet of this new guru.

One of these bodybuilders was Mike Mentzer, who went on to write for Joe Weider's *Muscle Builder & Power* en route to winning Mr. Amer-

In midset of incline dumbbell flyes.

ica, Mr. North America, Mr. Universe, and Heavyweight Mr. Olympia titles. Mentzer had his own version of Jones's system, which he christened "Heavy Duty." He authored a series of booklets on the program as well as a couple of books.

The Heavy Duty System obviously worked for Mike Mentzer because he was winning title after title, including two of the first few IFBB Pro Grand Prix events contested. He followed his own system religiously, training on a four-day split routine (twice per week for each half of his body), doing only 2–4 total sets per muscle group, and pushing every set he did to the absolute limit.

Typically he'd start a set of barbell preacher curls with about 180 pounds; his brother Ray—another physical prodigy—spotted him. On his own Mike Mentzer would grind out 6–8 full positive and negative reps, moving the weight relatively slowly and being careful not to bounce it in the bottom position, a point at which the lower biceps tendon is particularly vulnerable.

Even with 20-inch upper arms, it's obvious that Mentzer would fail somewhere within this set, say, about halfway up on the eighth rep. At that point Ray would jump into action and give him just enough of a nudge on the bar to allow 2–3 forced reps to be completed past the point of failure. By then Mentzer's biceps were almost completely done in, but they weren't yet finished with this set.

After the forced reps, Ray would literally lift the barbell up to the top position for his brother; Mentzer would do negative reps, slowly lowering it while resisting the downward momentum of the bar as strongly as possible. After 3–4 of these negative reps, however, he couldn't even slow the bar down. At that point the set was concluded.

It's obvious that a muscle trained this hard on a single set isn't going to be able to absorb too many more sets. For bis Mentzer might do only one more exercise, dumbbell concentration curls, and that for only one set. On a particularly energetic day he might have done three total sets for biceps.

Larger muscle groups were in for three or four total sets, the theory being that the larger the muscle mass, the more work it needed. For example, a typical chest routine would consist of two sets of incline presses at the bench-press station of a Universal Gyms machine, sitting on an incline bench that set the buttocks only 2–3 inches off the gym floor, and two sets of pec deck flyes. The same pattern of full positive and negative reps, followed by forced reps, and concluded by negatives held true for every set in each movement.

Many top bodybuilders have criticized the Heavy Duty System of Mike Mentzer, as well as Arthur Jones's even shorter workout programs, and we'll summarize their criticisms.

- The system works well for genetically gifted bodybuilders like Mike and Ray Mentzer, but progressively less well as a bodybuilder's genetic gifts fall off.
- While the system does build muscle mass in genetically talented individuals, it doesn't concurrently develop the type of muscular detail that wins bodybuilding contests.
- The relative absence of warm-ups in the program leads to injuries.
- It's impossible for beginners or intermediates to follow this type of routine because they lack the mental and physical drive to push a set as far as is necessary to get results from it.
- Lack of variety of exercise choice can make the program boring to follow after a few months.
- Mental burnout is common among bodybuilders who follow this type of system because each set takes such extreme concentration in order to get anything out of it.

The most salient facts for you, the reader of this book, are that the heavy-duty program will probably not work at all well for you, and you'll probably incur a debilitating injury if you follow it for very long.

The System That Will Never Die

Arthur Jones had a lot of disciples. One of the most ardent was Ellington Darden, Ph.D., who is still writing popular books on Jones's version of the program with a new frill thrown in now and then. This type of book appeals to younger bodybuilders who don't want to put in the type of time and energy that the vast majority of successful male and female bodybuilders have, so they opt for a program that supposedly guarantees them the same results in one-third of the time.

Obviously, this approach sells a lot of books for Darden, but we defy him to produce a single bodybuilder who has reached national-level prominence while training with his methods. The most highly touted bodybuilder supposedly using Nautilus methods was Casey Viator, who won Mr. America at the age of 19, a record that will probably stand for all time. But Viator was already a huge, highly muscular bodybuilder before he moved to Florida to train under Jones, and Viator admits that he'd probably never have won Mr. America if he hadn't sneaked out at night to local gyms and put in more normal workouts to supplement what Jones had given him during the day.

Viator was also the subject of the famed "Colorado Experiment" during which, under scientifically verifiable circumstances, he gained more than 60 pounds of muscle in a single month. This experiment is often pointed to as proof of how effective heavy-duty training happens to be. Unfortunately, few individuals have talked directly with Viator to learn some of the behind-the-scenes factors that are never reported in the experiment.

To begin with, Viator was at an artificially low body weight when he began the experiment. He'd severed half of one of his fingers in an industrial accident, and a bad reaction to antibiotics had caused massive weight losses. He hadn't been training for several months and was lighter than usual anyway. Jones had offered him a generous cash bonus for every pound of muscle he gained, so Viator also starved himself for a couple of weeks prior to heading to Colorado, to reduce even more muscle mass.

Once in Colorado Viator did train less than 60 minutes per week and did gain more than 60 pounds of muscle mass in one month. But is that a real gain? No, because muscle memory is very strong, and once you've had a certain degree of muscle mass and allowed it to dissipate due to no workouts and poor diet, it comes crashing back onto your frame as soon as you resume former training and nutritional habits. Since there was a bonus offered for every pound of muscle gained, Viator was not remiss to be on the juice while this experiment was being conducted.

It would have been more impressive if Jones had taken an untrained athlete to Colorado with him and put just 10 pounds of muscle on the man, preferably 10 pounds of muscle that wasn't at least partially steroid-induced. But that doesn't make as good a batch of news clippings as Casey Viator gaining more than two pounds of muscle per day over a one-month period, does it?

Incidentally, the information in the foregoing section is well verified. Viator trained for several years at Gold's in Venice and is a close friend of one of the authors. He also has written an article about the Colorado Experiment, "Casey Comes Clean," which was published in 1980 in *Muscle & Fitness* magazine.

The New Breed

There are a couple of top bodybuilders today who use modifications of the Heavy Duty System quite effectively. One of these is Lee Labrada, who has won every major title but Mr. Olympia and has placed second in that event twice behind Lee Haney. Mike Mentzer was in his heyday when Labrada began training, and Mike's many articles in *Muscle Builder & Power* influenced his training philosophy.

Labrada does do low sets, although much higher than Mentzer suggested. He pushes every set at least to the point of failure, and he trains each muscle group less than twice per week. The individual changes Labrada has made involve warming up thoroughly prior to beginning each body part. After the warm-up he jumps to his highest weight for the first movement, taking the set to failure. After about a 45- to 60-second rest, he does a second set of the same movement with about 10 percent less weight to compensate for the fact that his muscles are a bit weaker after pushing or pulling so hard that first set. If a third set is to be done he'll drop the weight another 10 percent and also take that set at least to failure. When pushing a set past the failure point, Labrada prefers forced reps.

As far as the number of sets performed for each body part is concerned, let's let Lee Labrada explain that for himself: "I don't do the numbers of sets that other top pros do. I normally do three exercises per muscle group, three sets of 10 reps per set. I rarely do more than 10 sets for any muscle group, but the back I make

Incline dumbbell flyes supersetted with incline barbell presses are guaranteed to muscle up the upper pecs with as few as one preex superset.

Maxed out alternate dumbbell curls.

an exception, the reason being that the back is comprised of so many different muscles that I felt I had to do more exercises and more total sets to train it properly.

"When it comes to back training many bodybuilders go wrong because they think only of lats or lats and traps when they train their backs. Besides the trapezius and latissimus dorsi, there are many other muscles to worry about. You have the teres major and minor, the rhomboideus major and minor, and the infraspinatus.

"Then you have to think about the muscles in the middle of the back and the spinal erectors of the lower back. There are also multiple layers of muscles in the back that give that impressive look of power and density when developed to the maximum.

"Anyway you look at it, there are at least three major areas of the back to concentrate on: the lats, the traps and upper back, and the lower back. Obviously you can't do just a few chins or pulldowns and rows and expect to train the total back properly.

"Even if you do train just lats you have to worry about upper lats, the middle or belly of the lats, and the lower lats. There is no single exercise that will work all sections of the lats completely, so you should see the need for more than one exercise when training the lats. Think of it this way. If you normally do 10 sets for pecs, 10 sets for delts, and 10 sets for abs, serratus, and intercostals, that comes out to 30 sets. So are you going to train your large back muscles for only 8–10 sets? No way. You have to give the back equal treatment, and this means at least 25–30 total sets. But I personally do 12 sets for lats each workout.

"The exercises I normally do for my lats are medium-grip lat pulldowns to the chest, close-grip pulldowns to the chest using the triangle handle that gives me a narrow, parallel hands grip, and seated cable rows. For the upper back I prefer bent-over barbell rows, T-bar rows, and one-arm dumbbell rows. For traps I like dumbbell shrugs and for the lower back I alternate between hyperextensions and deadlifts done in a power back with the bar set at knee height. I find doing my deadlifts in this way allows me to use only my lower back muscles without placing any harmful stress on my hamstrings, fascia, or connective tissues.

"I don't do all of the exercises listed above in the same workout. Training instinctively, I choose the exercises I feel I need to do, mixing them up for each workout. I constantly change the number of reps I do, and even my workout style. My normal exercise style is to do 1–2 light warm-up sets, start with my heaviest set for 10 reps, reduce the weight by 10 percent for the second set, and then reduce the weight by 10 percent again for my third set. Because the potential for injury is greater on back exercises, on rowing movements and deadlifts I sometimes pyramid up in regular style to reduce the risk of injury. *Pyramiding* means to increase the weight and decrease the number of reps performed with each succeeding set.

"To give you an idea of how a typical back workout would go, here's a sample session I recently completed. Keep firmly in mind the fact that every back workout since this one has been at least a little different, since I prefer to shake everything up each session to keep my muscles from adapting to a rigidly set type of training program.

"I began the workout with three sets of 10 reps of the seated pulley rows. I like to use a handle that permits a narrow grip with my palms facing each other, although sometimes I'll use a straight bar for variety. I allow the weight to pull my upper body forward until it is parallel to the gym floor and my lats feel a strong stretch. As I pull the handle to the top of my abs I arch my sternum up and drop my shoulders to contract my lats. I hold the handle at the abs for a count of two—pulling my elbows back as far as I can—before allowing my upper body to be pulled forward again. One thing I never do is lean back as I pull the weight into my stomach; my upper body is perpendicular to the floor. On this exercise I do the reverse pyramid, the heaviest set first, the second set with 10 percent less, and the third set with 10 percent less than that. I try for 10 reps on each of the sets.

"After the pulley rows come lat pulldowns to the chest using a medium grip, three sets of 10 reps using the reverse pyramid. I feel a medium grip allows for a greater range of motion and gives the lats a better stretch than a wide grip. Again I feel it is important to arch the chest up and keep the shoulders down in order to contract the lats. I tilt my head back and lean back a few degrees, but I never allow my upper body to lean back too far the way some bodybuilders do. I sometimes do these with a bar that allows for a parallel-hands grip.

"Sometimes I do chins to the front instead of the pulldowns. I used to chin a lot in the past, but now I prefer the pulldown because I get a great range of motion and a better contraction in the lats. I chin only 20 percent of the time now. Whenever I do chins, I still use a medium-width grip.

"After the pulldowns my third lat exercise is more often than not the one-arm bent-over row with my knee resting on a bench. Again I do three sets of 10 reps, starting with my heaviest set first. I pull the weight to my waist—not to my rib cage—as this isolates the lower lats better. It is also important to pull the dumbbell back slightly as it comes up—not just straight up and down—when trying to contract the lat.

"I finish off my lats with either barbell bent-over rows or T-bar rows, whichever I feel like doing on that particular day. I usually alternate these two exercises every other back workout. I try to pull the bar—or the plates—up to my upper chest to stress the upper lats. I do three sets of 10 reps. To keep stress off my lower back I keep my knees bent and pull the weight smoothly and fluidly, without heaving or excessive cheating.

"That makes 12 total sets for my lats. Then I move to my traps. I normally do dumbbell shrugs, 5–6 sets of 10–12 reps. One thing I like to do with my dumbbell shrugs is hold the dumbbells with my palms facing forward rather than backward or to the sides. This allows me to throw more stress on the lower part of my traps, where I feel I need it, instead of on the top part near the ears. I shrug the dumbbells straight up and lower them straight down. I concentrate on keeping my arms straight and shrugging as high as I can. I hold at the top for a brief pause before lowering.

"This leaves just my lower back to train before I move on to work my biceps. I'll either do three sets of hyperextensions or three sets of deadlifts with the bar set in a power rack at knee height. If I do the hypers I do three sets of 15 reps. If I do the deadlifts I use the same poundage for each set and do three sets of 15 reps. And that completes my entire back workout."

Another bodybuilder who has adapted heavy-duty programs quite intelligently is the big British bodybuilder Dorian Yates, who won the Night of the Champions IFBB pro show in 1991 after placing second the previous year in his first professional competition. At 5'10" in height Yates cuts out at 235 pounds currently and is a threat in any pro event he enters, including Mr. Olympia, where he placed second to Lee Haney on his first try in '91.

Not counting warm-ups Yates's entire chest workout comprises only six sets, which is closer to Mike Mentzer's ideal workout for the same body part. But Yates does several lighter warm-

Milos Sarcev knows the importance of consistently taking his Gold's Gym brand vitamin-mineral supplements to help him max out his muscle mass.

up sets at higher repetition levels than his building sets.

DORIAN YATES'S WINNING NIGHT OF THE CHAMPIONS CHEST-TRAINING PROGRAM

Exercise	Warm-Ups	Building Sets
Bench Press or Decline Press	2–3 × 12	2 × 6–8
Incline Barbell Presses	1–2 × 10	2 × 6–8
Dumbbell Flyes (flat bench)	1–2 × 10	2 × 8–10

This doesn't say much about how the sets are performed, however, so let's have Yates tell you how he works his chest: "Let's assume I'm doing barbell bench presses. I start with a moderate weight and do 12 reps for a warm-up. The poundage is increased quite a bit for a second 12-rep warm-up and even more for a third 12-rep warm-up if I feel I'm still not completely ready for my heavy work.

"Once I'm fully warmed up I jump the weight up to the heaviest level I'll do during the entire workout and literally *grind* out 6–8 reps. These are all very full, strict repetitions with no back arch, no bouncing the bar off my chest, and nothing else in the way of cheating. The exercise cadence is decidedly slow, and I tend to lower the weight a bit more slowly than I press it back up. Take note of the fact that the last repetition I perform in this set is literally the last one I could humanly complete. It's that heavy, and it sometimes takes 10–12 seconds to press that last rep from my chest to straight arms before setting it back in the rack.

"After a very brief rest—mainly to reduce the poundage by about 10 percent, so it's not more than about 45 seconds—I do a second set of bench presses, again to complete failure in 6–8 reps.

"I do my inclines on a 30-degree bench because I feel that isolates the stress more on the upper pectorals and off of the anterior deltoids, although practically speaking you really can't isolate out the deltoids; you can just reduce how much they work to push up the weight. Again I do one or two warm-up sets, this time 10 reps on such a set. If I do two warm-ups there's a substantial jump in weight from the first to the second warm-up set.

"Using a medium-wide grip, as I also do on benches, I do a set to failure on incline presses with the heaviest possible weight, failing at between 6–8 repetitions. I'll rest about 45 seconds as the weight is reduced by 10 percent and immediately start doing another set to complete failure with the somewhat lighter weight. As with bench presses there is no cheating, because I want the working muscles to get all of the benefit of each chest movement, not the rest of my body.

"My final chest movement is flat-bench dumbbell flyes, but I do them completely differently from the other two exercises. On flyes I like to do descending, or drop, sets, so I'll line up three pairs of dumbbells, one very heavy, one a little lighter, and the third pair even a little lighter than the second pair. After a warm-up set or two I'll do triple drops with these dumbbells. This involves grabbing the heaviest pair and squeezing out 8–10 reps to failure. Then I'll drop that pair, immediately grab the medium-weighted pair of dumbbells, lie back on the bench again, and force out another 8–10 reps to the failure point. Those weights are quickly discarded and the lightest dumbbells are picked up for a final grueling 8–10 reps to failure. For most blokes this would be enough, but I'll rest for a couple of minutes and repeat the same triple-drop scheme for flat-bench flyes. And *that* is the end of my chest workout."

Both Labrada and Yates have made sensible individual modifications of the Heavy Duty System of training for mass and strength. You can't fault either individual on mass or power because both possess the qualities in spades. Yates in particular is very strong, capable of doing 8 reps in the bench press with 440 pounds in ultrastrict form!

A Note on Nutrition

Mike Mentzer was well known for believing that a calorie was a calorie regardless of where it came from, and his precontest diet often featured such delicacies as cheese Danish and other forbidden goodies. While this eating system did work well for Mentzer because he could get as cut as anyone in his day, the new breed of heavy-duty athletes is much more scientific about their diets, particularly prior to competitions.

We'll be covering diet in detail in Chapter 11, and you can learn how serious bodybuilders eat when you read that chapter. For now, believe us, they don't eat cheese Danish during a peaking cycle!

7
The Newest Rage

IFBB Pro Mr. International Andreas Cahling has been most responsible for popularizing the routine in which each muscle group is trained only once per week. Let's have him tell you about it: "A whopping majority of bodybuilders are vitally concerned about packing on tons of quality muscle mass, and from deep impatience most would like to develop Olympian-level competitive physiques almost overnight!

"Certainly no one throughout the history of bodybuilding has been able to make such rapid gains. Rome wasn't built in a day, and neither is a quality physique. Granted, some men and women make faster gains than others who are less well-endowed genetically, but anyone can improve muscle mass and quality, albeit slowly, if he trains with weights and eats properly.

"Of course, while I'm still seeking an invitation to the Mr. Olympia, the crème de la crème of pro bodybuilding shows, any expert will tell

Bodybuilding knows no size or national limitations. Barely over five feet tall, France's Thierry Pastel has won IFBB Pro Grand Prix titles with ease. Those upper arms are nearly 20-inchers.

you I've already done exceptionally well in the world's most difficult sport considering the limited genetic talent I had when I started systematic bodybuilding. I still haven't given up on receiving an Olympia invitation, since I'm only 38 and have 10–15 more years of steady physical improvement to look forward to.

"The correct approach to achieving a great physique—particularly if you follow it consistently—can be reduced to this elementary mathematical formula:

$$T + N + M + R = G$$

In this formula T represents training, N nutrition, M mental approach, R recovery, and G muscle growth. It should be obvious that when you increase the values of T, N, M, and R—even a little at a time—the value of G goes up markedly, and often rapidly.

"*Flex* and other bodybuilding magazines have run scores of articles on training, nutrition, and mental approach, but most have almost completely neglected the recovery factor in the equation. Yet the R factor is probably the most important single component in your bodybuilding success formula. Unless you recover completely between training sessions, it is impossible to make gains in muscle mass. Let's discuss the R factor in sufficient detail for you to be able to utilize it productively in your own training programs."

Training Frequency

"The frequency with which he seriously pumps iron is a vital component in every champion bodybuilder's physical success formula," Cahling continues. "In the early weeks and months

Czechoslovakia's Pavol Jablonicky has yet to make his mark as a pro, but he has two IFBB amateur world titles to his credit, one as a light-heavyweight and another a year later in the heavyweight division.

of involvement in the activity a book, magazine article, or coach can take care of this question for you. Almost universally, however, the recommendation calls for three full-body training sessions per week with workouts scheduled on non-consecutive days such as Mondays, Wednesdays, and Fridays.

"Such a program works well at first—it's even worked acceptably for a handful of international-level competitive bodybuilders in recent years—because the muscles are thoroughly stimulated on each workout day and then allowed to rest for 48 hours or more for recovery and growth before that body part is hit again.

"Rest between workouts is vitally important because growth in muscle mass, quality, and strength occurs *only after* a trained muscle group has fully recovered from a hard session of iron. Because the muscles pump up become briefly enlarged from a greater-than-normal influx of blood—during a workout, a lot of beginning and intermediate bodybuilders mistakenly conclude that growth occurs in the middle of each iron-slinging session. Wrong! In reality growth only occurs two to three days later.

"Exercise physiologists have experimented thoroughly with the workout-muscle-hypertrophy cycle and concluded that new tissue growth begins about 48 hours after a workout, reaching a peak growth rate at 72 hours. The process usually completes itself after about 96 hours have elapsed. For this reason most top bodybuilders follow a very popular split routine in which separate areas of the body are trained over a three-day period, followed by one full day of rest before the cycle is repeated. This is popularly called the three-on/one-off split, and it allows approximately 96 hours of rest time between training sessions for each major muscle group.

"At the risk of sounding heretical I have evolved a very successful split routine in which I bomb each muscle complex only once per week on a six-day split—I take Sundays off. This adds up to 168 hours of rest between workouts for each muscle complex. Here's how I am currently splitting everything up for that type of routine:

Monday: back

Tuesday: delts, abs

Wednesday: quadriceps

Thursday: upper arms, forearms

Friday: chest, calves

Saturday: glutes, hamstrings, spinal erectors

"I created this split based on the theory that recovery ability slows with age, and I'm getting to be a middle-aged bodybuilder. But this 'lazy man's' split has worked very well for me. I used it after a full five-year layoff from the gym to devote myself to business affairs, and I was able to get into shape with this type of program in just over a year to place fourth in the IFBB Niagara Falls Pro Invitational.

"Anyway, let's get back to beginners and intermediates following a three-day-per-week full-body program. Training intensity must be gradually augmented in two ways—systematically increasing the amount of weight used in each exercise and/or progressively adding more sets to the total program. These methods should work well until you arrive at such an extensive training session that it requires more than 45–60 minutes to complete. Past the 45- to 60-minute point in the gym you'll simply begin to run out of stored training energy, and over the last few sets of your routine you will be forced to expend proportionately less energy than is possible on exercises nearer the beginning of the workout.

"You will usually reach this breaking point three to six months after taking up serious training with heavy iron, although the exact point at which it happens will vary from one individual to another. What you do need to know is that this point marks your intensity transition upward to a split routine in which you work out four days per week rather than three."

FOUR-DAY SPLIT

Monday/Thursday

Exercise	Sets	Reps
Hanging Leg Raises	3-4	15-20
Bench Presses	5	12-5*
Machine Incline Presses	5	12-5*
Parallel Bar Dips	3	maximum
Seated Low-Pulley Rows	5	15-6*
Front Lat Pulldowns	5	15-6*
Rotating Dumbbell Shrugs	4	15-20
Seated Alternate Dumbbell Curls	4	12-6*
Dumbbell Concentration Curls	4	12-6*
Incline Barbell Triceps Extensions	4	12-6*
Close-Grip Pulley Pushdowns	4	15-8*
Close-Grip Barbell Reverse Curls	4	12-6*
Donkey Calf Raises	5-6	15-20

Tuesday/Friday Exercise	Sets	Reps
Twisting Incline Sit-Ups	3–4	20–25
Seated Presses Behind Neck	6	15–5*
Seated Dumbbell Bent-Over Laterals	4	8–10
Standing Dumbbell Side Laterals	4	8–10
Cable Upright Rows	4	10–12
Leg Extensions	4	15–20
Angled Leg Presses	6	25–10*
Lying Leg Curls	4–5	12–15
Russian Hyperextensions	4	12–15
One-Arm Dumbbell Wrist Curls	4	15–20
Seated Calf Raises	5–6	10–15

*Pyramid reps and weights.

"In the four-day split each major muscle group is trained twice per week, versus three weekly training days on a full-body break-in program. This is a *very* significant factor because it results in longer rest and recuperation periods between bombing runs on each muscle complex. This factor alone—additional recovery time between body-part workouts—will accelerate your bodybuilding gains as long as you are training intensely while closely monitoring your nutritional intake.

" 'But who has won anything training only four days per week?' you might rightfully ask. The premier example of such a champion would be hypermassive Lee Haney, winner of the last eight Mr. Olympia titles! According to Large Lee, 'I made tremendous gains on a four-day split in 1982, right up to a couple of months before winning my Heavyweight/Overall Nationals and Heavyweight World Championships, thereby gaining a pro card and initiating a successful and lucrative bodybuilding career. Even today I'll occasionally slip in a few productive off-season weeks of four-day splitting. I know of no other split routine so conducive to fostering more complete recovery between workouts and thereby encouraging humongous muscle-mass development!' "

FOUR-DAY SPLIT ROUTINES

Alternative A

Monday/Thursday	Tuesday/Friday
Abdominals	Legs
Chest	Lower back
Upper back	Biceps
Shoulders	Forearms
Triceps	Calves

Alternative B

Monday/Thursday	Tuesday/Friday
Abdominals	Quadriceps
Chest	Hamstrings
Upper back	Lower back
Shoulders	Upper arms
Calves	Forearms

Cahling continues, "I've known scores of superstar bodybuilders who have spent years following a four-day split routine, and inevitably each has exceptional muscle mass to show for his efforts. For two years early in my own bodybuilding career I trained similarly using basic exercises. That period was superproductive and I strongly recommend a four-day-per-week split routine to all intermediate and low-advanced bodybuilders.

"Be patient enough to train hard and consistently on this program for a year or two, and you'll build the solid foundation of muscle mass and recovery ability that can ultimately result in a much more outstanding competitive physique than if you'd trained seven days per week relying mainly on isolation movements.

"There are many other split routines that offer dramatically higher training intensity, but unless you're in a position where you can train and rest literally all day, or you want to saturate your system with growth drugs, these more advanced splits will quickly break you down, lead to an overtrained state, and stop all of your gains in their tracks. These verboten routines include six-day splits in which muscle groups are trained either two or three times per week, and all double-split or triple-split programs.

"Unless you are trying to rip up for a competition, aerobic training will also retard gains in muscle mass regardless of how careful you are with your weight workouts, nutrition, recovery procedures, and mental approach. If you're the type who requires a lot of precontest aerobic training, hop on the bike for 10–15 minutes three days a week off-season to maintain at least a low level of aerobic conditioning. Then it won't hurt so badly when you work back up to a full precontest aerobics schedule once you're in a peaking cycle.

"One very sane off-season and precontest split is the three-on/one-off routine I have already mentioned. It is widely popular among successful competitors, providing undeniable evidence that

Canada's Nimrod King has won plenty of his own pro titles with his fine-boned, massive physique. Look at the difference between the girth of his tiny wrists compared with his massive upper arms.

Two young lions on the loose: Michael Ashley (L) and Shawn Ray have both won the Arnold Schwarzenegger Pro Classic held under IFBB auspices every spring in Columbus, Ohio. Ray has placed as high as third in Mr. Olympia.

it works well for almost all advanced bodybuilders. The reason it works so well is it allows just under 96 hours of recovery time between training sessions for each muscle group.

"A couple of variations exist for this three-on/one-off split. In the first an extra rest day is scheduled, making it a three-on/two-off program; in the other an extra workout day is added, making the program a four-on/one-off split routine. Both variations seem to work well for certain bodybuilders, though the three-on/two-off seems better suited for intermediate and advanced athletes. The four-on/one-off split works most effectively for very high-level contest competitors.

"For the sake of illustration, here is a typical three-on/one-off split routine used by many top bodybuilders at Gold's Gym in Venice where I train:

Day 1: chest, back, abs

Day 2: legs, calves

Day 3: shoulders, upper arms, forearms

Day 4: rest, then repeat cycle on Day 5

Obviously, this routine goes on and on, and many weekend days must be used for workouts, something that doesn't appeal to too many family-oriented bodybuilders."

How Heavy to Go?

Cahling goes on, "The solution to this question relies on answers to the following three queries:

- How relatively strong are you on basic exercises?
- How good is your muscular endurance on high-rep sets of either basic or isolation movements?
- How injury-prone are you, even when using perfect form on every set of every exercise?

"It's axiomatic that *you have to lift big to get big*. This contention is definitely true up to a point, just as long as you can remain free of injuries as you push or pull the really heavy iron. But it *is* possible to develop a great degree of muscle mass using only moderately heavy poundages if you use all of the high-intensity training techniques at your disposal.

"Regardless of how physically powerful you might be, *always* take care to thoroughly warm up prior to each heavy-iron pumping session. A good warm-up, a quick exercise pace—no more than 60–90 seconds of rest between sets—and perfect exercise form will keep you injury-free 99.9 percent of the time when you're hoisting heavy iron.

"When adding muscle to your frame it's wisest to rely primarily on basic movements, because they provide the most complete stimulation to the muscles. Assuming you are following a four-day split, virtually all of your movements can be basic exercises.

"As a bodybuilder matures he learns to get a lot more out of a set with a particular weight than a novice bodybuilder. He has also learned instinctively which rep ranges work best on each muscle group. All of my leg muscles, for example, respond best to reps of 15 or more, sometimes as many as 40–50 per set. Once I had learned this high-rep technique for leg work, I soon noticed that my knees ached less than when I had forced them unnecessarily to deal with heavy poundages, and the muscles grew like lightning.

"On the other end of the scale, my shoulder, chest, and arm muscles seem to respond to more 'normal' rep ranges of 8–10. The point is, it takes time to determine which repetition ranges will work best for your various body parts, but once you have found them you'll cut training injuries to their lowest possible level."

Other Factors Affecting Recovery

Andreas Cahling says, "Excessive numbers of sets for each body part are pure death to a hard-training, highly enthusiastic young bodybuilder seeking fast muscle gains. Because most younger men and women have their enthusiasm thermostats set too high, they end up performing two to three times the total sets necessary to properly stimulate a muscle group. A few days or weeks later they become overtrained from the excessive load volume and cease to make any gains in new muscle mass. In some cases they may become so overtrained that their development actually starts to regress!"

The trick to choosing set volumes to encourage between-workout recovery is to train hard and heavy but limit total sets between the parameters shown in the following table.

SET VOLUME

Body Part	Beginner	Intermediate	Advanced	Contest-Level
Quads	4–5	6–8	10–12	12–15
Hamstrings	2–3	3–4	5–6	6–8
Glutes	—	3–4	4–5	6–8
Erectors	3–4	4–5	6–7	8–10
Lats	4–5	6–8	10–12	12–15
Traps	2–3	3–4	5–6	6–8
Pectorals	4–5	6–8	10–12	12–15
Deltoids	3–4	4–5	6–7	8–10
Biceps	3–4	4–5	5–6	6–8
Triceps	4–5	5–6	6–7	8–10
Forearms	2*	3*	4*	5*
Abdominals	3	4–5	6–7	8–10
Calves	4	5–6	6–8	8–10

*On forearm movements do the indicated number of sets for *both* flexors and extensors.

Canadian Steve Brisbois won the IFBB World Bantamweight Championship as an amateur weighing only 140 pounds. As a pro, he competes successfully in the 165-pound range.

Bob Paris—overall NPC National Champion and IFBB Heavyweight World Champion—came out publicly recently as a homosexual bodybuilder with a "husband."

Milos Sarcev keeps his abs sharp.

"Lack of sleep and rest sabotages all rising bodybuilders at one time or another," Cahling continues, "particularly if they happen to be party animals who stay out until 3:00 A.M. dancing and drinking. Sleep recharges your energy batteries, enabling you to get a good workout the following day. Sleep is also the period of time when your muscles actually grow; human growth hormone levels are most highly elevated approximately two hours after one has fallen soundly asleep.

"If you don't train hard, you don't grow. If you train hard and fail to sleep and rest properly, you also don't grow. And if you train and sleep perfectly—but forget to eat—you also won't make appreciable gains in muscle mass and shape. In case no one has told you yet, successful competitive bodybuilders live dedicated, highly regimented lives or they just don't become good at their sport!

"Poor nutritional practices will sink any serious bodybuilder's boat. Ask 100 of the top stars in the sport, and virtually all will tell you that diet and training bear 50–50 responsibility for success or failure in competitive bodybuilding. Train all you want but fail to eat like a serious athlete, and you're unlikely to make even marginal gains. Eat all you want without monitoring your diet, and you have a good chance of ending up looking like Jabba the Hutt in the Star Wars film, *Return of the Jedi*.

"Several excellent nutrition books are available, including *Supercut* (Contemporary, 1985), the *Gold's Gym Nutrition Bible* (Contemporary, 1986), and *Sliced* (Contemporary, 1991). They can be found in quality bookstores or via mail-order ads in many muscle mags. As well, scores of specific nutrition articles are published monthly in *Flex* and a variety of other bodybuilding-oriented magazines.

Jan Tana Pro Classic winner Sue Gafner is recognizable from every angle, even when her face isn't in view.

"I could easily give you 100 pages of nutritional 'do's and don'ts,' but I'll limit my comments to the following key points:

DON'T

- Consume junk foods high in refined sugar and/or white flour
- Drink alcoholic beverages
- Eat excessive amounts of animal fats (have visible fat trimmed before you purchase the meat)
- Drink soft drinks (not even diet sodas)
- Fry foods (broiling is much better)

DO

- Investigate the ovo-vegetarian lifestyle, which has done wonders for me. Otherwise, eat a little protein several times a day. Consume eggs (particularly the whites), lean cuts of beef, fish, and poultry (never fried). Your body can digest and assimilate only about 20–25 grams of protein per feeding, so you need not take in huge protein meals each day.
- Eat fresh fruits and vegetables, as close to their raw state as possible
- Eat a little vegetable fat in the form of seeds, nuts, and safflower oil (about a

Benfatto gets serious on a set of leg extensions. Note how he dresses for the weather, it having been a tad cold in Gold's Venice at 6:00 one morning.

tablespoon per day) to maintain skin, hair, and nerve health

- Consume a chelated multiple-mineral and multiple-vitamin supplement with each meal (multipacks of these supplements are also good)
- Eat at least three meals per day, preferably five or six. Avoid large meals; smaller meals are digested and assimilated more efficiently by the body.
- Take one or two multipurpose digestive enzyme capsules or tablets each time you eat
- Drink plenty of pure water each day (at least 8–10 glasses full). For purity, I like steam-produced, distilled, mountain spring water best.

"It will take at least one or two years to work out a daily diet that helps you build quality muscle mass at the fastest possible rate. But once you've discovered it, you're well on your way to a superior physique!"

Using Your God-Given Mind

"Your mental approach can make or break you when it comes to packing on quality muscle mass," Andreas Cahling concludes. "It's actually possible to psych yourself into making fast gains in muscle mass if you keep a consistently positive mind, free of distractions. Keep calm, cool, collected, and confident, and mass will come. By worrying constantly about how fast you're making gains—or allowing outside stresses to intrude on your workout time—you can remain a pencilneck for the rest of time.

"I'd personally like to gain greater muscle mass, so I'm constantly confident and calm. What do *you* want? If it's added muscle mass, you know how to achieve it!"

Bob Cicherillo—seated pulley rows.

8
The Hard-Gainer Approach

Let's define a hard-gainer so you can see if you qualify as one. A hard-gainer is usually a naturally weak and ectomorphic (naturally skinny and small-boned) individual. He or she is also likely to be high-strung enough emotionally that nervous energy is constantly being burned off. And it's also very common for hard-gainers to be chronically busy men and women who habitually miss some of their scheduled meals.

Out of 100 bodybuilders who take up weight workouts, 10–15 percent will be moderate hard-gainers, and about 5 percent will be full-blown, severe hard-gainers. Both types of hard-gainers are usually seduced at some point by magazine articles or well-meaning, experienced bodybuilders to follow the complicated routines of champions who make easy gains. On such high-intensity, high-volume workouts, hard-gainers very quickly overtrain. They will never make gains in muscle mass and strength, regardless of how hard and religiously they train, until they have remedied the overtraining problem and follow a more sane approach to training.

Here's good news for hard-gainers: with the training and dietary programs outlined in this chapter, you will make acceptable gains in muscle mass and contour. You will also build up your recovery abilities between workouts. Once these basic training and nutrition programs have been mastered and followed consistently for six months to a year, you will no longer be classified as a hard-gainer. You will then have metamorphosed into an average bodybuilder who can actually make gains on a more normal training-nutrition schedule.

With time you might work up to the level at which you can begin to win or place high in contests—local affairs at first, then later state and regional shows, and perhaps even national events. *That* is something to look forward to!

Training Frequency

The training frequency of a true hard-gainer is based on the system Andreas Cahling outlined in Chapter 7, which consists of training each muscle group only once per week. But Cahling does six workouts per week, taking only Sundays off. This allows him to work only one major muscle group each training day; it works well for him, but it wouldn't allow sufficient recovery time between workout days for a hard-gainer, so we have to modify Cahling's system somewhat.

Like Cahling you should still train each muscle group once per week, but spread each group over only three nonconsecutive workouts each week, keeping weekends totally free of physically demanding activities. Here's one good way to split your routine for this type of hard-gainer training program:

Monday: chest, shoulders, triceps, calves

Wednesday: quads, hamstrings, lower back, buttocks

Friday: upper back, biceps, forearms, abdominals

If you carefully analyze each of these daily workouts you'll notice that you're training body parts that *should* be worked as a unit because they are all synergistic. You need your shoulders and triceps to do bench presses for your chest, and you require your biceps and forearms to do seated low-pulley rows for your lats. You won't make the mistake of working some muscle groups twice per week, as would be the case if you matched chest, delts, and biceps one day and back, triceps, and forearms another. Training something twice in one week very quickly leads to overtraining.

All Basic Movements

Your next decision as a hard-gainer is to pick only basic movements for use in your mass-building routines. Pick two for large muscle groups like chest, back, and legs, plus perhaps shoulders which are a little more complex, and one for smaller body parts like biceps, triceps, forearms, abdominals, and calves.

Do not under any circumstances get involved in doing foo-foo isolation exercises like concentration curls for your biceps, dumbbell side laterals for your deltoids, or leg extensions for your quadriceps.

Here is a good solid list of the best basic movements for each of your major body parts. (I exclude the neck because it seems to come up on its own as a result of hard training for adjacent areas such as shoulders and upper back or upper chest.)

Body Part	Basic Exercises
Quads-buttocks	Squats, Angled Leg Presses
Hamstrings	Stiff-Legged Deadlifts
Lower back	Deadlifts
Lats	Seated Low-Pulley Rows, Front Lat Machine Pulldowns
Traps	Barbell Shrugs
Delts	Standing Barbell Presses, Barbell Upright Rows
Pecs	Bench Presses, Incline Barbell Presses
Biceps	Standing Barbell Curls (medium to wide grip)
Triceps	Close-Grip Bench Presses
Forearms	Barbell Reverse Curls (medium to narrow grip)
Calves	Standing Calf Machine Toe Raises
Abdominals	Hanging Leg Raises

Keep Total Sets Down

To avoid overtraining you will have to do no more than three total sets of each movement in your routine. We suggest one moderately heavy poundage for 12 reps. Add weight to the bar and do a heavy weight for 10 reps, then add weight to the bar and force out a very heavy effort for 6–8 reps on the final set. Do this for every movement even when you do two for a complex muscle group.

You shouldn't have any trouble plugging the recommended basic movements into the three-day program presented earlier. Then just do three sets of each exercise, giving every set 110 percent effort, and you'll gain some muscle mass if your diet is also correct and your mental approach is consistently positive (see the discussion on mental approach in Chapter 12).

You'll need to be careful to plug unnecessary nervous-energy leaks and get sufficient rest throughout the day plus 8–9 hours of sleep each night so your body can recover and grow.

Strict Attention to High-Calorie Diet

You should attempt to eat a complete meal as often as possible, for a bare minimum of six times daily and preferably up to eight meals each day. If you're up for 16 waking hours, you can eat a well-planned meal every 2 hours, a total of eight for that day. Since it takes your stomach and digestive tract just about 2 hours to digest and make ready into assimilable form the food you consume at each sitting, eight meals is probably the maximum you will want to eat each 16-hour day.

Bev Francis, born in Australia and originally a world champion five consecutive years in power lifting, has placed both third and second many times in Ms. Olympia without winning. Here she shows her form on stiff-armed pulldowns. Bev owns her own Gold's Gym on Long Island, New York.

This may sound a little kinky, but if you're really dedicated you can set your bedside alarm clock to ring at two more well-spaced times during the night. Have two complete but quickly consumable meals ready at your bedside, and wake up specifically to eat a couple more times in the middle of the night. One nocturnal feeding would make quite a difference, but two would put your nutrition program into outer-space trajectory.

You'd wear out your teeth and gums if you attempted to consume 8–10 meals each 24-hour period, so many of your "meals" will be liquid in nature or, at worst, liquids washing down concentrated amino-acid-formula capsules. It's much easier to drink calories than it is to eat them, as you'd soon find out if you timed yourself drinking 1,000 calories of orange juice one evening, then timed yourself eating 1,000 calories' worth of whole oranges the following night. Yet the relative nutritional values of the orange juice and whole fruit have negligible differences in them as long as the juice is freshly squeezed.

Make up your mind right now that you aren't going to miss any more meals. If there is a chance in hell that you're going to miss a meal, mix up a tasty and nutritious protein shake to take along with you in a thermos bottle as a meal replacement. You'll find that when conveniently and quickly mixed in a blender, shakes will become one of your best friends in bodybuilding.

The protein powder of highest biological quality—and also the one which costs the most—is made exclusively from powdered egg albumen (egg whites). Probably a more economical, but still effective, protein powder would be one that mixed both milk and egg sources. Try to avoid vegetable-based protein powders such as those made from soybeans and sesame seeds.

Here's a great high-protein milkshake you can blend up and keep cool in a thermos bottle for most of the day:

- 8–10 ounces raw full-fat milk (raw milk is best, but pasteurized milk can be used in its absence)
- 2–3 heaping tablespoons of milk and egg protein powder
- 2–3 pieces of soft fruit (peach, pear, berries of various types) to add flavor

Hard-gainers will find that egg whites are first on the scale of protein assimilability, and they may want to add 2–3 whole eggs to their protein shakes from time to time. Just be careful to soft boil the eggs before blending them into the drink. Raw eggs destroy the vital B-complex vitamin called *avidin*, while soft boiling the eggs negates this problem. Soft-boiled eggs will give a nicer consistency to some of your shakes, particularly if you're not the type of bodybuilder who likes to blend ice cream into your concoctions.

For the most part your liquid of choice should be milk. The protein in milk (called *casein*) is nature's second-best form of protein in terms of its assimilability by the body.

Usually whole raw milk is the best choice, although low-fat and nonfat raw milk are also good substitutes, just lower in total calories than the full-fat variety. Pasteurized milk is lower on the scale of usefulness in a hard-gainer's digestive system than raw milk and raw-milk products such as cheese, cottage cheese, and yogurt.

Many individuals are allergic to milk and suffer from symptoms such as immediate lethargy and sleepiness, painful stomach bloating, sore joints and muscles (for no reason other than drinking the milk), and generally bloated tissues throughout the body. In this case the allergy is to lactose, the sugar found in milk, and the allergy occurs because an individual has lost the ability to manufacture sufficient lactase to digest the lactose. If this is the case and you insist on consuming milk, several over-the-counter preparations are available which contain lactase (the digestive enzyme) to help you easily digest milk.

Generally speaking, you'll be more allergic to milk if you are older or are of a darker race. In fact, the darker the race, the more likely you are to be milk intolerant. But even if you have an allergy, you can still consume hard cheeses, cottage cheese, and yogurt, all of which have the lactose removed when these foods are processed.

In the absence of milk, most hard-gainers prefer freshly squeezed juice—either fruit or vegetable is good—as a solvent to mix protein drinks and to swallow supplements.

Even with the shakes, eating can definitely become a chore for a hard-gainer. It's essential to thoroughly chew your food so it is mixed with enzymes from your mouth before it enters the digestive tract proper. Make mealtimes long enough so you can choose foods according to your appetite, because your body has an unerring way of choosing to be hungry for the precise nutrients that you require at a particular time.

You'll find it much easier to eat if you arrange your meals attractively and are sure that everything is as fresh as possible when it's placed on the table. Follow these rules and you should be able to consume enough calories at each meal to fuel your bodybuilding training efforts.

Even small hard-gaining women will require 4,000 calories of food per day every day. Smaller men can consume 5,000 calories, with larger individuals usually exceeding 7,000 calories daily. Gary Strydom has been eating a minimum of 7,000 calories daily for the past 5–6 years, so it can be done quite comfortably, particularly if much of your intake is in the form of food supplements.

Strydom consumes bottle after bottle of amino acids throughout the year and particularly large quantities of them during an 8- to 10-week peaking cycle. He consumes free-form aminos 30 minutes prior to each meal and ingests branched-chain aminos (which make up the bulk of muscle tissue and aid between-workout recovery) following every workout, whether it's with weights or an aerobic session, or even posing practice. Such heavy consumption of amino acids obviously would cost him a fortune, but he's always had a sponsorship, first from Weider and now from the WBF, whom he represents so ably.

Strydom is also big on vitamins, minerals, and enzyme supplements. At a minimum he recommends 2–3 multipacks of vitamins and minerals with meals each day, and he takes plenty of extra water-soluble vitamins with each meal. The water-soluble vitamins (B complex and C) are constantly eliminated from the body through the urinary tract, so they must be equally constantly resupplied in the diet. Strydom is also careful to take the electrolyte minerals calcium, potassium, and magnesium with each meal. Obviously, he doesn't need to take supplementary sodium, even though it's an electrolyte, because most diets have sodium in excess unless a bodybuilder is specifically controlling his or her intake over the last few days prior to competition.

Recommended solid foods include whole eggs, lean beef (preferably ground round, broiled, so you don't have to chew it so thoroughly), and broiled poultry (remove the overly fatty skin prior to cooking and stick to white meats, which are lower in fats than darker poultry meats). Unless he or she has a taste for it, no hard-gainer needs to waste time on fish, because it is so low in calories. If you choose to make specific room in a meal for fish, supplement it with higher-fat flesh foods.

Complex carbohydrates should be next on the list, and the best are baked potatoes (you can occasionally get away with butter or sour-cream topping, but be a real bodybuilder and consume them dry most of the time); yams; rice; and millet or whole grains such as wheat, rye, and corn, usually in the form of cereals (topped with milk and fruit) or breads. Cornmeal muffins are a great weight-gain food for hard-gainers, so we hope you can develop a taste for them.

More simple carbs can also be consumed in the forms of various fruits and vegetables with their calories stored in underground tubers (carrots, beets, radishes). At no time should you waste space in your digestive system on high-sugar junk foods, because they just take the place of a food that would actually aid in building muscle.

Hard-gainers have no reason to indulge in alcohol, even though it is high in calories, because it dulls the appetite and makes you a very foolish person in public. An occasional beer isn't going to kill you, but avoid wines and hard liquors, particularly when liquor is mixed into tasty cocktails with little umbrellas floating in them; you can drink them to excess almost without realizing you're inebriated until you try to stand up and walk normally. A man or woman drunk on alcohol usually has no thoughts of consuming real food for muscle-building purposes.

If you want junk food we recommend an occasional pizza or pasta excursion. Pizza, with all of its cheese, is particularly high in calories. Japanese and Chinese food, in contrast, is relatively low in calories, and when you eat it out you'll be hungry for real food within an hour.

Here is a suggested daily menu for 10 meals, including two for which you'll have to set your alarm in the middle of the night:

Meal 1: cheese omelette with whole eggs, whole-grain toast with butter, as much milk as you can comfortably drink, multipack of supplements

Meal 2: protein drink, water-soluble vitamins, electrolyte minerals

Meal 3: two or three homemade hamburgers with all the trimmings you like, potato

Despite being a slow gainer, Vince Taylor has placed third in the Mr. Olympia twice. He may win it soon, particularly if Lee Haney now retires with his eight consecutive Olympia victories.

salad, all the milk you can drink, multipack of supplements

Meal 4: protein drink, water-soluble vitamins, electrolyte minerals. (This should be the preworkout meal, so it's quickly and easily digested; you might like to mix in more fruit than usual in this protein drink for the simple carbs needed in a workout.)

Meal 5: homemade pizza with plenty of extra cheese and lots of ground meat on top, all the milk you can drink, multipack of vitamins and minerals

Meal 6: ham-and-cheese omelette with whole eggs, hot whole-grain cereal with fruit and milk, all the milk you can drink, electrolyte minerals, water-soluble vitamins

Meal 7: cold cuts (particularly cooked meat left over from previous meals), boiled or deviled eggs, all the milk you can comfortably hold, final multipack of vitamins and minerals for the day

Meal 8: another meat-and-cheese omelette or meat and cheese sandwiched on whole-grain bread, all the milk you can hold, water-soluble vitamins, electrolyte minerals

Meal 9 (middle of the night): protein drink

Meal 10 (also middle of the night): another protein drink

One final food supplement I haven't mentioned yet are digestive enzymes, which *must* be taken with every meal or protein drink. These should be mixed enzymes, particularly with papain and bromelain in them but also with peptide hydrochloric acid included if possible. Digestive enzyme tablets (you'll need to take 3–4, depending on the amount of food consumed) will help you process and make ready for assimilation into muscle tissue much more protein, as well as more carbohydrates to fuel your workouts.

As you've no doubt noticed, when you are a hard-gainer you really have to eat a lot and at set intervals during the day or you'll end up being a no-gainer in the long run. If you can form good eating habits, however, you're halfway to developing the type of physique that you dream about. Soon your digestive system will become so efficient and your recovery ability will improve to the point where you may be able to move up to the four-day split routine Lee Haney recommends. Then you can take the "hard-gainer" sign from around your neck and become a real bodybuilder who makes gains like most of the rest in the sport. It's a time well worth working for!

A legend meets a legend. Eight-time Mr. Olympia Lee Haney gets some sage words of advice from Reg Park, the first man to win four Mr. Universe titles.

9
Key Exercises

Thirty-four key mass- and power-building exercises are fully described and precisely illustrated in this chapter. Almost every key movement has at least one variation.

Carefully study the descriptions and photos of each exercise presented in this chapter. This is important since even experienced bodybuilders may have picked up little ways of cheating on movements which can greatly reduce their effectiveness. Beginners should attempt to do the exercises correctly from the very first, because it is difficult to break bad habits two, three, or more years down the road.

We are talking about optimum biomechanics with each key exercise—the precise form that places the maximum possible productive stress on the intended muscles and minimum possible harmful stress on the rest of the body. If you follow to the letter the directions we give you, you will always have safe, productive workouts with minimum risk of injury.

Leg Exercises

Squats

Values: The squat is probably the greatest single mass- and power-building movement in existence. It directly stresses the quadriceps muscles on the fronts of your thighs, the buttocks, and the spinal erectors. Secondary stress is placed on the hamstrings, the abdominal muscles (which help support the torso when under a heavy load), and the trapezius muscles. Heavy squatting places so much stress on your metabolic system that it can turn your metabolism anabolic, not only in your legs but also in your upper body. And the heavy breathing induced by high-rep squatting has a beneficial effect on expanding your rib cage.

Starting Position: Place a barbell on a squat rack so the bar rests 4–6 inches lower than shoulder level and load up the bar with an appropriate number of plates. Be sure to place the collars tightly on each end of the bar to keep the weights from shifting during the movement. Step under the bar and position the middle of it across your shoulders even with the top of your deltoid muscles. You'll find that the bar will rest more comfortably in this position if you squeeze your shoulder blades together and hump up your trapezius muscles to make a pad for the bar. Set your feet about shoulder-width apart directly beneath the bar and grasp the bar with your hands midway between your shoulder and the

Squat—start/finish.

Squat—midpoint.

inner plates on each side. Straighten your legs to remove the bar from the rack and step one pace backward with the load across your shoulders. Set your feet about shoulder-width apart again, with your toes angled slightly outward. Tense all of the muscles of your back and abdomen in order to keep your torso as erect as possible during the movement. Pick a point on the wall in front of you at head level and focus your eyes on it during the movement to keep your head up and back straight.

Movement Performance: Keeping your thigh muscles tensed throughout the movement, slowly sink down into a full squatting position. Be sure that your knees extend forward and directly over your toes. Without bouncing in the bottom position, slowly extend your legs and return to the starting point. Repeat the movement for the suggested number of repetitions. Be sure to return the bar safely to the rack at the conclusion of your set.

Training Tips: Once you're using fairly heavy weights, you'll probably find that you need to use a weight-lifting belt fastened tightly around your waist to improve midsection stability. If you have an old knee injury, you will probably want to wrap the joint with an elastic knee band; don't come to depend on these elastic wraps if you aren't injured, however, because they tend to help you lift the weight and take some of the beneficial stress off your leg muscles. When you are lifting poundages near your maximum, be sure to have a spotter standing behind you (alternatively, you can have one at each end of the bar). A spotter can give you a bear hug around the torso and help you up with a weight that's a little too heavy for your present capabilities.

Variations: Some bodybuilders feel the movement more if they take a more narrow stance, say, one with their heels set about 12 inches apart. Others prefer a wider stance, with the feet set 4–6 inches wider than the shoulders on each side. Other variations involve the depth of squat performed. There are several partial squats: quarter squats (going a quarter of the way down), half squats, parallel squats (going down until the thighs are parallel with the floor), and bench squats (squatting down astride a flat exercise bench until your buttocks lightly touch the bench before you resume the fully erect position).

Squat—variation (going down to just above a position with legs parallel to the gym floor).

Squat—variation (astride bench, which limits downward path of hips while squatting).

Angled Leg Presses

Values: This exercise has most of the values of a squat movement but does not place undue stress on the lower back. Thus, if you have a lower-back injury, you can probably still do leg presses when you can't do squats. Leg presses place primary stress on the quadriceps and buttocks, with second emphasis on the hamstrings, most of the back muscles, and the forearm flexors.

Starting Position: Lie back with your butt lodged in the angle created by the two main pads of the angled leg-press machine. Your back should extend straight up the rear angled pad. Bend your legs and place your feet about shoulder-width apart on the moving platform of the machine with your toes angled slightly outward. Extend your legs and rotate the stop bars on each side of your hips to release the slide. Grasp the handles by the sides of your hips to steady your torso in place as you do the movement.

Movement Performance: Slowly bend your legs as fully as possible, until your knees actually contact your shoulders, if you can. Without bouncing in any way in the bottom position, slowly extend your legs until you have returned

Angled leg press—finish.

Seated leg press—midpoint.

to the starting position. Repeat the movement until you have performed the suggested number of repetitions. Be sure to lock the stop bars and gently lower the machine slide down to the stops before you terminate your set and exit the machine.

Training Tips: Don't hold your breath as you perform this movement. Doing so can build up terrific intrathoracic pressure that could cause you to faint, after which you are completely at the mercy of the weight on the machine slide. Breathe in as you lower the weight, out as you

raise it. Sometimes you'll have to take a few panting breaths between reps, usually when your legs are straight and you're near the end of a set. Always keep your spine as straight as possible, because it's easy to allow your head to come forward and hunch your shoulders; this can lead to compression in your thoracic and cervical vertebrae.

Variations: The weight slides on the original leg-press machines ran vertically up two rails; an angled pad was placed beneath the slide, and a bodybuilder positioned his or her hips directly

Vertical leg press—start/finish.

beneath the slide before putting their feet against the underside of the slide. It was very easy to incur a lower-back injury if you placed your hips beyond a position directly beneath the slide, e.g., farther away from the head end. Many gyms still have vertical-slide leg-press machines, which you can use profitably as long as you remember where to position your hips. Nautilus and Universal Gyms both came out with horizontal leg-press machines in which a bodybuilder sat erect, held on to handles at the sides of the seat, and pushed the pedals relatively parallel with the gym floor. There are many copies of this type of machine; one of the best is a curved-back leg-press machine that for some reason tends to place a greater proportion of stress on the muscles just above the knees. Regardless of the type of leg-press machine utilized, you should experiment with various widths of foot placement, from a position in which your feet almost touch each other to one as wide as the machine slide allows. Each different foot stance places a uniquely different stress on the quadriceps and glutes.

Vertical leg press—midpoint.

Leg extension—start.

Leg Extensions

Values: For the most part, when building mass and power you will want to use compound movements (those that work a large muscle group in conjunction with other large or small groups). Some isolation exercises, such as leg extensions and leg curls, do have value. Leg extensions isolate stress almost solely on the quadriceps muscles at the fronts of your thighs.

Starting Position: There are scores of different leg-extension machines available, and some big gyms like Gold's in Venice have 5–10 from which to choose. All are operated in the same way, although some machines have unique adjustments to better suit your body. Sit on a leg-extension machine with your knees over the edge of the pad toward the lever arm of the apparatus.

Hook your toes and insteps under the roller pads attached to the end of the lever arm; these pads will be in such a position at the start of a movement that your legs will be bent to or sometimes slightly past a 90-degree angle once you have hooked your toes under them. Lean back against the back rest and grasp the handles at the sides of your hips. Be sure to remain sitting erect throughout the set.

Movement Performance: Slowly straighten your legs completely; hold this peak contracted position for a slow count of two, and slowly lower yourself back to the starting point. Repeat for the suggested number of repetitions before exiting the machine.

Training Tips: Avoid jerking the weight up—the movement should always be smooth in both

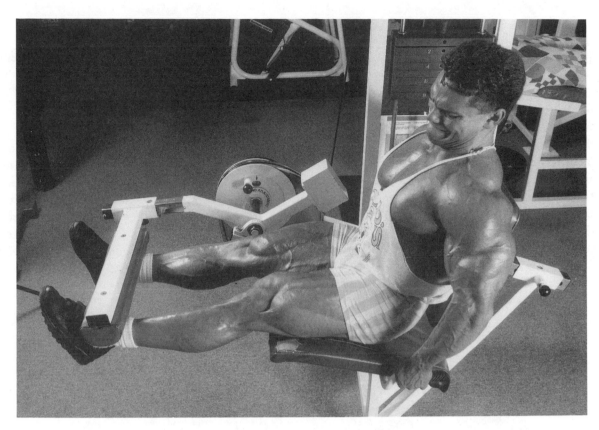

Leg extension—finish.

Leg extension—finish (detail).

upward and downward arcs, with a pause at the top and no pause at the bottom. One interesting training technique you can use on leg extensions, called *21s*, consists of doing seven half reps from the bottom, seven half reps from the midpoint up to the finish, and finally seven complete repetitions. These 21s are guaranteed to put a blowtorch to your quads.

Variations: This movement can also be performed one leg at a time as long as you're sure to do the same number of sets and reps with each limb. You'll probably find it easier to concentrate on the exercise when you do it one leg at a time, because your mental focus won't be split between the two limbs.

Stiff-Legged Deadlifts

Values: This is a highly effective movement for intensely stressing the hamstrings, lumbar muscles, and buttocks. Secondary stress is placed on the forearm flexors and trapezius muscles.

Starting Position: In order to achieve a maximum range of motion on stiff-legged deadlifts, you must perform the movement while standing on a thick block of wood or a flat exercise bench. (If you did it on the floor, the large-diameter Olympic plates would touch the gym floor and terminate the movement far short of its potential range; standing on a bench or block allows you to lower the weight downward another 6–8

Stiff-legged deadlift—start/finish.

inches before the bar itself touches the bench or block, stopping the movement.) Place a moderately weighted barbell across the block or bench so you can stand with your toes just touching it. Bend your legs and torso so you can comfortably take a shoulder-width over-grip on the bar. Flatten your back and extend your legs to stand erect with the bar across your upper thighs. Your arms should be held perfectly straight throughout the movement, but your knees should always be bent slightly to remove potentially harmful stress from your lower back. Strictly speaking, this isn't a stiff-legged deadlift at all, but an almost-stiff-legged deadlift.

Movement Performance: Keeping your back as flat as you can, slowly bend forward at the waist until the bar touches your toes. Without bouncing, slowly return to an erect position. Repeat the movement for the suggested number of reps.

Training Tips: While you should keep your back as flat as possible, there will be some rounding as you approach the bottom position. This does put your spine in a bad mechanical position, but as long as you do the movement slowly and evenly, you will avoid back injury. Generally speaking, you should do relatively high reps—in the range of 10–20—on stiff-legged deadlifts and fairly low reps—usually 5–8—on regular deadlifts, which will be described later.

Stiff-legged deadlift—midpoint.

Variations: With light weights you can do the movement with your legs completely straight, but the heavier you go the more bent your legs should be. True stiff-legged deadlifts can be best used after a series of leg-curl sets as a means of stretching out your hamstrings. Two other movements that have a similar effect on the hams, buttocks, and lower back are "good mornings" (in which you bend from an erect position to one in which your torso is parallel with the floor while a light barbell rests across your shoulders behind your neck) and glute-ham hyperextensions (which are performed like normal hyperextensions except that they are done with the upper thighs rather than the pelvic structure resting on the horizontal pad).

Lying Leg Curls

Values: There are three types of leg curls—lying, seated, and standing—and all three place isolated stress on the biceps femoris muscles (hamstrings) at the backs of the upper legs. The most common type of leg curl is done lying facedown on a lying leg-curl machine.

Starting Position: Lie facedown on the flat padded surface of the machine with your legs straight, and slide toward the foot end until you can comfortably hook your heels beneath the roller pads at the end of the lever arm. Situate yourself so your knees are still on the horizontal pad while your heels are under the rollers. Grasp the handles at the sides of the machine, or the

Lying leg curl—start.

Lying leg curl—finish.

sides of the pad if handles aren't provided. Fully straighten your legs.

Movement Performance: Keeping your hips constantly in contact with the horizontal pad, use biceps femoris strength to bend your legs as completely as possible. Hold the peak contracted position for a count, and slowly lower back to the starting point. Without bouncing at the starting point, begin a second repetition. Continue until you have finished the prescribed number of reps.

Training Tips: If you need to cheat up a rep or two, it is permissible to lift your hips from the padded surface of the machine, but be certain that you do a series of strict repetitions first. Try shifting from a position with your toes pointed straight at the floor to one where your toes point inward or outward at 45-degree angles. Your foot should always be flexed rather than extended; doing leg curls with toes pointed like a ballet dancer gets too much calf into a movement which is intended to isolate the hamstrings.

Seated leg curl—midpoint.

Variations: You can do leg curls on a seated machine, which tends to stress the hamstrings more near their upper insertion, where they meet the buttocks. With either lying or seated leg curls, you can do the movement with one limb at a time. Standing leg curls are normally performed one leg at a time and tend to stress more of the lower section of the hamstrings. Only lying leg curls tend to stress the entire length of the biceps femoris muscle.

Back Exercises

Barbell Shrugs

Values: Shrugs can be done with a barbell, two dumbbells, or on a variety of machines, but all types of shrugs place direct stress on the trapezius muscles. Indirect emphasis is on both the forearm flexors and the deltoids. Since the traps can become very massive when worked with heavy weights on shrugs, the movement is important for mass and power building.

Starting Position: Place a moderately heavy barbell on the floor and step up to it so your shins are touching the bar. Your feet should be set about shoulder-width apart, your feet approximately parallel to each other. Take a shoulder-width over-grip on the bar. Straighten your arms and keep them straight throughout the movement. Flatten your back and dip your hips to achieve a basic pulling position, and slowly stand erect so the weight rests across your upper thighs. If you have the correct type of rack available, you will need to lift the bar only a few inches up to the starting point, rather than all of the way from the floor. Once you are standing erect, allow the weight to pull your shoulders as far downward and forward as is comfortably possible.

Barbell shrugs—start (note use of grip-reinforcing straps).

Movement Performance: Use only trapezius strength to shrug your shoulders simultaneously upward and backward as far as possible. Often bodybuilders are urged to try to touch their shoulders to their ears, but this results in a movement that goes directly upward and downward. A shrug that stresses the trapezius muscles properly must go both upward and backward. Hold this peak contracted position for a moment, then slowly lower back to the starting point. Repeat for the suggested reps.

Training Tips: You'll be able to work up quickly to using substantial weights in this movement, so you should learn to use canvas straps to reinforce your grip on the bar. Eventually your traps will become so strong that you could shrug with a weight that you literally couldn't hold in your hands unassisted. You'll get the most benefit from shrugs by doing relatively high reps, something in the 10–15 range being optimum.

Variations: In comparison to barbells, dumbbells are unwieldy and difficult to handle when

Barbell shrugs—finish.

doing shrugs, but many bodybuilders like using dumbbells because it allows them to shrug their shoulders in a circular fashion. You can also use the bench-press station at a Universal Gyms machine—or any similar machine with a bench-press station—to do shrugs. Just stand between the handles, grasp them, and shrug to your heart's content.

Barbell Bent-Over Rows

Values: This and similar machine and dumbbell movements are keys to developing maximum muscle mass and strength in the upper back. Primary stress is on the latissimus dorsi, rhomboids, posterior deltoid, brachialis, biceps, and forearm flexor muscles. Secondary emphasis is on the lower-back muscles.

Starting Position: Place a moderately heavy barbell on the gym floor. Set your feet about shoulder-width apart approximately two feet back from the bar. Bend over and take a shoulder-width over-grip on the bar. Keep your knees unlocked throughout your set to remove potentially harmful stress from your lower back. Arch your back and with your arms straight lift the weight just off the floor, so it hangs downward directly below your shoulder joints at straight-arm's length. Attempt to keep your torso motionless throughout the movement.

Barbell bent-over row—start.

Barbell bent-over row—finish.

Movement Performance: Being sure that your upper arms move upward at about a 45-degree angle from your torso, slowly bend your arms and pull the weight up to touch the lower part of your rib cage. Hold this peak contracted position for a moment, then lower slowly back to the starting point. Repeat.

Training Tips: When you're using weights heavy enough to have the 45-pound plates on the ends of an Olympic bar, you will have to stand on a thick block of wood or a flat exercise bench in order to allow a full stretch at the bottom

Barbell bent-over rows (narrow-grip variation)—midpoint.

point of the rowing motion. With heavy weights you might also need to reinforce your grip on the bar with straps.

Variations: On barbell bent-over rows, the main source of variation is in the width of your grip. Your grip can be as narrow as one with your hands touching in the middle of the bar, or as wide as the length of the Olympic bar will allow. Other possible variations involve pulling the bar up to touch other points on your rib cage, either in the middle or up toward your shoulder joints.

Seated pulley row—start.

Seated pulley row—finish.

Seated Pulley Rows

Values: Seated pulley rows are similar to barbell bent-over rows, but with greater involvement of the spinal erector and trapezius muscles. Primary emphasis is still on the lats, rhomboids, posterior deltoid, brachialis, biceps, and forearm flexor muscles, as well as the traps and erectors. All rowing movements—including seated pulley rows—tend to develop thickness more than width in the upper-back muscles. However, seated pulley rows tend to develop both thickness and width in that area.

Starting Position: To the end of the cable running through the floor pulley, attach a handle that allows you to take a narrow grip with your hands set close together. Place your feet against the foot restraint and sit down on the seat attached to the pulley apparatus. At the start of the movement your arms should be straight and your legs slightly bent to keep potentially harmful stress off your lower back. Allow the weight to pull your shoulders forward so your torso is inclined as far forward as is comfortably possible.

Movement Performance: Keeping your legs slightly bent throughout the movement, simultaneously pull the handle in to touch your upper abdomen and sit back until your torso is perpendicular to the floor. As you pull the handle in to your torso, your arms should be close to your sides. Hold this peak contracted position for a moment, then slowly reverse the procedure and return to the starting point. Repeat for the suggested number of repetitions.

Training Tips: Never allow yourself to sit back past the recommended perpendicular position, because this will allow you to pull harder with your very powerful trapezius muscles, in turn robbing the lats and other midback muscles of some of the stress they should be receiving. On all rowing movements, it is prudent to do one or two light, high-rep warm-up sets before tackling maximum poundages. It is even better to pyramid your reps and poundages, starting with a set of high reps at a light weight and then progressively increasing the poundage and reducing the reps with each succeeding set.

Variations: A wide variety of handles can be attached to the end of the cable. The narrow-parallel-grip handle is most commonly used. There is also a handle that allows a shoulder-width parallel grip, which gives an effect somewhat different from the narrow-grip handle. A straight bar handle can be used with either an over- or an under-grip of varying widths. There are individual loop handles that attach to the central cable and allow you to pull your hands backward along any arc you choose, rather than restricting you to the arcs allowed by other types of handle arrangements.

Seated pulley row (under-grip variation)— midpoint.

One-arm dumbbell bent row—start.

One-Arm Dumbbell Bent-Over Rows

Values: This movement hits the same muscles as barbell bent-over rows but avoids overstressing the lower back. As a result, you can often do one-arm dumbbell rows when you have a sore back and can't do either barbell rows or seated pulley rows. One-arm dumbbell rows place primary stress on the lats, rhomboids, rear delts, brachialis, biceps, and forearm flexors. Secondary stress is on the traps.

Starting Position: Place a moderately heavy dumbbell on the gym floor near the side of a flat exercise bench. Orient yourself so you will be pulling on the dumbbell with your right arm. First kneel on the bench with your left knee and place your left hand on the flat surface of the bench about 12–14 inches ahead of your knee.

One-arm dumbbell bent row—finish.

Reach down with your right hand and grasp the dumbbell, turning it so the axis of the dumbbell is parallel to your torso throughout the movement. Lift your right shoulder just enough to move the dumbbell free of the floor, and hold it in this position for a moment, stretching all of the back muscles on the right side of your body.

Movement Performance: Keeping your elbow close to your side, bend your arm and pull the dumbbell upward until it touches the side of your rib cage. As you pull the weight upward you'll find that your shoulder naturally rises until it is at the same level as your left shoulder. Reverse the procedure to lower the weight back to the starting point, and repeat the movement for the required number of reps. Be sure to perform the same number of sets and reps with each arm.

Two-dumbbell bent-over row—midpoint.

Training Tips: Be sure to do the movement relatively slowly and smoothly to avoid torquing your lower back and injuring it. With heavy dumbbells you'll undoubtedly need to use straps to reinforce your grip.

Variations: Try starting some sets with the dumbbell handle perpendicular to your torso, then rotate your hand as you pull it upward until the handle is parallel with your torso in the top position. This movement can also be done with two dumbbells simultaneously, making it very analogous to barbell bent-over rowing.

T-Bar Rows

Values: T-bar rows are a great all-around back exercise, and you'll seldom see a bodybuilder with a great back who hasn't slaved away on the T-bar. The movement places great stress on the spinal erectors from their lowest insertions right up into the middle of your back. Strong primary stress is also placed on the lats, traps, biceps, brachialis muscles, and the forearm flexors. T-bar rows build little in the way of back width, but they're awesome when it comes to developing back thickness.

Starting Position: Stand astride the T-bar with your feet set solidly on the platforms on each side of the bar. T-bars have numerous types of attached handles, but the most common is a bar handle angled backward at both ends so a nearly parallel-hands grip can be taken at about shoulder width. Some T-bars also come with handles that provide a much narrower parallel-hands grip. Regardless of the handle attached, take your favorite grip, straighten your arms, flatten your back, keep your knees slightly bent throughout your set, and raise your shoulders just enough to lift the weight from the gym floor. Try to stretch your lats completely in this flat-backed, straight-armed position.

T-bar row—start.

Movement Performance: Attempting to keep your torso motionless, bend your arms and pull the bar up to touch the plates on your chest. Keep your upper arms close to your sides as you pull the bar upward. Hold the peak contracted position for a moment, then slowly lower back to the starting point. Repeat.

Training Tips: Resist the temptation to raise your head and upper torso as you pull the weight upward, since this removes some of the valuable stress from your mid- and upper-back muscles. If possible, experiment with a variety of grip widths and types (over-grip, parallel-hands grip) on the T-bar. To increase the range of motion, try using smaller diameter plates such as 25s or 35s instead of the standard 45s. Obviously, very strong bodybuilders will be stuck with the 45s because they simply won't be able to load enough weight on the end of the bar with smaller plates. But plates of smaller diameter do allow a longer range of motion.

Variations: One drawback to T-bar rows is that they are murder if you have a sore lower back. Gym equipment designers have taken this into consideration and developed a T-bar apparatus with a narrow angled pad on which you can place your torso for complete support as you do the movement. Even if you don't have a back problem, it's a good idea to switch off to this different piece of equipment from time to time.

T-bar row—finish.

T-bar row (machine-supported variation)—finish.

Chins (front variation/medium over-grip)—start.

Chins (front variation/medium over-grip)—finish.

Chins

Values: Chins are the basic width-building movement for lats. Strong emphasis is placed on the biceps and brachialis muscles, forearm flexors, lats, and other upper-back muscles that impart a rotational movement to the scapulae. Chins performed behind the neck tend to work the upper lats harder, while front chins tend to work lower lats more intensely.

Starting Position: Place a small stool directly beneath a chinning bar. Step up on the stool so you can most easily take an over-grip on the bar with your hands set 3–5 inches wider than your shoulders on each side. Tip the stool over so you can hang at straight-arm's length directly beneath the bar. Arch your back slightly and cross your ankles while bending your legs at about a 90-degree angle.

Movement Performance: From the fully stretched position, pull yourself up to the bar until it touches your upper chest, then slowly lower back to the starting point. Repeat the movement.

Training Tips: Most bodybuilders find it necessary to wear straps to reinforce their grip on the chinning bar. If you don't have sufficient strength to do at least 6–8 chins, you'll have to work hard on lat-machine pulldowns until you develop sufficient strength to do chins. We've seen many women doing set after set of chins in their back workouts and men doing the movement with 50–60 pounds of weight strapped around their waists to make the movement progressively more difficult.

Chins behind neck—near finish.

Chins (narrow parallel-grip variation)—midpoint.

Variations: Many variations of chins exist; the first, called *chins behind the neck*, is to chin upward so the bar touches your trapezius muscles behind your neck. With both front chins and chins behind the neck, you can use a wide variety of grip widths on the chinning bar. For front chins, however, it is much easier to use narrow grip widths, something that is basically impossi-

ble to accomplish when doing chins behind the neck. A triangular chinning handle fits over the bar and allows a narrow parallel-hands grip; you will find it best to lean back as you do the chin, pulling yourself upward with your torso angled at about 45 degrees from the gym floor, touching the middle of your chest to your hands at the top point of the movement.

Chins (medium under-grip variation)—midpoint.

Lat-Machine Pulldowns

Values: This movement is analogous to chins both in effect on the torso muscles and in terms of the number of variations available to a bodybuilder, but you can use poundages lighter than your body weight when doing pulldowns. Lat-machine pulldowns are a basic width-building movement for the lats. Strong emphasis is placed on the lats, other upper-back muscles that impart a rotational movement to the scapulae, biceps, brachialis muscles, and forearm flexors. Pulldowns behind the neck tend to work the upper lats harder, while pulldowns to the front tend to work the lower lats more intensely.

Starting Position: Stand facing the lat machine; reach up and take an over-grip on the pulley-bar handle with your hands set 3–5 inches wider than your shoulders on each side. Straighten your arms and use your weight to pull your body downward until you can wedge your knees beneath the restraint bar. Once in this position, allow the weight to pull your shoulders upward to fully stretch your lats.

Movement Performance: Arch your back and keep it arched throughout the movement. Use upper-back and arm strength to pull the bar down to touch your upper chest. Hold this peak contracted position for a moment, then slowly return to the starting point. Repeat the movement for the desired number of reps.

Front lat machine pulldowns (normal over-grip)—start.

Front lat machine pulldowns (normal over-grip)—finish.

Lat machine pulldowns behind neck—near finish.

Front lat machine pulldowns (parallel-hands grip at shoulder width)—start.

Front lat machine pulldowns (parallel-hands grip at shoulder width)—finish.

Training Tips: Heavy weights require straps to reinforce your grip. With weights at or near your body weight, you will probably require a training partner to pull you down until you can wedge your knees beneath the restraint bar.

Variations: The main variation is to pull the bar down to touch your trapezius muscles behind your neck, a movement called *pulldowns behind the neck*. On front pulldowns you can vary your grip outward as wide as possible or inward until your hands touch in the middle of the bar; you can also use an under-grip on the bar—again, with various grip widths possible. On pulldowns behind the neck you'll be able to vary your grip only from one about shoulder-width outward to one as wide as the bar permits. Two handles are available that allow you to take a parallel-hands grip, one in which your hands are set at approximately shoulder width, the other in which your hands will be set close together.

Lat machine pulldowns (narrow parallel-hands grip variation)—finish.

Stiff-armed lat machine pulldowns—midpoint.

Deadlifts

Values: The deadlift is one of the most fundamental tests of physical power, demonstrating literally how much weight you can lift off the floor and up to the tops of your thighs as you stand erect with the weight hanging at straight-arm's length down from your shoulders. When doing deadlifts as an exercise, primary stress is on the spinal erectors, all of the muscles of the hip girdle, quadriceps, trapezius muscles, and forearm flexors. Strong secondary stress is placed on almost every other muscle of the human body, but particularly the remaining muscles of the back, shoulders, and arms.

Starting Position: When deadlifting, you will use what is called a *mixed grip*, or one in which one palm faces forward and the other faces the rear as you do each rep. With a mixed grip you can lift much more weight than when using a normal over-grip on the bar. Load up a heavy barbell lying on the gym floor and step up to it so your shins literally touch the bar. Bend over and take a shoulder-width mixed grip on the bar. Straighten your arms, flatten your back, and dip your hips to assume the basic pulling position.

Deadlift—start/finish.

Deadlift—midpoint.

Movement Performance: Start pulling the weight from the gym floor by first straightening your legs, then following through by straightening your back. As you stand erect, pull your shoulders back to complete the movement. Reverse the procedure to lower the weight back to the floor, and start another repetition. Repeat until you have finished a heavy set of 5–8 repetitions.

Training Tips: If you find it more comfortable to use a normal over-grip, reinforce your grip with straps. It's also possible to do your deadlifts from the hang position, but be sure you don't allow the bar to actually touch the gym floor until your set has been completed. This type of movement builds incredible starting power into your deadlifts.

Variations: Some bodybuilders do partial deadlifts in a power rack, lifting the weight three-fourths, one-half, or one-fourth of the way up to the finish position. Three-time Mr. Olympia Frank Zane gave top deadlifts (the last quarter of the movement) a great deal of credit for developing the last degree of ultimate mass and detail in his back.

Chest Exercises

Bench Presses

Values: Bench presses are sometimes called the *upper body squat*, since they affect nearly all of the muscles of the torso and arms. Primary stress is placed on the pectorals, anterior and medial deltoids, triceps, and those upper-back muscles that impart rotational movement to the scapulae. Significant secondary stress is placed on the posterior deltoids, the lats, and even the lower-back muscles that stabilize your body on the bench as you perform the movement.

Starting Position: Always have a spotter when you are doing maximum poundages in the bench press. Load up the bar with a moderately heavy poundage as it lies on the bench-pressing rack. Lie back on the bench and set your feet solidly on either side of the bench, your legs bent at 90-degree angles. Your head should be almost directly beneath the racked barbell when you are oriented correctly on the bench. Reach up and take an over-grip on the bar with your hands set 4–6 inches wider than your shoulders on each side. Have your training partner lift the weight off the rack up to straight-arm's length directly above your shoulder joints.

Bench press—start.

Movement Performance: Keeping your elbows almost directly out to the sides throughout the movement, slowly lower the weight down to touch the middle of your chest. Be sure to keep tension in your pecs, delts, and triceps so you won't be tempted to bounce the weight off your chest. Instead, simply reverse direction with the bar and push it strongly back to the starting point. Repeat until you have fully exhausted your pushing muscles, then have your spotter help you rack the weight before you get up from the bench.

Training Tips: Never hold your breath as you are pressing the weight, because this can cause sufficient intrathoracic pressure to impede blood flow to and from your brain, which in turn can cause you to black out with no warning. If that happens and your spotter is not alert, you can be badly injured, perhaps even killed. Inhale as you lower the weight and exhale as you press it out. To be sure you are exhaling, you might consider growling a bit as you press the bar out. If you're feeling out of breath you can take several breaths at the top point of the movement before you initiate your next rep. As you press the weight upward it's essential that your hips stay in contact with the bench. Arching your back to bring your stronger lower-pec muscles into play is cheating and should be avoided at all costs. Besides, it can cause a painful cramp in your spinal erectors if you're not careful.

Variations: The main variations of barbell bench presses involve the width of your hand spacing on the bar. The wider you go with your grip (and only the length of the bar limits grip width outward), the more you shift stress to the lower and outer sections of the pectorals. The more you move your hands in toward each other, the more you move stress from your pectorals to your triceps. Many bodybuilders actually do narrow-grip bench presses as a triceps exercise. When using a normal grip on the bar, some bodybuilders like to lower the bar down to touch the base of their neck, a practice that lengthens the range of motion over which the pectorals must contract and places greater-than-normal stress on the upper pecs.

Dumbbells can be quite unwieldy, but many bodybuilders use very heavy dumbbells to do their bench presses. They can lower the dumbbells farther than they can lower a barbell whose bar contacts the chest to halt the downward

Machine bench press—start.

movement short of its potential full range of motion. With very heavy dumbbells, you'll need a training partner on each side of you to hand you the weights either at chest level or preferably at straight-arm's length above your chest. We have frequently seen hypermassive Bertil Fox (four-time Mr. Universe) do flat-bench presses with a pair of 200-pound dumbbells for a minimum of 10 reps per set. Each of the five sets he does with these massive weights forces his training partners to lift the huge dumbbells up to a position where he can take them at straight-arm's length. It takes more than a puppy to lift that heavy of a dumbbell that high by himself—it takes a real man!

Many equipment manufacturers have developed machines that mimic the effect of doing bench presses on a flat bench. Each machine has a different effect on the muscles, and you alone can determine which machines are best for you by experimenting with every one available in the gym where you train. If it's a Gold's Gym, there should be plenty of bench-pressing machines from which to choose.

Barbell Incline Presses

Values: When you lie back on a bench inclined to an angle somewhere between 30 and 45 degrees, you shift stress from the lower and outer pecs to the upper section of your pectoral muscle complex, as well as to the showy pec-delt tie-ins.

There is still terrific stress on the deltoids and triceps, but less on the upper-back muscles used so strongly in presses on a flat bench.

Starting Position: Load up a moderately heavy barbell resting on the rack attached to an incline pressing bench. Have your training partner stand on the little step built into the head end of the bench. Sit down on the bench's seat and reach up to take an over-grip on the bar with your hands set 4–6 inches wider than your shoulders on each side. Have your training partner assist you in removing the barbell from the rack to a supported position at straight-arm's length directly above your shoulder joints.

Barbell incline press—start.

Barbell incline press—midpoint.

Movement Performance: Keeping your elbows as far back as possible during the movement, maintain tension in your pecs, deltoids, and triceps as you slowly lower the weight downward until it touches your upper pectorals. Without bouncing the barbell off your chest, reverse its direction and slowly press the weight back to the starting point at straight-arm's length. Repeat the movement for the required number of repetitions for that particular set.

Training Tips: On bench presses, incline presses, and decline presses, your training partner can give you 2–3 forced reps at the end of a set to push your muscles past the point of normal failure, thus inducing an even greater degree of ultimate hypertrophy. Again, inhale as you lower the barbell and exhale as you press it back to the starting point. Be sure to keep yourself seated on the bench's seat so you avoid arching your back and cheating the weight up. In the long run you'll get much more out of strict-style training than from cheating workouts.

Barbell incline press—finish.

Variations: You can vary your grip width on the barbell handle from one about shoulder-width apart outward to one as wide as the length of the bar allows. Again, dumbbells can be used in place of barbells. With lighter weights you won't have much trouble cleaning them up to your shoulders, but heavier poundages will have to be handed to you. We have repeatedly seen 145-pound Debby McKnight (Overall U.S. Champion and currently a hot pro bodybuilder) lift one 85-pound dumbbell up to her shoulder with both hands and have the other one handed to her at shoulder level, after which she does a perfect set of 8–10 repetitions with these monster weights. There are many varieties of incline pressing machines which you can explore. Generally speaking, tracked machines are somewhat easier to use because they relieve you of the responsibility of balancing a barbell or two heavy dumbbells.

Dumbbell incline press—start/finish.

Dumbbell incline press—midpoint.

Smith machine incline press—near finish.

Barbell decline press—start.

Barbell Decline Presses

Values: When you lie back on a decline bench set at an angle between 30 degrees and about 15 degrees and do barbell bench presses on it, you shift stress primarily to the lower and outer sections of the pectorals, the anterior deltoids, the triceps, and the lats and other upper-back muscles that rotate the scapulae. The combination of incline, flat, and decline presses with a barbell, two dumbbells, or various machines hits every area of your pectoral muscles.

Starting Position: Load up a moderately heavy barbell lying on the rack at the head end of a decline bench. Have your spotter stand at that end of the bench to protect you from accidentally dropping the weight on your face or neck. Lie back on the bench, slip your feet beneath the foot restraint (which will keep you from sliding down the bench at an inopportune time), and reach up to take an over-grip on the barbell handle with your hands set 4–6 inches wider on each side than your shoulders. Have your partner assist you in removing the bar from the rack to a supported position at straight-arm's length directly above your shoulders.

Movement Performance: Keeping your elbows back as you do the movement, bend your arms and slowly lower the bar down to touch the lower edge of your pectoral muscles. Without bouncing the weight off your chest, slowly press it back up to straight-arm's length. Repeat for the desired number of repetitions.

Training Tips: Some bodybuilders like to lower the bar to the base of their neck rather than to the lower edge of the pectorals, a movement that increases the range over which your pectorals must contract. This in turn gives you better development in the long run. Inhale as you lower the weight and exhale as you press it back to the starting point.

Variations: As with bench presses and incline presses, you can do decline presses either with two dumbbells or on the decline-pressing machine of your choice.

Smith machine decline press—midpoint.

Parallel Bar Dips

Values: Dips are like bench presses in that they work virtually all of the upper-body muscle groups in concert. Primary emphasis is on the pectoral muscles (particularly the lower and outer sections), the deltoids (particularly the anterior and medial heads), the triceps, and the lats.

Starting Position: Jump up between the parallel bars so you are supported on your hands and straight arms, with your body straight and your torso above the level of the bars. Tuck your chin into your chest and flex slightly at the waist so your torso is angled somewhat forward and your feet are directly beneath your face.

Movement Performance: Slowly bend your arms and allow your body to sink down between

Parallel bar dips (weighted variation)—start/finish.

the bars as far as is comfortably possible. Without bouncing in this bottom position, slowly straighten your arms and press back up to the starting position. Repeat.

Training Tips: Within a few months you'll be able to do so many reps with your body weight that you will have to add weight to the movement after 1–2 warm-up sets. Hang a dumbbell in a large loop of rope or webbing placed around the waist so the dumbbell hangs in the bottom part of the loop where you can grasp it between your legs.

Variations: Most gyms are equipped with parallel bars that are not actually parallel but are angled inward at one end. This type of setup allows you to use different grip widths for your dips, narrowing the grip width as you progress down the bars toward the narrow end.

Parallel bar dips (weighted variation)—midpoint.

Flat-bench dumbbell flyes—start/finish.

Dumbbell Flyes

Values: Compared to bench presses, dumbbell flyes performed on a flat bench are an isolation movement. Flyes isolate stress primarily on the pectoral muscles and anterior deltoids, with minimum stress on the remainder of the deltoid-muscle complex and the triceps. When performed on a flat exercise bench, flyes stress the center and outer sections of the pectorals; when done on an incline bench, stress is switched to the upper sections of the pecs; and, when performed on a decline bench, the lower and outer sections of the pectorals receive most of the stress. Therefore, by altering the angle at which you do your sets of flyes, you can selectively stress the weaker areas of your pectoral complex, bringing them up to par with the rest of the chest muscles.

Starting Position: Grasp two moderately

Flat-bench dumbbell flyes—midpoint.

weighted dumbbells and sit at the end of a flat exercise bench. Place your feet solidly on the floor on either side of the bench and then lie back on the flat surface of the bench, extending your arms straight upward from your shoulders. Rotate your wrists so your palms are facing each other and press the dumbbells together directly above your chest. Bend your arms at approximately 15-degree angles, and maintain them in this rounded posture throughout your set.

Movement Performance: Keeping your arms rounded, slowly lower the dumbbells directly out to the sides and downward in semicircular arcs until they are below the level of your chest and your pectoral muscles are stretched to the limit. Reverse the movement of the dumbbells, using pectoral strength to pull them back along the same arcs to the starting point. Repeat the movement for an appropriate number of repetitions.

Incline dumbbell flyes—start.

Decline dumbbell flyes—midpoint.

Training Tips: This movement is sometimes performed with the arms held straight, but stiff-arm flyes tend to put unnatural strain on the ligaments of the inner elbows. When doing bent-armed flyes, the object of the movement is to lower your elbows as far below the level of your chest as is comfortably possible, fully stretching the pectorals before returning the dumbbells to the starting point.

Variations: As mentioned earlier under Values, flyes can be performed on various degrees of incline and decline benches. On both incline and decline benches, the movement is performed identically to the flat-bench version; the dumbbells always travel in arcs that are perpendicular to the floor when viewed from the side.

Shoulder Exercises

Standing Barbell Presses

Values: This is the most basic of shoulder-girdle movements. It places intense stress on all three heads of the deltoids (but particularly the anterior and medial heads) and on the triceps, with secondary stress on the upper-chest and upper-back muscles.

Starting Position: To initiate this movement you must first clean a moderately weighted barbell from the floor to your shoulders. Place the barbell on the gym floor and stand up to it so your shins touch the bar. Place your feet about shoulder-width apart, then bend over and take an over-grip on the bar with your hands set 3–5 inches wider on each side than your shoulders. Straighten your arms, flatten your back, and dip your hips to assume the basic pulling position. With coordinated movement to the legs, back, and arms, quickly whip the bar off the floor and catch it at your shoulders. Rotate your elbows directly beneath the bar, and you are in position for a set of standing barbell presses.

Standing barbell press—start.

Movement Performance: Without leaning backward at the waist, push the barbell directly upward past your face to straight-arm's length directly overhead. Lower slowly back to the starting point, and pause for a second to prevent bouncing the weight off your shoulders. Repeat the movement for the required number of repetitions.

Training Tips: On all heavy overhead lifts, you should wear a weightlifting belt buckled tightly around your waist to prevent potential back or abdomen injuries. Some bodybuilders prefer to do this movement while seated on an exercise bench, particularly one with a backboard set at about 80 degrees to support the torso as the movement is performed.

Variations: A very similar movement can be performed holding two dumbbells rather than a barbell in your hands. The dumbbells can be pressed up either simultaneously or alternately in seesaw fashion, one going up as the other is coming down.

Standing barbell press—finish.

Seated press behind neck—start/finish.

Barbell Presses Behind Neck

Values: Like standing barbell presses from the front of the neck, presses behind the neck stress all three heads of the deltoid (particularly the anterior and medial heads) and the triceps with equal intensity. Secondary stress is placed on the upper-back muscles.

Starting Position: While this exercise can be performed while standing erect, it is most frequently done while seated astride a flat exercise bench, particularly one with an upright padded surface against which you can brace your back. Clean a moderately weighted barbell to your shoulders and push it up over your head so it

Seated press behind neck—midpoint.

comes to rest across your trapezius muscles behind your neck. Sit down astride the bench and rotate your elbows to a position directly beneath the barbell bar.

Movement Performance: Slowly straighten your arms to press the barbell directly upward to straight-arm's length. Lower slowly back to the starting point, avoid bouncing the weight off your traps, and initiate another rep. Repeat the movement until you have completed the desired number of repetitions, then return the barbell safely to the floor of the gym.

Training Tips: You'll find that you'll need to use a somewhat wider grip on the bar than you use for standing barbell presses, say, 4–6 inches wider than your shoulders on each side rather than 3–5 inches. On both presses behind the neck and standing barbell presses, you can experiment with various grip widths to see how each affects your shoulder muscles.

Variations: For the sake of variety, try alternating reps from the front of your neck, from the back, from the front, and so on until you have completed your set. This will give you the best of each type of pressing movement.

Machine Presses

Values: Machines offer a substitute for free weights, and many overhead-pressing machines are available. Like barbell presses from the front or back of the neck, machine presses in front or behind the neck stress all three heads of the deltoid (particularly the anterior and medial sections) and the triceps with equal intensity. Secondary stress is placed on the upper-chest and upper-back muscles.

Starting Position: We'll describe front presses

as performed on a Smith machine, because this movement most closely resembles other machine overhead-pressing exercises. Place a flat exercise bench (preferably one with a back support) between the uprights of a Smith machine so it is perpendicular to the middle of the bar when viewed from above. Sit astride the bench and reach up to take an over-grip on the bar with hands set 4–6 inches wider than your shoulders on each side. Unhook the bar from the horizontal pins attached to the machine uprights and fully extend your arms.

Movement Performance: Slowly lower the bar down past your face until it lightly touches your shoulders, then reverse the movement and slowly press the bar back to straight-arm's length. Repeat the movement for the required number of reps.

Training Tips: A bench with a back support works better than a flat bench in this case. If you use the flat bench, you also might want to wear a weightlifting belt to support the middle of your body.

Variations: You can also do presses behind the neck on a Smith machine. On both front presses and presses behind the neck, you can experiment with a variety of grip widths.

Seated dumbbell press—start.

Seated dumbbell press—finish.

Smith machine front press—start.

Barbell upright row—start.

Upright Rows

Values: Upright rows place primary stress on the entire deltoid complex and the trapezius muscles. Secondary emphasis is on the biceps, brachialis muscles, and forearm flexors.

Starting Position: Place a moderately weighted barbell on the gym floor and stand up to it with your feet about shoulder-width apart. Bend over and take a narrow over-grip on the bar (there should be 4–6 inches of space between

Barbell upright row—finish.

your index fingers). Stand erect with your arms hanging straight down from your shoulders and your hands resting on your upper thighs.

Movement Performance: Be sure to keep your elbows above the level of your hands at all times. Slowly pull the barbell directly upward 2–3 inches away from your body until the backs of your hands touch the underside of your chin. At the top point of the movement, squeeze your shoulder blades together and roll your shoulders back as far as possible. Lower slowly back to the starting point and repeat the movement.

Training Tips: The biggest mistake most bodybuilders make when doing upright rows is dropping the bar too quickly from the top point of the movement back to the starting position. Lower it a bit more slowly than you raised it, because emphasizing the negative (downward) cycle of the movement gives just as much muscle-building benefit as raising the weight in the first place. To reduce stress on your traps and transfer it more to the medial deltoids, try doing upright rows with a shoulder-width grip. You'll discover that you can't pull the bar much higher than the bottom edge of your pecs, but wide-grip upright rows still fry the medial delts.

Variations: Other than grip width changes, the main variations of upright rows are performed with either two dumbbells or a short bar handle attached to a cable running through a floor pulley. You might find dumbbells give you pain-free movement while barbell upright rows hurt your shoulders. Cable upright rows offer a more continuous form of tension on the working muscles than either barbell or dumbbell upright rows.

Dumbbell upright row—finish.

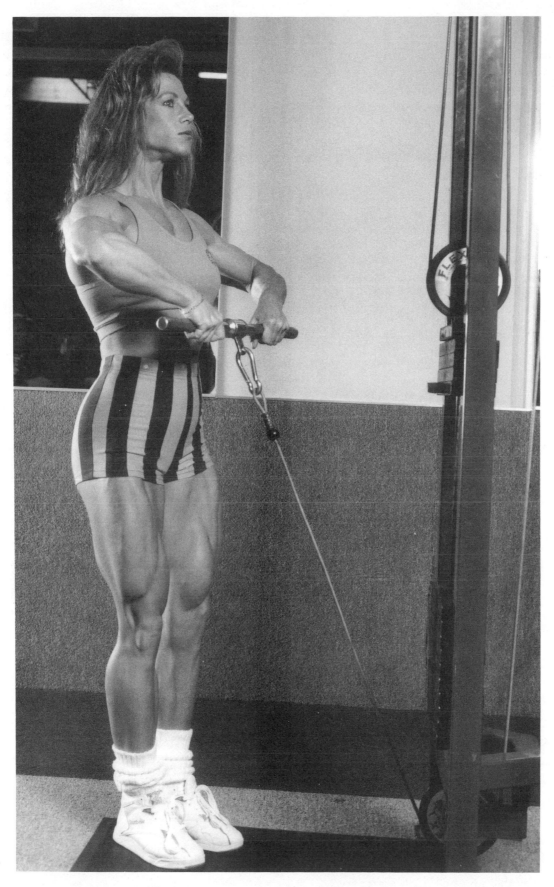

Cable upright row—midpoint.

Arm Exercises

Barbell Curls

Values: This is the most basic biceps movement. Secondary stress is placed on the brachialis muscles and forearm flexors.

Starting Position: Place a moderately weight-ed barbell on the gym floor and stand up to it with your feet set about shoulder-width apart. Bend over and take an under-grip on the bar with your hands set 3–4 inches wider on each side than your shoulders. Stand erect with your arms down at your sides and the bar resting

Standing barbell curl—start.

across your upper thighs. Pin your upper arms to the sides of your rib cage and keep them motionless in this position as you do the exercise.

Movement Performance: Use biceps strength to slowly curl the barbell in a semicircular arc from your thighs to a point just beneath your chin. As the bar passes the halfway point, you will probably find it most natural to flex your wrists as you finish each repetition. Reverse the procedure used to raise the weight in order to lower it back along the same semicircular arc to the starting point. Repeat.

Standing barbell curl—midpoint.

Training Tips: To lessen the amount of forearm involvement when performing barbell curls, try keeping your wrists straight throughout the movement, rather than flexing them for the second half of the curl. For even less forearm involvement, try doing the entire movement with your wrists bent backward in the direction opposite from the position they occupy when flexed. Unless you are trying to cheat up a rep, your torso should not sway forward and backward as you do your barbell curls. If swaying becomes a problem, try performing your curls with your

Standing barbell curl—finish.

Standing barbell curl (narrow-grip variation)—midpoint.

Barbell curl (EZ-curl bar variation)—start.

Standing barbell curls (wide-grip variation)—midpoint.

back pressed against the gym wall and your feet 1½ feet from the wall to isolate your lower body from the movement.

Variations: By changing the width of your grip on the bar, you can vary the effect on your working biceps. Narrow-grip barbell curls (with your hands set 4–6 inches apart) tend to stress the inner head of the muscle more intensely. Narrow-grip barbell curls were a favorite movement of Rick Wayne, the former Mr. World who once edited *Flex* magazine. Wide-grip curls (with your hands set 6–8 inches wider than your shoulders) place greater emphasis on the outer head of the biceps. Wide-grip curls were a favorite biceps exercise of Arnold Schwarzenegger during the years when he was winning seven Mr. Olympia titles.

Alternate dumbbell curls—position 1.

Standing Alternate Dumbbell Curls

Values: Since you can supinate your hands when using dumbbells for curls, alternate dumbbell curls actually place a better quality of stress on the biceps, which accomplishes both arm flexion and hand supination. Secondary stress is placed on the brachialis and forearm flexor muscles.

Starting Position: Place two moderately weighted dumbbells on the gym floor and stand between them with your feet set about shoulder-width apart. Squat down and grasp the dumbbells, then stand erect with your arms down at your sides and your palms facing your thighs. Pin your upper arms to the sides of your rib cage and keep them motionless in this position throughout the movement.

Alternate dumbbell curls—position 2.

Movement Performance: Start curling the dumbbell in your left hand forward and upward in a semicircular arc until it reaches shoulder level. As you curl the weight upward, simultaneously turn your palm so it faces upward for the entire second half of the movement. Turning your palm upward like this is called *supination*, while turning it downward is called *pronation*. As you begin to lower the weight in your left hand, start to curl the dumbbell in your right hand upward. As your left hand lowers, pronate your hand during the lower half of the movement so your palm again faces your leg. Continue curling in seesaw fashion until you have completed the suggested number of repetitions with each arm.

Training Tips: You'll find it a bit difficult to concentrate with sufficient intensity to remember to supinate each hand as the weight goes up and pronate it as you lower the dumbbell. Do your first two or three workouts of dumbbell curls simultaneously rather than alternately. It's easier to master the supination-pronation movements doing both arms at once, after which it becomes easy to supinate and pronate when curling the dumbbells alternately. Doing curls alternately makes it almost impossible to cheat during the movement.

Variations: Gary Strydom, who won the first WBF competition in June 1991, uses a variation of alternate dumbbell curls. He does an entire set of curls with one arm, then an entire set with the other, rather than curling them in seesaw fashion. This way Strydom can alternate from one arm to the other until he completes his assigned sets with each arm before putting down the dumbbells. Alternate dumbbell curls can also be done while seated on a flat exercise bench.

One-arm cable curl (variation on dumbbell curls)—midpoint.

Close-grip bench press—
start/finish.

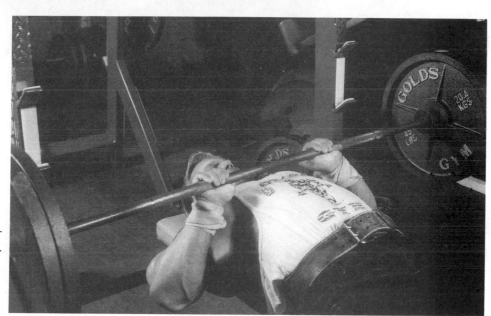

Close-grip bench press—
midpoint.

Close-Grip Bench Presses

Values: Doing bench presses with a close grip switches primary emphasis to the triceps, with secondary stress on the anterior deltoids and inner pectorals, where the chest muscles meet in the middle of the sternum.

Starting Position: Load a bar resting on a bench-press rack with a moderately heavy weight. Lie back on the bench with your face directly beneath the racked bar and place your feet solidly flat on the gym floor to balance your body securely on the bench. Reach up and take a narrow over-grip on the bar, leaving 4–6 inches between your index fingers. Straighten your arms and lift the weight off the rack to a supported position at straight-arm's length directly above your shoulder axis.

Movement Performance: Bend your arms to slowly lower the barbell until your fists touch the middle of your chest. As the barbell is lowered and raised, your upper arms should form about a 45-degree angle with your torso. Without bouncing the weight off your chest, slowly extend your arms to return the barbell to the starting position. Repeat the movement.

Training Tips: Don't let your hips leave the bench, because arching your back is cheating the weight up. If you have a problem with this, try lifting your feet off the floor and curling your legs up over your hips.

Variations: You can vary the width of your grip inward until your hands touch each other and outward until your hands reach shoulder width.

Incline Barbell Triceps Extension

Values: This is one of the best isolation exercises for the triceps, particularly for the long inner head of the muscle group.

Starting Position: Place a moderately weighted barbell at the foot of a 30- to 45-degree incline bench. Stand astride the bench and take a narrow over-grip on the middle of the barbell

Incline barbell triceps extension—start/finish.

handle so 4–6 inches of space show between your index fingers. Stand erect and pull the bar up to chest level, rotating your elbows under it. Lie back on the incline bench and sit down on the bench's seat. Extend your arms straight up from your shoulders.

Movement Performance: Without moving your upper arms, slowly lower the bar to the rear and downward in a semicircular arc from the starting point until the backs of your hands touch your forehead. Slowly return the barbell back along the same arc to the starting point using triceps strength only. Repeat the movement for the suggested number of repetitions.

Training Tips: Do not bounce the weight off your forehead (someone once undoubtedly did, because many bodybuilders call this movement *skull crushers*). You can vary the width of your

Incline barbell triceps extension—midpoint.

Pulley pushdowns—start/finish.

Pulley pushdowns—midpoint.

grip both inward and outward for different effects on your triceps.

Variations: Incline triceps extensions can also be done with a floor pulley set behind the head end of the bench. In this case a short incline bench (one with the seat near the gym floor) is usually used. A variety of handles can be attached to the end of the cable. The most popular one at Gold's in Venice is shaped so the ends angle slightly downward from the middle toward the ends, but any short bar-type handle can be used.

Lying EZ-curl triceps extension—start/finish.

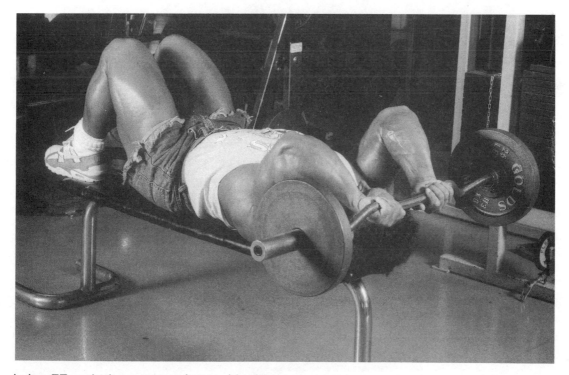

Lying EZ-curl triceps extension—midpoint.

Barbell Reverse Curls

Values: When performing barbell reverse curls, primary emphasis is on the brachialis and forearm supinator muscles. Secondary stress is placed on the biceps and forearm flexors.

Starting Position: Place a light barbell on the gym floor at your feet and step up to it, placing your feet about shoulder-width apart. Bend over and take an over-grip on the barbell handle with your hands set about shoulder-width apart. Stand erect with your arms straight down at your sides and the bar resting across your upper thighs. Press your upper arms against the sides of your rib cage and keep them motionless in this position throughout the movement.

Barbell reverse curls—start.

Barbell reverse curls—midpoint.

Barbell reverse curls—finish.

Movement Performance: Slowly curl the barbell upward in a semicircular arc from your thighs to a position directly beneath your chin. Slowly lower it back along the same arc to the starting point, and repeat the movement.

Training Tips: Vary your grip inward to one as narrow as having your hands touch each other in the middle of the bar; you probably won't be able to move your hands outward, however.

Variations: You can also do reverse curls with a straight bar handle attached to the end of a cable running through a floor pulley.

Barbell Wrist Curls

Values: Performed with the palms facing upward, wrist curls develop the forearm flexor muscles. Done with palms facing downward, barbell wrist curls build up the forearm extensors.

Starting Position: Take a narrow under-grip on a moderately weighted barbell and sit astride a flat exercise bench. Your forearms should run along the surface of the bench so your wrists and fists are off the end of the bench. Allow the weight to pull your hands as far toward the gym floor as possible.

Movement Performance: Use forearm strength to curl the weight upward in a small semicircular arc to as high a point as possible. Lower back to the starting point and repeat.

Barbell wrist curls—start.

Barbell wrist curls—finish.

Training Tips: You can also use a shoulder-width grip and do this movement with your forearms running down your thighs as you are seated, so your wrists and hands hang out into space. You can also perform the movement with either a pair of dumbbells or a single dumbbell.

Variations: This wrist-curl movement is referred to as *reverse wrist curls* when done with the palms facing downward.

Barbell reverse wrist curls—start.

Barbell reverse wrist curls—finish.

Dumbbell wrist curls (bench-supported variation)—start.

Dumbbell wrist curls (bench-supported variation)—finish.

Calf Exercises
Standing Calf Raises
Values: This is the most basic gastrocnemius exercise, and it gives you that much desired upside-down heart on the back of your lower legs.

Starting Position: Step up to a standing calf machine and dip your shoulders under the machine's yokes. Then carefully place the toes and balls of your feet on the calf block with your heels hanging off the edge. Your feet should be about 12–14 inches apart and your toes should

Standing calf raise—start.

be pointed straight ahead. Stand erect to bear the weight of the machine pressing down on your shoulders. Allow the weight to push your heels as far below the level of your toes as possible, fully stretching your calves prior to the start of a repetition.

Movement Performance: Use calf strength to rise up as high as possible on your toes. Hold this peak contracted position for a moment, then slowly lower back to the fully stretched position. Repeat the movement for the required number of repetitions.

Standing calf raise—finish.

Standing calf raise—detail (toe's
pointed inward)—midpoint.

Training Tips: Try varying toe positions
(straight ahead, angled outward at 45 degrees,
and angled inward at 45 degrees) as well as the
width of your feet placement on the calf block.
Each change of foot angle or placement will
affect your calves somewhat differently.

Standing calf raise—detail (wide
foot stance)—midpoint.

Variations: If you don't have a standing calf
machine available, it is possible to perform this
movement with a moderately heavy barbell resting across your shoulders. It takes a great deal of
balance, but standing calf raises with a barbell
can be done if you work at it.

Seated Calf Raises

Values: When you do calf raises with your knees bent at a 90-degree angle, you transfer stress from the gastrocnemius to the broad, flat soleus muscle lying beneath it. The soleus gives you most of your calf width, so it's essential that you don't neglect seated calf work.

Starting Position: Sit down on the seat of a seated calf machine. Adjust the height of the knee pads so you still have resistance on your

Seated calf raises—start.

knees when your heels are in the lowest possible position. Place your toes and the balls of your feet on the cross bar provided for them; your feet should be set about 12–14 inches apart with the toes pointed straight ahead. Pull the knee pads over your knees, push up with your toes, and release the lever arm of the machine by pushing the stop bar forward. Once weight is on your knees, allow it to push your heels as far below the level of your toes as possible to prestretch your calf muscles prior to each repetition.

Movement Performance: Use calf strength to

Seated calf raises—finish.

Seated calf raises—detail (greater foot flexibility)—start.

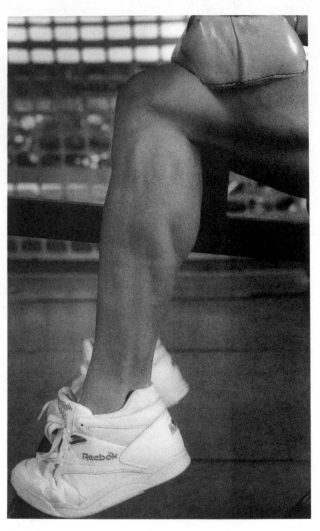

Seated calf raises—detail (greater foot flexibility)—finish.

push against the machine's weight to rise up as high as possible on your toes. Hold this peak contracted position for a moment, then lower back to the fully stretched position. Repeat the movement for the suggested number of repetitions.

Training Tips: Try varying your toe angle (straight ahead, outward, or inward), as well as the width of your foot placement on the toe bar.

Variations: If a seated calf machine isn't avail-

able, you can do seated calf raises like body-builders performed them prior to the invention of a machine to simplify the movement. Place a calf block about a foot from the end of a flat exercise bench. Roll a heavy towel around the middle of a moderately heavy barbell to pad it. Sit down on the end of the bench and place your toes and the balls of your feet on the block. Have a training partner lift the weight up to rest on your knees, where you can balance it as you do the movement by grasping the bar out near the plates.

Calf presses (45-degree machine)—start.

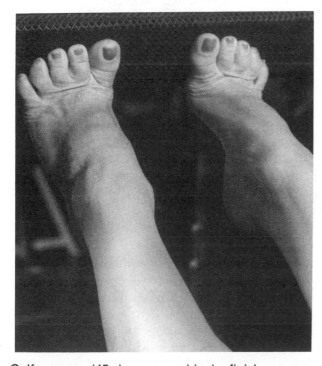

Calf presses (45-degree machine)—finish.

Calf Presses

Values: This is a good secondary movement for the gastrocnemius. It can be performed on any type of leg-press machine.

Starting Position: Let's describe the movement as done on a 45-degree angled leg-press machine. Sit back in the seat and recline your back against the back support. Place your toes and the balls of your feet on the foot board on the machine with your heels hanging out in space. Your feet should be about 12–14 inches apart, and your toes should be angled directly forward. Straighten your legs to take the weight on the machine and allow that weight to push your toes as far toward your face as possible, thereby prestretching your calf muscles prior to your first repetition.

Movement Performance: Use calf strength to completely extend your feet. Hold this peak contracted position for a moment, then return to the starting position. Repeat.

Calf presses (vertical machine)—start.

Training Tips: Vary your toe angle (straight ahead, outward, or inward) and the width between your feet as they are placed on the board.

Variations: This movement can also be conveniently performed on seated and lying leg-press machines.

Abdominal Exercises

Hanging Leg Raises

Values: This is a very intense movement that affects the entire rectus-abdominis muscle wall, giving a washboard appearance to your midsection.

Starting Position: Jump up and take a shoulder-width over-grip on a chinning bar. Hang straight down from the bar and bend your knees slightly to keep unnecessary pressure off your lower back; keep them bent like this for the entire set.

Hanging leg raises—start.

Hanging leg raises—finish.

Movement Performance: Slowly raise your feet in a semicircular arc from the starting point to a position just above the level of your hips. Hold this peak contracted position for a moment, then return to the starting point. Repeat the movement for the desired number of repetitions.

Hanging leg raises (variation with elbow straps)—start.

Training Tips: You'll probably find it difficult to kill your swing back and forth beneath the bar when you first start including hanging leg raises in your program. If you have a problem with swing, have a training partner hold the sides of your hips stationary as you perform the

Hanging leg raises (variation with elbow straps)—finish.

movement. Many gyms are now equipped with padded loops in which you can comfortably rest your elbows to support yourself when doing leg raises. Muscle-film star Brad Harris invented these loops and advertises them for sale in most bodybuilding magazines from time to time.

Variations: There is an easier variation of hanging leg raises called *frog kicks*. You simply pull your knees up to your chest while simultaneously bending your legs fully.

Incline Sit-Ups

Values: This is another intense rectus-abdominis movement, particularly for the upper half of the muscle wall. If you perform it in twisting fashion, it also stresses the intercostal muscles.

Starting Position: Set the incline sit-up board to an appropriate angle. Hook your feet beneath the roller pads at the top end of the bench, and point your head toward the lower end. Bend your knees about 30 degrees to remove unwanted stress from your lower back; keep them bent like this throughout the movement. Interlace your fingers behind your head or neck to immobilize your arms during the exercise.

Movement Performance: Slowly curl first your head, then your shoulders, upper back, and finally your lower back off the board to sit upward until your torso is perpendicular to the floor. Lower slowly back to the starting point, reversing the procedure used to sit upward, and repeat the movement for the suggested number of repetitions.

Incline sit-ups—start.

Incline sit-ups—finish.

Training Tips: The higher the end of the bench, the greater the amount of resistance placed on the abdominal muscles as you perform incline sit-ups. Once the board is at about a 45-degree angle, raising it further becomes impractical, and you should begin to add more resistance by holding a light barbell plate behind your head.

Variations: Try twisting as you perform your incline sit-ups. Do the first repetition straight ahead, the second twisting your torso to the left, the second straight ahead, the next twisting your torso to the right, and so on, until you have thoroughly exhausted your abdominal muscles.

Crunches

Values: Crunches intensely stress the entire rectus-abdominis muscle wall at the front of your midsection. If you do the movement twisting from side to side, you can also stress the intercostals at the sides of your waist.

Starting Position: Lie on your back on the gym floor with your lower legs draped over a flat exercise bench so your thighs are perpendicular to the gym floor. Place your hands behind your head and keep them there throughout the movement.

Movement Performance: You must do four things at once to perform a perfect rep of the crunch movement: use lower abdominal strength to lift your hips from the floor; use upper ab-

Crunches (variation with feet over bench)—start.

Crunches (variation with feet over bench)—finish.

dominal strength to lift your shoulders from the floor; attempt to shorten the distance between your shoulders and your hips by contracting your abdominal muscles to pull the two toward each other; and sharply exhale. If you perform these functions correctly, you will feel a satisfyingly intense contraction in your frontal abdominal muscles. Relax and repeat the movement.

Training Tips: Be sure you don't do a leg-curl movement to lift your hips from the floor. That lift must come entirely from tensing your lower ab muscles. And don't throw your shoulders up-

ward; instead, lift them using upper-ab strength.

Variations: If you don't have an exercise bench handy, you can do this movement by placing your feet flat against the gym wall so your shins are parallel with the floor and your thighs are perpendicular to it. You can also try twisting crunches in which you do one rep straight ahead, the second twisting as far as possible to the left, the third straight ahead, the fourth twisting as far as possible to the right, and so on, until you have exhausted your abdominal muscles for that set.

Crunches (variation with feet over bench)—twisting to one side.

Suggested Routines

Now that you know all of the best mass-building exercises, you'll need some routines to follow. The three that appear here were contributed by Lee Haney, history's only eight-time Mr. Olympia winner. Haney trained at Gold's Gym during 1983–84, the year leading up to his first Mr. Olympia victory, and many of his photos were used to illustrate *The Gold's Gym Training Encyclopedia* (Contemporary, 1984). We know you want the best programs for building mass and power, so we've gone to the best of the best to get them for you. Good luck with your workouts, and always THINK HUGE!

Three of the greats reveal their secrets in one mega-seminar: Diana Dennis (L), IFBB Pro World Champion; Lee Haney, eight-time Mr. Olympia; and Mike Christian, another Pro World Champion. It is essential to attend these training and nutrition seminars—the champions always share the latest bodybuilding information.

MR. OLYMPIA'S SUGGESTED MASS-BUILDING ROUTINES

Routine A

Monday/Thursday Exercise	Sets	Reps
Hanging Leg Raises	3–4	15–20
Leg Extensions (warm-up)	2–3	15–20
Squats	6	15–5*
Stiff-Leg Deadlifts	5	20–10*
Seated Low-Pulley Rows	5	15–6*
Medium-Grip Front Lat Pulldowns	5	15–6*
Standing Barbell Curls	4	12–6*
Seated Incline Dumbbell Curls	4	12–6*
Seated Calf Machine Toe Raises	5–7	12–10*

*Pyramid

Tuesday/Friday Exercise	Sets	Reps
Floor Crunches	3–4	20–30
Barbell Bench Presses	6	15–5*
Incline Dumbbell Presses	5	15–6*
Barbell Upright Rows	5	15–6*
Seated Presses Behind Neck	5	15–6*
Incline Barbell Triceps Extensions	4	15–8*
Barbell Pullover and Press	4	15–8*
Barbell Reverse Curls	3–4	8–10
Barbell Wrist Curls	3–4	12–15
Standing Calf Machine Toe Raises	5–7	20–10*

*Pyramid

Routine B

Monday/Thursday

Exercise	Sets	Reps
Twisting Incline Sit-Ups	3–4	20–25
Leg Extensions (warm-up)	2–3	15–20
Angled Leg Presses	6	15–5*
Hyperextensions (weighted)	5	20–10*
Barbell Bent Rows (on block)	5	15–6*
Wide-Grip Pulldowns Behind Neck	5	15–6*
Seated Dumbbell Curls	4	12–6*
Pulley Preacher Curls	4	12–6*
One-Leg Toe Raises	5–7	15–20

*Pyramid

Tuesday/Friday

Exercise	Sets	Reps
Pulley Crunches	3–4	20–30
Barbell Incline Presses	6	15–5*
Dumbbell Bench Presses	5	15–6*
Cable Upright Rows	5	15–6*
Seated Smith Machine Front Presses	5	15–6*
Flat-Bench Barbell Triceps Extensions	4	15–8*
Pulley Pushdowns	4	15–8*
Hammer Curls	3–4	8–10
Dumbbell Wrist Curls	3–4	12–15
Donkey Calf Machine Toe Raises	5–7	20–10

*Pyramid

Routine C

Monday/Thursday

Exercise	Sets	Reps
Knee-Ups (hanging from bar)	3–4	20–25
Leg Extensions (warm-up)	2–3	15–20
Hack Squats	6	15–5*
Good Mornings	5	20–10*
One-Arm Dumbbell Bent Rows	5	15–6*
Close-Grip Front Lat Pulldowns	5	15–6*
Barbell Preacher Curls	4	12–6*
Standing Alternate Dumbbell Curls	4	12–6*
Calf Presses (on leg press machine)	5–7	15–20

*Pyramid

Tuesday/Friday

Exercise	Sets	Reps
Roman Chair Sit-Ups	3–4	30–40
Parallel Bar Dips (weighted)	6	15–5*
Low-Incline Barbell Presses	5	15–6*
Behind-Back Barbell Shrugs	5	12–15
Seated Dumbbell Presses	5	15–6*
Close-Grip Bench Presses	4	12–6*
Standing One-Arm Dumbbell Triceps Extensions	4	12–6*
Preacher Barbell Reverse Curls	3–4	8–10
Behind-Back Barbell Wrist Curls	3–4	12–15
Hack Machine Toe Raises	5–7	12–15

*Pyramid

After winning his eighth-straight Mr. Olympia title in the Fall of 1991 at Orlando, Florida, Lee Haney addresses the audience while master of ceremonies Reg Park looks on.

Humongous Lee Haney, winner of eight consecutive Mr. Olympia titles between 1984 and 1991, gives a mean training seminar. If he's appearing in your area, he's worth at least double the price of admission.

10
The Recovery Cycle

"The most fundamental and important aspect of gaining muscle mass is a complete understanding of the recovery cycle," reveals eight-time Mr. Olympia Lee Haney, one of the most massively muscular men of all time. "It should be noted that very few young bodybuilders give recovery a moment's thought and thus fail to make good gains simply because they neglect between-workout rest and recuperation practices.

"It's axiomatic that muscles increase in mass and power *following* a workout, during the period when the body is allowed to rest. Muscles may get temporarily pumped up during a training session, but growth doesn't occur during the course of a workout. Rather, muscle growth takes place during the two- to four-day break between workouts for a particular body part."

A complete understanding of the recovery cycle is the true key to success when it comes to building larger and more powerful muscles. But in their zeal to buff up, young bodybuilders often become so completely concerned with their

Canadian Paul Dillett prepares his hypervascular arms for a set of dumbbell curls.

workouts—and perhaps also with what they eat—that they completely ignore proper recovery. Their workouts become longer and longer, until their bodies are unable to fully recuperate between training sessions. They become chronically fatigued, so fatigued and overtrained that they can't make good gains—indeed, any gains at all—regardless of how hard and highly intense their workouts happen to be.

In many ways bodybuilding magazines contribute to massive numbers of overtrained young bodybuilders. These publications concentrate on the routines and training methods of the sport's elite athletes, men and women who have spent many years developing outstanding powers of recovery and as a result can profit from long, hard, heavy workouts.

Great competitive bodybuilders didn't always train the way they say they do in magazine articles, however. While they might be doing 15–20 total sets per muscle group now, they once did only 3–4 sets for each body part. Muscle magazines neglect to write about the types of routines elite athletes followed on the way to the top of the bodybuilding pyramid; in doing so they mislead thousands of highly enthusiastic young men and women who want to become great bodybuilders as quickly as humanly possible.

Successful bodybuilders patiently build up the ability to recover between workouts. Over a period of years they progress from a three-day-per-week beginners routine to a four-day-per-week program. Over the same extended period they progress from doing 3–4 sets per body part up to 8–10 and ultimately even higher. During this process they are patient, understanding that a championship physique can take years to achieve, and they are careful to undertrain rather than overtrain.

"Overtraining is the biggest enemy a young bodybuilder can face," explains Lee Haney, "because it negates his efforts in the gym. Muscle growth will not and cannot occur when an athlete is in an overtrained state; in extreme cases of overtraining a bodybuilder can actually lose mass, tone, and strength. Finally, in all cases of overtraining a bodybuilder is more injury-prone and open to infectious illnesses."

Training Frequency

Haney says, "Overtraining occurs as a result of two factors: overly frequent training sessions and excessively long workouts. For most bodybuilders I suggest a four-day split routine—twice a week for each muscle group—when in a mass-building phase. That's the same type of program I personally followed until the last three months before I won the Heavyweight and Overall NPC National and Heavyweight IFBB World Championships in 1982, two years before my first Mr. Olympia victory. For the very advanced bodybuilder, good gains in muscle mass as a result of optimum recovery can occur by following a three-on/two-off split routine."

The most basic four-day split routine involves working half of the body on Mondays and Thursdays, the other half on Tuesdays and Fridays. This split leaves Wednesdays and weekends free for complete rest.

EXAMPLES OF THE FOUR-DAY SPLIT

Alternative 1

Monday/Thursday	Tuesday/Friday
Abdominals	Abdominals
Chest	Legs
Deltoids	Arms
Back	Calves

Frank Hillebrand—leg extensions.

Alternative 2

Monday/Thursday	Tuesday/Friday
Abdominals	Abdominals
Chest	Legs
Shoulders	Back
Arms	Calves

Alternative 3

Monday/Thursday	Tuesday/Friday
Abdominals	Abdominals
Legs	Back
Chest	Delts
Calves	Arms

Note how abdominals can be trained each of the four workout days if desired. No direct neck exercises are included because the neck grows large and powerful simply as a result of the training you do for peripheral muscles like traps, delts, chest, and even upper arms.

Lee Haney also mentions a three-on/two-off split routine for more advanced bodybuilders.

EXAMPLES OF THE THREE-ON/TWO-OFF SPLIT

Alternative 1

Day 1	Day 2	Day 3	Days 4-5
Chest	Legs	Shoulders	Rest
Back	Calves	Arms	
Abdominals	Abdominals	Calves	

Alternative 2

Day 1	Day 2	Day 3	Days 4-5
Chest	Back	Legs	Rest
Shoulders	Biceps	Calves	
Triceps	Abdominals	Abdominals	

Lee Haney says, "In both of the foregoing types of splits, emphasis is placed on taking relatively few workouts each week. Very few bodybuilders can make any gains in mass when training six days per week. Long experience—both personally and through the young men and women I coach—has demonstrated conclusively that a four-day-per-week split yields the optimum number of weekly workouts when shooting for additional muscle mass."

Older bodybuilders and hard-gainers recover more slowly than most, and these individuals

Career army Sarge Joe Dawson won two NPC National Amateur championships.

Tim Belknap has become history's most famous diabetic bodybuilder, but what a bodybuilder! He's won the Mr. America, Mr. World, and Mr. Universe titles.

often make their best gains from training each muscle complex only once per week. Andreas Cahling, IFBB Pro Mr. International, pioneered this type of training program. It worked wonders for Cahling when he decided to make a competitive comeback in his late thirties after taking more than five years completely off regular workouts to concentrate on business affairs.

"This type of split routine works best for me if I train six days per week," Cahling notes, "but it's also great for four- and three-day programs. Since I have six full days of rest between workouts for a particular body part, I can do lengthy sessions for each muscle complex—certainly longer workouts than if I trained body parts two or three times each week.

"I felt the back was my weakest muscle group prior to making my comeback, so I decided to specialize on developing that area, particularly trying to bring out the width of my back. I did 40–45 total sets for my upper and middle back each time I trained it over the last few months prior to competition.

"The lower back was trained separately. Of these 40–45 total sets, 20 sets were chins. My training partner and I did five sets each of four different bar grips on chins, which are excellent for developing width in the back. We trained relatively slowly, so that each workout took about 1½ hours. It was by far the longest workout of the week. In comparison, we did arms and forearms—strong points for both of us—in only 20 minutes.

"My back program worked better than I could have visualized it in my wildest dreams. As I went through my free-posing routine at the Niagara Falls Pro Invitational, I knew my back had improved so radically that it was no longer a weak point. Instead, it was a strong point.

"Training each muscle group only once per week works best for bodybuilders who can't seem to make gains in any other manner. This is because the program allows a very intense workout for each individual muscle group, followed by a maximum recovery period of six days. Hard-gainers almost always begin to gain strength and muscle mass on this program, particularly if they work out only three days per week."

Following is an example of the type of routine Cahling recommends for hard-gainers.

Monday	Wednesday	Friday
Chest	Quadriceps	Back
Shoulders	Hamstrings	Biceps
Triceps	Calves	Forearms

"Hard-gainers don't usually require abdominal training," Cahling says. "For each large muscle group I recommend 10–12 total sets, but less—usually 6–8 sets each—for biceps, triceps, and forearms. Stick to basic exercises only, and have a training partner help you get 2–3 forced reps past failure on the last set of each movement. Train relatively quickly so your workouts last no more than 45–60 minutes each.

"Advanced bodybuilders past 35 years of age tend to recover somewhat more slowly than their younger counterparts. They will make great gains working one muscle group each day for six full days until the entire physique has been trained once. Then Sunday can be taken as a full rest day."

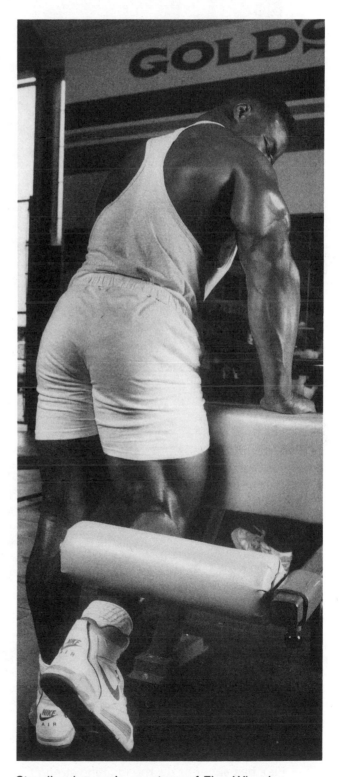

Standing leg curls courtesy of Flex Wheeler.

Flex has superior overhead lifting strength.

Flex Wheeler manhandles 315 pounds for presses behind the neck at a body weight of about 225 pounds.

Here is how Andreas Cahling splits up his body parts for the type of split routine he follows:

Monday: chest

Tuesday: quadriceps

Wednesday: back

Thursday: shoulders

Friday: arms, calves

Saturday: hamstrings, buttocks, lower back

Sunday: rest

The Saturday workout involves three interrelated muscle groups that are difficult to train individually. Cahling also rarely trains abdominals, fitting them in 2–3 times per week anywhere convenient in his program over the final 6–8 weeks leading up to a competition.

Total Sets

"Yet another way to avoid overtraining," says Lee Haney, "calls for keeping under control the total number of sets performed for a muscle group in a workout. I've always done significantly fewer total sets per body part than most comparable bodybuilders, a primary reason why I have been so successful in building muscle mass. I perform no more than about 15 total sets for large muscle groups and fewer than 10 for smaller ones when on a mass-building cycle. This contrasts dramatically with the 20–30 sets per body part many top men do.

"If *I* do 10–15 total sets per muscle group, then a relatively less experienced bodybuilder should perform even fewer if he wishes to avoid the overtraining syndrome that will hold back his progress. For most bodybuilders I recommend 10–12 total sets for large muscle groups such as legs, back, chest, and shoulders and 6–8 for smaller, less complex body parts. Beginners should do even fewer sets—generally speaking, no more than 3–5 sets per muscle group.

"There are exceptions to the preceding parameters. Perhaps 5–10 percent of all bodybuilders would fall into the category called *hard-gainer*. They find it easy to overtrain yet difficult to gain mass. Hard-gainers should *never* work out more than four days per week, while reducing the recommended number of sets for each muscle group by about 25 percent.

"Anyone who follows proper recovery and training procedures can pack on muscle mass if he wants to. Interestingly, no one ever gains muscle body weight as quickly as he would like. Put simply, it's a slow process, slow enough that most advanced and contest-level bodybuilders are overjoyed to gain 5–6 pounds of solid muscle per year. The point is, be patient. Always keep in mind the fact that you *will* make good gains if you are highly motivated and disciplined enough to stick to a proper mass-building program 100 percent of the time."

Sleep and Rest

The main way your body restores itself is through sound sleep each night. "Sleep and rest are essential elements of between-workout recuperation and recovery," says Berry de Mey, a former World Games Champion who now competes in the WBF. "Recovery won't take place unless you obtain sufficient rest and sleep each day.

"By rest I mean maintaining a low-energy-loss approach to each day. Avoid doing much aerobic training when in a weight-gaining phase. Stay calm and collected all day, train hard, then get a good night's sleep.

"The amount of sleep each night is highly individualized, varying from 6 hours in some

Sue Gafner—U.S. Lightweight Champ and now a successful IFBB pro via her 1991 victory in the IFBB Pro Jan Tana Classic.

cases to as many as 12 hours per day. Whatever the length, the object is to sleep long enough each night to feel completely rested the following day. You can arrive at appropriate amounts of sleep for you through experimentation. Once you have discovered the correct amount of sleep for your individual mind and body, you should stick to it. If you don't sleep enough one night, make it up the next one.

"Also, most of the best bodybuilders in the world take naps during the day to recharge their batteries. Twenty to 30 minutes of sleep during the afternoon works miraculous wonders in encouraging optimum recuperation between training sessions."

Glycogen Loading/Depleting

Long experience has taught top bodybuilders that they need to load up on carbohydrates in the days and hours prior to a workout so their muscles will be completely full of glycogen to fuel a hard, heavy, weight-gaining workout. Long experience has also taught them that they should not fully deplete the glycogen in their

Frank Hillebrand is one of the many Europeans who spend the summer in California training at Gold's in Venice, known far and wide as the Mecca of bodybuilding.

Upright rows.

bodies each workout, because that tends to make it much more difficult to load up fully for the next workout.

For optimum glycogen loading, you should include many sources of complex carbohydrates in your daily diet. These foods include potatoes, yams, rice, whole-grain cereals and breads, and vegetables. It's particularly advisable to consume a high complex-carb meal about two hours prior to each workout. Since foods rich in complex carbohydrates digest slowly and release their energy over a sustained period of time, you can supplement the glycogen stored in your muscles and liver with new sugars from the digesting complex-carbohydrate foods.

To make sure your carbohydrate foods digest efficiently, try to avoid consuming any type of meat or other protein foods at the same meal. And try consuming at least three types of complex carbohydrate foods in that meal, e.g., rice, potatoes, and yams.

About 30 minutes prior to your workout, you can consume some simple carbs in the form of fruit. Fruit will release its energy more quickly than complex carbs but in releasing that energy will give your workout a good blast-off. Pick your favorite fruit.

To keep blood-sugar levels high during a workout, many bodybuilders now drink high-carb beverages in the middle of a training session. Most of these drinks are made with glucose polymers, which break down at a rate about halfway between those of complex and simple carbs. Taking a sip every few sets is helpful in maintaining a workably high level of glycogen in the working muscles.

Overtraining

You've already read Lee Haney's statement that overtraining is caused by excessively frequent and/or long workouts. But how can you recognize when you've become overtrained, and what can you do about the problem to remedy it?

Following are the most frequently observable symptoms of an overtrained state.

- Lack of enthusiasm for training
- Persistently sore joints and/or muscles
- Poor motor coordination
- Nervousness
- Lethargy
- Constant lack of energy
- Sleeping excessively or sleeplessness
- Elevated morning pulse rate
- Elevated morning blood pressure
- Frequent infectious illnesses

If you are experiencing more than one or two of these symptoms, you are no doubt overtrained. As soon as you recognize this fact, you should cease gym workouts for at least one or two weeks. But don't stop exercising completely. Instead, indulge in favorite physical activities unrelated to bodybuilding, such as scuba diving, mountain hiking or biking, swimming, or playing any of several racket sports. This is what Russian exercise scientists call *active rest*, and it will keep you in shape while your body recovers from its overtrained state.

You'll usually know precisely when you're ready to get back into the gym, because you'll begin to think about it all of the time. Once back into your workout pattern, alter your sessions somewhat. It's a good idea to get away from the type of training schedule that caused you to overtrain in the first place. Reduce the number of workouts you perform each week, while concurrently reducing the total number of sets per body part. If possible, however, you should try to increase the intensity of each workout.

Experienced bodybuilders recognize the fact that there is an almost knifelike edge between optimal training and overtraining, and it's relatively easy to slip over that knife edge. Keep vigilant, and once you observe any symptoms of the overtraining syndrome, take some rest from the gym and make appropriate changes in your training routines. In this way, you can continue to make gains in muscle mass and strength at an optimum rate of speed without ever becoming so overtrained that you might injure yourself.

Neal Spruce, author of most of Chapter 11. Obviously, he knows what he's talking about.

11 Nutrition for Mass and Power

Authors' Note: This chapter was researched and written almost completely by Neal Spruce, Director of the Nutritional Products Division for Gold's Gym Enterprises, Inc. Spruce is a former competitive bodybuilder who has placed in the top five at more than one national-level competition. He remains active as a frequent guest lecturer on nutrition and physical fitness across the country. For more information, contact the Gold's Gym Nutritional Products Division at (800) 457-5357 or (310) 392-3005.

Serious bodybuilders simply don't dispute the importance of proper nutrition in the muscle-gaining process. Most agree that training and diet are a 50–50 process at worst, and many feel that nutrition is responsible for 70–75 percent of the success they experience in packing on quality beef.

Nutrition and bodybuilding training, though, doesn't affect just the elite members of the sport. Did you know that 70 percent of all people who join a gym quit after only six weeks? Why? No results! This is almost always due to improper diets—consuming too few calories, skipping meals, having meal nutrients unbalanced—and/or due to the cooking and processing of foods. These incomplete diets make it virtually impossible to get all of the nutrients your body needs in order to make the cosmetic changes you desire.

The typical American diet lacks the complete and proper combination of vitamins, minerals, and other essential nutrients your body needs to function at an optimum level. Without these essentials (vitamins, minerals, and nutrients) your body will be unable to synthesize as much muscle, burn as much fat, or have as much energy as it could if it were supplied with complete nutrition. If you are training without the proper balance of nutrients, vitamins, and minerals, you will guarantee yourself frustration from not achieving the results you intend.

By providing your body with the proper supplementation, you are accomplishing two things. First, you are providing your body with the nutrients it needs to recover from the workout you're giving it (i.e., daily workouts, stress, etc.). With these nutrients your body can recover or respond to that workload by building more muscle and losing more fat. If you choose not to give your body these nutrients, it will not fully respond and you will see very little or no results.

Constant depleting of nutrients—both liquid and solid—during a hard workout must be compensated for via meals both between and often during workouts. WBF superstar Gary Strydom towels off in midworkout.

Second, supplements provide your body with the required nutrients and contain little or no calories. This allows you to synthesize and/or tone muscle while losing fat at the same time. Remember, if you don't enhance your nutrition, you can't enhance your physique or your performance!

The key to achieving your desired goal is to supply your body with the proper number of calories and food combinations. Adding sensible supplementation to your diet will help you cover all of your nutritional bases. This is the only way to achieve maximum results from your efforts with heavy iron in the gym.

Don't be a gym dropout. Give your body the nutrition it needs so that every workout makes a difference in your relative muscle mass and strength levels.

Milos Sarcev has won a Mr. Universe title through intelligent training and nutrition. Here he gears up for a hard workout with a quick meal on the front steps of Gold's in San Diego.

Macronutrients

Macronutrients include protein, carbohydrates, fats, and water. On the other hand, micronutrients include vitamins, minerals, trace elements, and enzymes.

Protein

A champion bodybuilder pays more attention to the protein in his or her diet than to any other nutrient because protein is the primary nonwater constituent of skeletal muscles. In their quest for bigger and more defined muscles, bodybuilders around the world have made private experiments in the consumption of protein foods and protein concentrates and/or amino acids.

Protein builds muscle tissue. Unlike some nutrients, protein cannot be stored in your body. It must be consumed in adequate supplies throughout the day in order to provide the tissue-build-ing needs your workouts have stimulated. The protein you consume must be of high biological quality so that a maximum amount of it is used each time you eat.

Protein consists of 22 basic building blocks called *amino acids*. Nine amino acids cannot be manufactured within your body and therefore must be consumed in food throughout the day; these are called *essential* amino acids. The remaining 13 aminos—called *nonessential* amino acids—can be manufactured within your body from the foods you consume in the course of a day.

The 22 amino acids can be combined in a large number of configurations—over 1,600—within your body. When those proteins containing all of the essential amino acids are nearly in the same conformation as the proteins in your body's tissues, the protein food has high biological quality. In general, protein from animal sources (fish, poultry, beef, eggs, milk products)

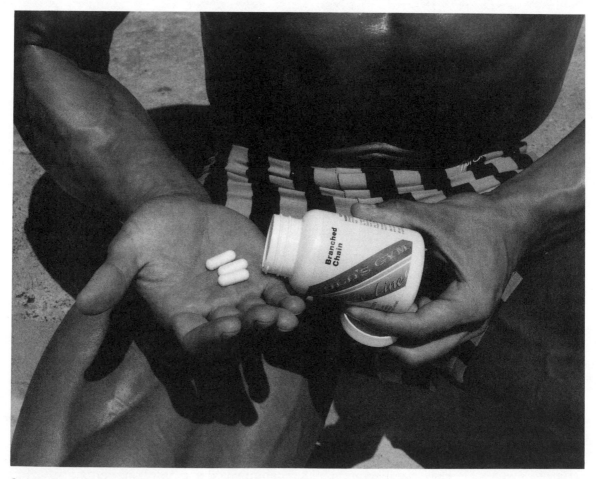

Gold's Gym brand branched-chain amino acids are great for postworkout recovery and building solid muscle tissue.

is of significantly higher biological quality than protein from vegetable sources.

Virtually all serious bodybuilders consume drinks made from concentrated proteins, and Gold's Gym has a complete line of protein supplements. These drinks are used for two main reasons: to supplement (or increase) the amount of protein in your diet or to act as a replacement for a meal that might otherwise have been missed.

Later in this chapter we have included a series of suggested weight-gain diets and menu plans for 2,000-, 2,500-, 3,000-, 3,500-, 4,000-, 4,500-, 5,000-, 5,500-, and 6,000-calorie days. One primary constituent of these weight-gain menus is a protein drink made with Gold's Gym Weight Gainer Formula.

RECIPES FOR MEAL SUBSTITUTE OR MEAL SUPPLEMENT

Recipes are based on Gold's Gym Weight Gainer Formula. All recipes may include ice.

500-Calorie Formula	Cal
2 scoops Weight Gainer mix	290
1½ cups low-fat milk	135
1 banana	100
	525

750-Calorie Formula	Cal
3 scoops Weight Gainer mix	435
2 cups low-fat milk	180
1 banana	100
1 cup strawberries	50
	765

975-Calorie Formula	Cal
3 scoops Weight Gainer mix	435
2 cups low-fat milk	180
1 banana	100
2 whole eggs	160
2 cups frozen strawberries	100
	975

Heavy-Duty Gainer	Cal
4 scoops Weight Gainer mix	580
3 cups low-fat milk	270
2 tablespoons peanut butter	190
1 banana	100
2 whole eggs	160
	1300

At the elite level of competitive bodybuilding, amino-acid supplements are also essential. These come in two types: free-form aminos, which help to enhance your body's critical nitrogen balance, and branched-chain aminos, which are useful for accelerated muscle recovery between workouts as well as for muscle growth. The three branched-chain amino acids (leucine, isoleucine, and valine) make up a disproportionately large part of each skeletal muscle.

Muscles are high in nitrogen content, and keeping your body's basic nitrogen ratio, or balance, on the plus side is essential if you intend to get as much out of your hard mass-building workouts as you should. The way to keep your nitrogen balance high is to follow a high-protein diet supplemented with protein concentrates (in the form of drinks) and/or amino acids.

Carbohydrates

Carbohydrate foods are a vital element in any serious bodybuilder's diet because they provide the fuel for forceful muscle contractions during a high-intensity workout. Indeed, the correct choice of carbohydrate foods and the manner in which they are eaten can literally make or break you as a competitive bodybuilder.

Carbohydrate molecules all contain various combinations of elemental carbon (chemically represented by the letter C) and water (H_2O), giving carbohydrates a chemical structure of CH_2O. The energy boost you feel when you've consumed a carbohydrate food comes from breaking up the energy bonds that hold the carbon, hydrogen, and oxygen atoms together to form the carbohydrate molecule. The amount of energy received and the speed with which that energy is released depend on the complexity of various carbohydrate molecules.

Carbohydrate foods are classified as either simple or complex. That classification refers to the complexity of the food's molecule. Simple carbs are easily and quickly digested and are turned into glucose, which can be stored in the muscles and liver as glycogen for later use or for immediate use, if necessary. Junk foods made from simple sugars (primarily sucrose) are the worst type of carbohydrates a serious bodybuilder can consume; eating sugar results in a very quick energy peak and an equally quick energy valley as insulin is secreted to drive the blood-sugar level back to normal.

Most serious bodybuilders stick to complex carbohydrate foods, which are broken down more slowly and provide a lower—but much more sustained—amount of energy to the sys-

A constant sight at Gold's Gym, toweling off between sets . . .

. . . and replenishing fluids shortly thereafter.

tem. Favorite complex carbohydrate foods include potatoes, rice, yams, legumes, grains, and vegetables.

If you do feel the need for simple carbs in your diet, you should obtain them from fruit, particularly fruit high in water content (e.g., watermelon and other melons) and relatively low in sugar content. Eating this type of simple carbohydrate will give you fewer energy peaks and valleys.

One of the newest types of food supplements available to bodybuilders are carbohydrate drinks, which consist of glucose polymers in powder form. The powder is mixed with pure water and carried around during a workout in a squeeze bottle. Glucose polymers do not break down as quickly as a sugar-laden soft drink would, however, so you should begin to drink them about 30 minutes prior to your workout and take a sip here and there throughout your session with the weights.

Fats

In modern industrial countries we have developed quite a taste for dietary fats. Indeed, the average American consumes three to four times

as many calories in fat as in either protein or carbohydrates.

Bodybuilders, however, are tremendously conscious of the fat content in their diets. Sometimes bodybuilders monitor their dietary fat consumption to the point where they possibly cause temporary danger to their health. In general, bodybuilders approach an ideal caloric ratio of 60–25–15 (off-season) in carbohydrates, protein, and fats. These ratios, incidentally, vary a bit according to oxidative type.

Polyunsaturated fats from vegetable sources are a vital component in your diet. They are necessary for healthy conformation and function of your nerves, skin, and hair. Linoleic acid, arachidonic acid, and linolenic acid (called *essential fatty acids*) are necessary for proper metabolism of body-fat stores. Fats are also necessary for transportation of the fat-soluble vitamins— A, D, E, and K.

The saturated fats found in animal flesh, egg yolks, and milk products, however, have no useful function in a bodybuilder's diet. They do provide some of the taste found in animal protein foods, but saturated fats also provide more than twice as many calories per gram than either protein or carbohydrates.

Cholesterol and triglycerides have been implicated in heart and vascular disease. Cholesterol is an essential dietary factor necessary for the manufacture of vitamin D in the body, formation of cell walls and nerve sheaths, and production of a variety of hormones. But excess cholesterol can be deposited in your arterial system, gradually narrowing and then eventually completely closing the bore of the arteries.

Very little cholesterol is required for healthy bodily function. Even a vegetarian diet, inherently very low in cholesterol content, will provide sufficient cholesterol for the health of cells and nerves and for the production of hormones. Therefore, a diet of skinned chicken and turkey meat, fish, egg whites, nonfat milk products, grains, seeds, nuts, fruits, and vegetables will limit cholesterol intake and help prevent formation of plaques in your arterial system.

About 80 percent of the fat in a bodybuilder's diet consists of molecules called *triglycerides*, which have also been implicated in cardiac disease by some researchers. You can limit your intake of triglycerides by avoiding the fats found in ice cream and other junk foods.

Much has been written lately about high-density lipoproteins (HDLs), a beneficial form of cholesterol that makes up about 30 percent of the cholesterol in your diet. When you take anabolic steroids, however, you dramatically reduce the ratio of HDLs in your blood, allowing more harmful LDLs (low-density lipoproteins) to gain the upper hand.

Water

Despite the fact that water is a nutrient almost universally ignored by hard-training bodybuilders, it is essential to the maintenance of life itself. Roughly 70 percent of a champion's body weight is water, and 70 percent of his or her muscle weight is water as well. Blood has a very high water content, and fatty tissues also contain water, although not as much by percentage as

At the IFBB San Jose Pro Invitational, Albert Beckles, Milos Sarcev, and Steve Brisbois compare front double-bi shots in the compulsory-poses round. The trio all are Gold's Gym members.

does muscle tissue. Even bone tissues contain about 25 percent water, and teeth slightly less than 10 percent water.

Nutritionists refer to water as the universal solvent within the human body. It is involved in myriad chemical reactions within the body and also helps regulate body temperature during hot days—and heavy workouts—through the evaporation of perspiration. The temperature-regulating properties of water are vital to hard-training bodybuilders, so you should never be afraid to take occasional swallows of water in midworkout.

Other functions of water within your body include its use as a joint and muscle lubricant; use as a solvent in primary and secondary digestion of food; use as a vehicle for transportation of toxins from your body in urine, feces, and perspiration; use as the "filler" in each cell of your body; and use as a means of transporting electrolyte minerals between cells to encourage powerful and sustained muscle contractions. When you grow weak and overly fatigued in the middle of a workout, chances are good that you haven't been drinking sufficient water and/or consuming enough supplementary electrolytes.

One of the most important functions of water is its action as a natural cleanser within your body. Concentrations of toxic elements can be broken up, suspended in water, and excreted from your body. That's why you should drink 8–10 large glasses of pure water every day.

SUMMARY CHART OF NUTRIENTS

Macronutrients

Protein: Necessary for growth and development. Acts in formation of hormones, enzymes, and antibodies. Maintains acid-alkali balance. Source of heat and energy

Carbohydrates: Provide energy for body functions. Assist in digestion of food

Fats: Provide energy. Act as a carrier for fat-soluble vitamins (A, D, E, K). Provide essential fatty acids needed for growth, health, and smooth skin

Water: Part of blood, lymph, body secretions. Aids digestion, regulates body temperature. Transports nutrients and body wastes

Vitamins

A: Necessary for growth and repair of tissue. Important to eyes. Fights bacteria and infection. Aids in formation of bone and teeth

B Complex: Necessary for carbohydrate, fat, and protein metabolism. Helps functioning of nervous system. Maintains muscle tone in gastrointestinal tract. Maintains health of skin, hair, eyes, mouth, and liver

B_1 (Thiamine): Necessary for carbohydrate metabolism. Maintains health of nervous system. Stabilizes appetite. Stimulates growth and good muscle tone

B_2 (Riboflavin): Necessary for carbohydrate, fat, and protein metabolism. Aids formation of antibodies and red blood cells. Maintains cell respiration

B_6 (Pyridoxine): Necessary for carbohydrate, fat, and protein metabolism. Aids in formation of antibodies. Helps maintain balance of sodium and phosphorus

B_{12} (Cyanocobalamin): Essential for normal formation of blood cells. Essential for carbohydrate, fat, and protein metabolism. Maintains healthy nervous system

B_{13} (Orotic Acid): Needed for metabolism of some B vitamins

Bioflavonoids: Help increase strength of capillaries

Biotin: Necessary for carbohydrate, fat, and protein metabolism. Aids in utilization of other B vitamins

C: Maintains collagen. Helps heal wounds, scar tissue, and fractures. Gives strength to blood vessels. Produces resistance to infections. Aids absorption of iron

Choline: Important to normal nerve transmission. Aids metabolism of fats. Regulates liver and gall bladder

D: Improves absorption and utilization of calcium and phosphorus required for bone formation. Maintains stable nervous system and normal heart action

E: Protects fat-soluble vitamins and red blood cells. Essential for cellular respiration. Inhibits coagulation of blood by preventing blood clots

F: Important for vital respiration of organs. Helps maintain resilience and fabrication of cells. Regulates blood circulation. Essential for normal glandular activity

Folic Acid: Important in red blood cell formation. Aids metabolism of proteins. Necessary for growth and division of body cells

Inositol: Necessary for formation of lecithin. Vital for hair growth. Indirectly connected to metabolism of fats, including cholesterol

K: Necessary for formation of prothrombin. Needed for blood coagulation

Laetrile (B_{17}): Has been linked to cancer prevention

Niacin: Necessary for carbohydrate, fat, and protein metabolism. Maintains health of skin, tongue, and digestive system

PABA: Aids bacteria in producing folic acid. Acts as a coenzyme in breakdown and utilization of proteins. Aids in formation of red blood cells

Pangamic Acid (B_{15}): Helps eliminate hypoxia. Promotes protein metabolism. Stimulates nervous and glandular system

Pantothenic Acid: Participates in release of energy from carbohydrates, fats, and proteins. Helps in

Andrian Batho travels from Australia to compete
in IFBB pro events all over the planet.

utilization of some vitamins. Improves body's
resistance to stress

Minerals

Calcium: Necessary for development and
maintenance of strong teeth and bones. Assists in
normal blood clotting and nerve and heart function

Chlorine: Regulates acid-base balance. Maintains
osmotic pressure. Stimulates production of

hydrochloric acid. Helps maintain joints and tendons

Chromium: Stimulates enzymes in metabolism of
energy and synthesis of fatty acids, cholesterol,
and protein. Increases effectiveness of insulin (RDA
is 50–200 mcg. per day.)

Cobalt: Functions as part of vitamin B_{12}. Maintains red
blood cells. Activates many enzymes (No RDA.)

Copper: Aids in formation of red blood cells. Works

with vitamin C to form elastin (RDA is 2 mg. per day.)

Fluorine: May reduce tooth decay by discouraging growth of acid-forming bacteria (Depending on water source, RDA is 1.5–4.0 mg. per day.)

Iodine: Essential part of hormone thyroxine. Necessary to prevent goiter. Regulates production of energy and rate of metabolism. Promotes growth

Iron: Necessary for hemoglobin and myoglobin formation. Helps in protein metabolism. Promotes growth

Magnesium: Acts as catalyst in utilization of carbohydrates, fats, proteins, calcium, phosphorus, and possibly potassium

Manganese: Enzyme activator. Plays part in carbohydrate and fat production. Necessary for normal skeletal development. Maintains sex-hormone production (RDA is 2.5–5.0 mg. daily.)

Molybdenum: Acts in oxidation of fats and aldehydes. Aids in mobilization of iron from liver reserves (No RDA. Intake should be 0.15–0.5 mg. daily.)

From Arizona, Michael Ashley competes in pro shows totally drug-free, a philosophical choice which requires strict attention to nutritional practices.

Nickel: Known to activate several enzyme systems. Also present in ribonucleic acids (No RDA.)

Phosphorus: Works with calcium to build bones and teeth. Utilizes carbohydrates, fats, and proteins. Stimulates muscular contraction

Potassium: Works to control activity of heart muscles, nervous system, and kidneys

Selenium: Works with vitamin C. Preserves tissue elasticity (RDA is 50–200 mcg. per day.)

Sodium: Maintains normal fluid level in cells.

Maintains health of nervous, blood, lymph, and muscular systems

Sulfur: Part of amino acids, B vitamins. Necessary for tissue formation and collagen synthesis

Vanadium: Inhibits cholesterol formation (No RDA. Intake of 0.1–0.3 mg. per day suggested.)

Zinc: Component of insulin and male reproductive fluid. Aids in digestion and metabolism of phosphorus. Aids in healing (RDA is 15 mg. per day; for pregnant women, 20–25 mg. daily.

England's massive Selwyn Cottrell.

The Concept of Individuality

There is no such thing as a generic diet, a diet that works for every individual. You can't look at what someone else in the gym is doing, copy his nutritional program, and expect to obtain the same results. Variables such as height, weight, lean body mass, age, sex, weight training and aerobic activity levels, oxidative type, and food allergy sensitivities change the equation from one individual to the next.

Individualized diets *can* be computer generated using the Nutritionalysis computer program. Nutritionalysis is based on an extensive questionnaire that compiles individual data for computer input. The program then generates a diet that matches the needs of an individual bodybuilder.

Nutritionalysis is an exclusive Gold's Gym feature, and at the time of writing it was available at 115 Gold's Gyms in the United States alone. If you have a Gold's Gym in your area, a quick phone call will tell you whether or not it can computer-analyze your nutritional program and tailor one to fit your individual needs.

If Nutritionalysis is not available, the general rules of sound nutrition apply to almost all bodybuilders. This chapter will supply you with a starting point in terms of weight-gain diet. Everyone will have individual quirks nutritionally, however, and they can only be determined and adjusted through experience and study of nutrition. Most bodybuilding magazines carry regular features on bodybuilding nutrition. The more you know about how to feed your body, the more quickly you'll be able to gain muscle mass.

SUGGESTED MEAL PLANS AT VARIOUS CALORIC LEVELS

2,000-Calorie Diet

Meal 1

Menu Selection	Cal	Pro (g)	Carbs (g)	Fats (g)
⅕ cup raisins	96	0.82	25.60	0.1
1 cup orange juice	122	2.00	29.00	0.2
2 cups oatmeal	264	9.60	46.04	5.6
2 eggs, any style	164	6.50	0.50	6.5
	646	18.92	101.14	12.4

Meal 2
500-Calorie Weight Gainer Formula

Meal 3

Menu Selection	Cal	Pro (g)	Carbs (g)	Fats (g)
1 small banana	86	1.06	22.20	0.2
2 slices whole-wheat bread	112	4.80	22.00	1.4
6 ounces water-packed tuna	191	42.00	0.00	1.2
	389	47.86	44.20	2.8

Meal 4

Menu Selection	Cal	Pro (g)	Carbs (g)	Fats (g)
Large mixed green dinner salad	120	0.00	30.00	0.0
1½ cups cooked spaghetti	225	7.50	48.00	0.8
6 ounces chicken breast, baked	246	41.20	0.00	9.0
	591	48.70	78.00	9.8

Eat Meal 1 first, then arrange the remaining meals to fit your lifestyle and schedule. You may have water, coffee, tea, or a diet drink with each meal.

Meal Substitute

You may substitute any missed meals with the Weight Gainer Formula of equivalent calorie level. Do not substitute more than half of the day's calories unless medically supervised.

2,500-Calorie Diet

Meal 1

Menu Selection	Cal	Pro (g)	Carbs (g)	Fats (g)
⅕ cup raisins	96	0.82	25.60	0.1
1 cup orange juice	122	2.00	29.00	0.2
2 cups oatmeal	264	9.60	46.04	5.6
2 eggs, any style	164	6.50	0.50	6.5
	646	18.92	101.14	12.4

Meal 2
500-Calorie Weight Gainer Formula
Meal 3

Menu Selection	Cal	Pro (g)	Carbs (g)	Fats (g)
2 slices whole-wheat bread	112	4.80	22.20	0.2
6 ounces water-packed tuna	191	42.00	0.00	1.2
½ tablespoon mayonnaise	23	0.10	0.15	2.5
	326	46.90	22.35	3.9

Meal 4
This menu or 500-Calorie Weight Gainer Formula

Menu Selection	Cal	Pro (g)	Carbs (g)	Fats (g)
1 small banana	86	1.06	22.20	0.2
2 slices whole-wheat bread	112	4.80	22.20	0.2
6 ounces water-packed tuna	191	42.00	0.00	1.2
	389	47.86	44.40	1.6

Meal 5

Menu Selection	Cal	Pro (g)	Carbs (g)	Fats (g)
Large mixed green dinner salad	120	0.00	30.00	0.0
1½ cups cooked spaghetti	225	7.50	48.00	0.8
6 ounces chicken breast, baked	246	41.20	0.00	9.0
	591	48.70	78.00	9.8

Eat Meal 1 first, then arrange the remaining meals to fit your lifestyle and schedule. You may have water, coffee, tea, or a diet drink with each meal.

Meal Substitute

You may substitute any missed meals with the Weight Gainer Formula of equivalent calorie level. Do not substitute more than half of the day's calories unless medically supervised.

3,000-Calorie Diet

Meal 1

Menu Selection	Cal	Pro (g)	Carbs (g)	Fats (g)
1 cup apple juice	118	0.20	29.50	0.0
½ cup raisins	240	2.05	64.00	0.2
2½ cups oatmeal	330	12.00	57.55	7.0
2 eggs, any style	164	13.00	1.00	12.0
½ cup whole milk	80	4.25	6.00	4.4
	932	31.50	158.05	23.6

Meal 2
500-Calorie Weight Gainer Formula
Meal 3

Menu Selection	Cal	Pro (g)	Carbs (g)	Fats (g)
1½ cups pineapple	270	1.80	66.00	0.6
2 slices whole-wheat bread	112	4.80	22.00	1.4
6 ounces water-packed tuna	191	42.00	0.00	1.2
½ tablespoon mayonnaise	23	0.10	0.15	2.5
	596	48.70	88.15	5.7

Meal 4
This menu or 500-Calorie Weight Gainer Formula

Menu Selection	Cal	Pro (g)	Carbs (g)	Fats (g)
2 ounces tomato sauce	54	2.25	12.25	0.3
1 cup white pasta, cooked	150	5.00	32.00	0.5
6 ounces chicken breast, baked	246	41.20	0.00	9.0
	450	48.45	44.25	9.8

Meal 5

Menu Selection	Cal	Pro (g)	Carbs (g)	Fats (g)
1 ounce tomato sauce	27	1.13	6.23	0.1
6 ounces mixed vegetables	66	3.75	15.00	0.0
2 cups white pasta, cooked	300	10.00	64.00	1.0
6 ounces chicken breast, baked	246	41.20	0.00	9.0
	639	56.08	85.23	10.1

Eat Meal 1 first, then arrange the remaining meals to fit your lifestyle and schedule. You may have water, coffee, tea, or a diet drink with each meal.

Meal Substitute

You may substitute any missed meals with the Weight Gainer Formula of equivalent calorie level. Do not substitute more than half of the day's calories unless medically supervised.

3,500-Calorie Diet

Meal 1

Menu Selection	Cal	Pro (g)	Carbs (g)	Fats (g)
1 cup apple juice	118	0.02	29.50	0.0
½ cup raisins	240	2.20	64.00	0.2
2½ cups oatmeal	330	12.00	57.55	7.0
2 eggs, scrambled	164	13.00	1.00	12.0
½ cup whole milk	80	4.25	6.00	4.4
	932	31.47	158.05	23.6

Meal 2

This menu or 500-Calorie Weight Gainer Formula

Menu Selection	Cal	Pro (g)	Carbs (g)	Fats (g)
1 banana	86	1.06	22.20	0.2
2 slices whole-wheat bread	112	4.80	22.00	1.4
6 ounces water-packed tuna	191	42.00	0.00	1.2
½ tablespoon mayonnaise	23	0.10	0.15	2.5
	412	47.96	44.35	5.3

Meal 3

Menu Selection	Cal	Pro (g)	Carbs (g)	Fats (g)
1½ cups pineapple	270	1.80	66.00	0.6
2 slices whole-wheat bread	112	4.80	22.00	1.4
6 ounces water-packed tuna	191	42.00	0.00	2.5
	573	48.60	88.00	4.5

Meal 4

This menu *and* 500-Calorie Weight Gainer Formula (Total Cal = 928)

Menu Selection	Cal	Pro (g)	Carbs (g)	Fats (g)
2 ounces tomato sauce	54	2.25	12.25	0.3
1 cup white pasta, cooked	150	5.00	32.00	0.5
6 ounces chicken breast, baked	246	41.20	0.00	9.0
	450	48.45	44.25	9.8

Meal 5

Menu Selection	Cal	Pro (g)	Carbs (g)	Fats (g)
1 ounce tomato sauce	27	1.13	6.23	0.1
6 ounces mixed vegetables	66	3.75	15.00	0.0
2 cups white pasta, cooked	300	10.00	64.00	1.0
6 ounces chicken breast, baked	246	41.20	0.00	9.0
	639	56.08	85.23	10.1

Eat Meal 1 first, then arrange the remaining meals to fit your lifestyle and schedule. You may have water, coffee, tea, or a diet drink with each meal.

Meal Substitute

You may substitute any missed meals with the Weight Gainer Formula of equivalent calorie level. Do not substitute more than half of the day's calories unless medically supervised.

4,000-Calorie Diet

Meal 1

Menu Selection	Cal	Pro (g)	Carbs (g)	Fats (g)
⅕ cup raisins	96	0.82	25.60	0.1
1½ cups orange juice	183	3.00	43.50	0.3
3 cups oatmeal, cooked	396	14.40	69.05	8.4
3 eggs, boiled	246	19.50	1.50	18.0
2 tablespoons butter	66	0.20	0.00	8.0
¾ cup low-fat milk	91	6.09	8.78	3.5
	1,078	44.01	148.43	38.3

Meal 2

750-Calorie Weight Gainer Formula

Meal 3

Menu Selection	Cal	Pro (g)	Carbs (g)	Fats (g)
2 ounces tomato sauce	54	2.25	12.25	0.3
1 small banana	86	1.06	22.20	0.2
2½ ounces whole-wheat pasta, dry	350	17.50	68.25	0.1
6 ounces chicken breast, baked	246	41.20	0.00	9.0
	736	62.01	102.70	9.6

Meal 4

This menu or 950-Calorie Weight Gainer Formula

Menu Selection	Cal	Pro (g)	Carbs (g)	Fats (g)
4 ounces mixed vegetables	44	2.50	10.00	0.0
1 cup pineapple	180	1.20	44.00	0.4
2 cups rice, cooked	316	6.00	72.00	0.4
6 ounces lean ground beef	306	36.00	0.00	16.5
	846	45.70	126.00	17.3

Meal 5

Menu Selection	Cal	Pro (g)	Carbs (g)	Fats (g)
Mixed green dinner salad	100	0.00	25.00	0.0
2 cups rice, cooked	316	6.00	72.00	0.4
4 ounces lean ground beef	204	24.00	0.00	11.0
	620	30.00	97.00	11.4

Eat Meal 1 first, then arrange the remaining meals to fit your lifestyle and schedule. You may have water, coffee, tea, or a diet drink with each meal.

Meal Substitute

You may substitute any missed meals with the Weight Gainer Formula of equivalent calorie level. Do not substitute more than half of the day's calories unless medically supervised.

4,500-Calorie Diet

Meal 1

Menu Selection	Cal	Pro (g)	Carbs (g)	Fats (g)
⅕ cup raisins	96	0.82	25.60	0.1
1½ cups orange juice	183	3.00	43.50	0.3
3 cups oatmeal, cooked	396	14.40	69.06	8.4
3 eggs, boiled	246	19.50	1.50	18.0
2 tablespoons butter	66	0.20	0.00	8.0
¾ cup low-fat milk	91	6.09	8.78	3.5
	1,078	44.01	148.44	38.3

Meal 2

750-Calorie Weight Gainer Formula

Meal 3

Menu Selection	Cal	Pro (g)	Carbs (g)	Fats (g)
2 ounces tomato sauce	54	2.25	12.25	0.3
1 small banana	86	1.06	11.20	0.2
2½ ounces whole-wheat pasta, dry	350	17.50	68.25	0.1
6 ounces chicken breast, baked	246	41.20	0.00	9.0
	736	62.01	91.70	9.6

Meal 4

This menu *and* 750-Calorie Weight Gainer Formula (Total Cal = 1,596)

Menu Selection	Cal	Pro (g)	Carbs (g)	Fats (g)
4 ounces mixed vegetables	44	2.50	10.00	0.0
1 cup pineapple	180	1.20	44.00	0.4
2 cups rice, cooked	316	6.00	72.00	0.4
6 ounces lean ground beef	306	36.00	0.00	16.5
	846	45.70	126.00	17.3

Meal 5

Menu Selection	Cal	Pro (g)	Carbs (g)	Fats (g)
Mixed green dinner salad	100	0.00	25.00	0.0
2 cups rice, cooked	316	6.00	72.00	0.4
4 ounces lean ground beef	204	24.00	0.00	11.0
	620	30.00	97.00	11.4

Eat Meal 1 first, then arrange the remaining meals to fit your lifestyle and schedule. You may have water, coffee, tea, or a diet drink with each meal.

Meal Substitute

You may substitute any missed meals with the Weight Gainer Formula of equivalent calorie level. Do not substitute more than half of the day's calories unless medically supervised.

5,000-Calorie Diet

Meal 1

Menu Selection	Cal	Pro (g)	Carbs (g)	Fats (g)
⅕ cup raisins	96	0.82	25.60	0.1
1½ cups orange juice	183	3.00	43.50	0.3
3 cups oatmeal, cooked	396	14.40	69.06	8.4
3 eggs, boiled	246	19.50	1.50	18.0
2 tablespoons butter	66	0.20	0.00	8.0
¾ cup low-fat milk	91	6.09	8.78	3.5
	1,078	44.01	148.44	38.3

Meal 2
750-Calorie Weight Gainer Formula

Meal 3

Menu Selection	Cal	Pro (g)	Carbs (g)	Fats (g)
2 ounces tomato sauce	54	2.25	12.25	0.3
1 small banana	86	1.06	22.20	0.2
2½ ounces whole-wheat pasta, dry	350	17.50	68.25	0.1
6 ounces chicken breast, baked	246	41.20	0.00	9.0
	736	62.01	102.70	9.6

Meal 4
This menu *and* 750-Calorie Weight Gainer Formula (Total Cal = 1,596)

Menu Selection	Cal	Pro (g)	Carbs (g)	Fats (g)
4 ounces mixed vegetables	44	2.50	10.00	0.0
1 cup pineapple	180	1.20	44.00	0.4
2 cups rice, cooked	316	6.00	72.00	0.4
6 ounces lean ground beef	306	36.00	0.00	16.5
	846	45.70	126.00	17.3

Meal 5

Menu Selection	Cal	Pro (g)	Carbs (g)	Fats (g)
Mixed green dinner salad	100	0.00	25.00	0.0
2 cups rice, cooked	316	6.00	72.00	0.4
4 ounces lean ground beef	204	24.00	0.00	11.0
	620	30.00	97.00	11.4

Eat Meal 1 first, then arrange the remaining meals to fit your lifestyle and schedule. You may have water, coffee, tea, or a diet drink with each meal.

Meal Substitute

You may substitute any missed meals with the Weight Gainer Formula of equivalent calorie level. Do not substitute more than half of the day's calories unless medically supervised.

5,500-Calorie Diet

Meal 1

Menu Selection	Cal	Pro (g)	Carbs (g)	Fats (g)
⅕ cup raisins	96	0.82	25.60	0.1
1½ cups orange juice	183	3.00	43.50	0.3
3 cups oatmeal, cooked	396	14.40	69.06	8.4
3 eggs, boiled	246	19.50	1.50	18.0
2 tablespoons butter	66	0.20	0.00	8.0
¾ cup low-fat milk	91	6.09	8.76	3.5
	1,078	44.01	148.42	38.3

Meal 2
This menu *and* 750-Calorie Weight Gainer Formula (Total Cal = 1,537)

Menu Selection	Cal	Pro (g)	Carbs (g)	Fats (g)
2 ounces tomato sauce	54	2.25	12.25	0.3
1 small banana	86	1.06	22.20	0.2
3½ ounces whole-wheat pasta, dry	350	17.50	68.25	0.1
6 ounces chicken breast, baked	246	41.20	0.00	9.0
½ tablespoon margarine	51	0.05	0.05	5.7
	787	62.06	102.75	15.30

Meal 3

Menu Selection	Cal	Pro (g)	Carbs (g)	Fats (g)
2 ounces tomato sauce	54	2.25	12.25	0.3
1 small banana	86	1.06	22.20	0.2
3½ ounces whole-wheat pasta, dry	350	17.50	68.25	0.1
6 ounces chicken breast, baked	246	41.20	0.00	9.0
	736	62.01	102.70	9.6

Meal 4
This menu *and* 750-Calorie Weight Gainer Formula (Total Cal = 1,596)

Menu Selection	Cal	Pro (g)	Carbs (g)	Fats (g)
4 ounces mixed vegetables	44	2.50	10.00	0.0
1 cup pineapple	180	1.20	44.00	0.4
2 cups rice, cooked	316	6.00	72.00	0.4
6 ounces lean ground beef	306	36.00	0.00	16.5
	846	45.70	126.00	17.3

Meal 5

Menu Selection	Cal	Pro (g)	Carbs (g)	Fats (g)
Mixed green dinner salad	100	0.00	25.00	0.0
2 cups rice, cooked	316	6.00	72.00	0.4
4 ounces lean ground beef	204	24.00	0.00	11.0
	620	30.00	97.00	11.4

Eat Meal 1 first, then arrange the remaining meals to fit your lifestyle and schedule. You may have water, coffee, tea, or a diet drink with each meal.

Meal Substitute
You may substitute any missed meals with the Weight Gainer Formula of equivalent calorie level. Do not substitute more than half of the day's calories unless medically supervised.

6,000-Calorie Diet

Meal 1

Menu Selection	Cal	Pro (g)	Carbs (g)	Fats (g)
⅕ cup raisins	96	0.82	25.60	0.1
1½ cups orange juice	183	3.00	43.50	0.3
3 cups oatmeal, cooked	396	14.40	69.06	8.4
3 eggs, boiled	246	19.50	1.50	18.0
2 tablespoons butter	66	0.20	0.00	8.0
¾ cup low-fat milk	91	6.09	8.78	3.5
	1,078	44.01	148.44	38.3

Meal 2
This menu *and* 500-Calorie Weight Gainer Formula (Total Cal = 1,287)

Menu Selection	Cal	Pro (g)	Carbs (g)	Fats (g)
2 ounces tomato sauce	54	2.25	12.25	0.3
1 small banana	86	1.05	22.20	0.2
3½ ounces whole-wheat pasta, dry	350	17.50	68.25	0.1
6 ounces chicken breast, baked	246	41.20	0.00	9.0
½ tablespoon margarine	51	0.05	0.05	5.7
	787	62.05	102.75	15.30

Meal 3

Menu Selection	Cal	Pro (g)	Carbs (g)	Fats (g)
2 ounces tomato sauce	54	2.25	12.25	0.3
1 small banana	86	1.06	22.20	0.2
3½ ounces whole-wheat pasta, dry	350	17.50	68.25	0.1
6 ounces chicken breast, baked	246	41.20	0.00	9.0
	736	62.01	102.70	9.60

Meal 4
This menu *and* 500-Calorie Weight Gain Formula (Total Cal = 1,346)

Menu Selection	Cal	Pro (g)	Carbs (g)	Fats (g)
4 ounces mixed vegetables	44	2.50	10.00	0.0
1 cup pineapple	180	1.20	44.00	0.4
2 cups rice, cooked	316	6.00	72.00	0.4
6 ounces lean ground beef	306	36.00	0.00	16.5
	846	45.70	126.00	17.3

Meal 5

Menu Selection	Cal	Pro (g)	Carbs (g)	Fats (g)
Mixed green dinner salad	100	0.00	25.00	0.0
2 cups rice, cooked	316	6.00	72.00	0.4
4 ounces lean ground beef	204	24.00	0.00	11.0
	620	30.00	97.00	11.4

Meal 6

950-Calorie Weight Gainer Formula

Eat Meal 1 first, then arrange the remaining meals to fit your lifestyle and schedule. You may have water, coffee, tea, or a diet drink with each meal.

Meal Substitute

You may substitute any missed meals with the Weight Gainer Formula of equivalent calorie level. Do not substitute more than half of the day's calories unless medically supervised.

In the accompanying table you will find nine suggested weight-gain daily meal plans, ranging from 2,000–6,000 calories per day. Find your weight group below and the number of calories to go with it, and match these calories to a diet program. As the weeks go by, use the adjustment procedure that follows to make increases or decreases in your diet according to weight gain.

Weigh yourself only once each week. Daily weight can fluctuate considerably.

STARTING CALORIC LEVELS FOR WEIGHT GAIN

Current Weight	Starting Calories
90–120 lbs.	2,000–2,500
120–50	2,500–3,000
150–80	3,000–3,500
180–210	3,500–4,000
210–40	4,000–4,500
240–70	4,500–5,000
270 and up	5,000–8,000

If you don't see a weight gain in the first two weeks, add another 500-Calorie Weight Gainer Formula to your daily diet. Continue this process until you are gaining weight consistently. You should be gaining 1–4 pounds a week in the beginning, but this will eventually slow down to 1 pound every two weeks.

Remember, this process can only continue as long as you keep adding food and proper exercise. You cannot upgrade your physique without upgrading your nutritional level, just as you cannot build a bigger house without adding new materials.

After you have gained 10 pounds of muscular weight, your weight will probably begin to stabilize. It is then time to raise your calories again. Add another 500-Calorie Weight Gainer For-

mula or more nutritious food or both to your daily diet. Every time you gain muscular body weight and your weight becomes stuck, you must add calories to feed the new muscle tissue. If your weight is still going up on your current calorie level after a 10-pound increase, then wait until your weight stabilizes before adding another 500 calories.

If you think you are putting on fat, the best way to lose fat is to add 20–40 minutes of aerobic work (on a bike, Stairmaster, treadmill) three or four days a week. This will allow you to continue to build new muscle tissue by continuing your high calorie intake and to burn fat at the same time.

Make sure you are doing enough resistance training to make your muscles grow. If all else fails, lower your calorie intake slowly until your weight gain slows slightly.

Losing Fat and Building Muscle Simultaneously

Everyone has a weight-regulating system in his or her brain. The job of this weight-regulating system is to maintain the fat content of your body at a certain level, which we call the *fat set point*. The body is a homeostatic organism; that is, it's designed to reach a state of equilibrium in most of its functions and to work to maintain that equilibrium. The fat set point is one example of this.

Once the body becomes accustomed to maintaining a certain level of fat retention, it will try to maintain this level. As a result, when you diet in an attempt to lose weight, your body will resist your efforts, and you'll find it all too easy to gain that weight back again. The level of this set point results from a number of factors.

The first factor to consider is genetics. Some people are born with the propensity to become fatter than others. There are naturally skinny ectomorphs. Some individuals are given more fat cells by heredity, some fewer. In individuals designed by nature to be fatter than normal, the function of various metabolic pathways and the levels of various enzymes and hormones predispose the body to store a relatively high percentage of calories in the form of body fat. In a slender individual, food tends to be converted directly into energy in greater proportions.

The fat set point is affected by environment and behavior as well as heredity. Your genetics determine certain limits to what level of leanness or fatness you'll be able to maintain under normal circumstances, but this range can often be quite wide. Within these limits, however, you can vary your set point considerably depending on what and how you eat, as well as what kind and how much exercise you do.

Once you've reached adulthood, your body, as a homeostatic organism, will do everything it can to "trick" you into maintaining your fat set point. On one level, it will vary your perception of whether you want to eat or not, as well as what kind of foods you want and in what quantity. This mechanism is called *appetite*, and appetite is much more of a psychological experience than a simple physiological sensation. Hunger, in other words, is often more of an indication of what you feel rather than an indication of whether or not your body is actually in need of food.

Your body also works to maintain your set point by varying the activity of various glands, the output of hormones and production of enzymes, and the rate of overall metabolism as well. Most dieters have experienced one example of this; you diet in order to force the body to burn stored fat for energy, but the more assiduously you diet and the less energy you consume, the slower your metabolism functions, and the less energy you use.

Fat-Storage Mechanism

When you look at the evolutionary history of the human body, this isn't hard to understand: Throughout most of history, human beings have been highly vulnerable to famine and starvation. As a result, in order to maximize its chances of survival in adverse conditions, the human body has become a highly efficient fat-storage mechanism.

During times of famine, survival is generally more a matter of being able to live for relatively long periods on stored energy than of expending large amounts of energy through muscular effort. In times of starvation the body tends to hold on to energy—to store it as body fat and maintain the highest possible levels of body fat—and to sacrifice muscle to do so. During a famine, muscle tissue is more valuable for the calories it can provide to sustain life and vital functions rather than for the physical effort it can produce. A state of physical lethargy is a normal and valuable response of the body to starvation.

In practical terms, you don't have to be in a state of starvation for your body to shift into a starvation mode. For the body to perceive itself in a state of deprivation, you just have to miss a couple of meals. When this occurs, the body very quickly begins to preserve body fat as much as possible, sacrifice muscle for caloric energy, and slow down its metabolic rate to conserve overall energy expenditure.

Balancing Act

Take a 200-pound man whose set point is at about 20 percent relative body fat and who lives on some 4,000 calories a day. Since his body has various mechanisms it can employ to maintain its equilibrium, he can most likely cut back his food intake to 3,500 calories or raise it to 4,500 or 5,000 without any long-term change in his set point or body weight. In simple terms, if he eats less, his body will tend to conserve energy to maintain his weight; if he eats more, his body will begin to convert more of this caloric intake into energy.

This balancing act can only take place within certain prescribed limits, however. If, instead of merely varying his caloric intake by a few hundred calories one way or the other, this individual drastically reduces his calories—say, to 2,000 or even fewer—other mechanisms will come into play. After following this regimen for a while he will likely observe an overall loss of body weight when he steps on the scales. But he may not be at all satisfied with the results.

For example, since under these conditions of deprivation the body perceives itself as starving and reacts accordingly, a very high proportion of the lost weight will be muscle tissue rather than fat. It's entirely possible to lose a considerable amount of body weight and find that your relative body-fat percentage has hardly gone down at all. In some cases—and this has frequently been observed in victims of anorexia nervosa—the relative fat percentage may actually go up! Such an individual, for example, can weigh as little as 85 or 90 pounds, with 60 percent or more of that weight being stored body fat.

Under these semistarvation conditions, the body will do everything it can to conserve energy and to return its weight back to the original set point. For example, it will learn to do with the available 2,000 or so calories what it once did with 4,000. How? One way is by reducing muscle mass. Muscle burns calories, so when you have less muscle, you burn less caloric energy. Another way is by making the dieter feel tired and fatigued, the early stages of the total lethargy you see in victims of extreme starvation.

Tim Belknap's return to pro competition in 1991 after five years completely out of training.

When you're tired, obviously you're less active and you metabolize less energy.

Appetite also comes into play as part of this scenario. Strict dieters often find themselves thinking about food. They frequently dream about food. They begin to develop food cravings, often developing an appetite for the kinds of foods they would normally never have any desire to eat.

Under the pressure of this two-pronged physiological and psychological onslaught, it's no wonder that most dieters succumb and eventually eat their way back up to their original set point level. However, since a large proportion of the weight they lost was muscle and almost all the weight they gain back is fat, when they return to their original body weight their body composition may have changed considerably. At the same weight, they're much fatter.

This situation, while undesirable for most people, is totally unacceptable to bodybuilders. Bodybuilders are not merely concerned with reducing body fat, but they also need to continue to build and maintain maximum muscle mass. They can't afford to follow diet programs that deplete needed muscle tissue. In fact, since it takes excess calories to build muscle, bodybuilders actually can't afford to diet in the traditional sense at all.

Take 1990 Pro Arnold Schwarzenegger Classic winner Mike Ashley, for example. In the past Ashley tried to stay in decent shape all year by maintaining a daily diet of about 3,000 calories. As a result, he looked good when he guest posed and even better when he showed up at a contest, but his muscle mass gains from year to year were minimal. As the result of following a new diet program, Ashley showed up in Columbus a full 10 pounds bigger than ever before and ripped to shreds as well.

How did he do it? The answer is not very complicated. Mike Ashley changed his metabolic set point so that he could diet on a full 4,000 calories per day or more. This caloric intake allowed him to build maximum muscle while at the same time stimulating his body's ability to burn fat for fuel so that he got big and cut at the same time. Ashley learned that, just as you can cause your body to adapt and build big muscles by proper training, there are also ways of dieting and exercising so the body adapts and learns to burn large amounts of fat for fuel as well.

Demand-Supply

It's important to realize to what degree the body works on a "demand-supply" basis. For example, you can eat all the protein you want, but this protein won't be used to make additional muscle tissue unless a demand for it is created—specifically, by stimulating it with bodybuilding-type weight training. The body works on the same demand system when it comes to energy. When you do anaerobic exercise (such as bodybuilding, for example), the majority of the energy expended comes from stored carbohydrates in the form of glycogen. When you do aerobic exercise, on the other hand, your body is able to use fat to supply the needed energy.

For your body to burn large amounts of fat efficiently, you have to specifically develop and stimulate its fat-metabolizing capacities. This has been proved by a host of studies done on endurance athletes such as marathon runners and triathletes. These athletes have developed their aerobic systems so fully that their bodies have learned to use fat directly for energy, even in some cases in preference to glycogen.

Actually, the body never confines itself to one kind of fuel except in the most extreme conditions. For example, the body's metabolism almost always uses some combination of amino acids, carbohydrates, and fats for energy. You can't prevent your body from metabolizing all three of these food elements virtually all the time, but you can make substantial changes in the *proportion* of each nutrient the body prefers to use. You can decrease the proportion of amino acids metabolized for energy or increase the proportion of calories derived from fat.

Burning fat efficiently for energy is the *opposite* of the starvation-response situation in which the body conserves fat and metabolizes amino acids. You can eat more, because excess calories will be metabolized to provide energy rather than stored as fat. Since you're eating more, your metabolism speeds up rather than slows down, again resulting in more energy expended and less energy conserved as fat. Specifically, for bodybuilders eating more means that your body will be able to build the maximum amount of muscle tissue in response to your bodybuilding workouts.

But how exactly do you arrive at this situation? By doing a sufficient amount of calorie-consuming, aerobic-type exercise over a long enough period that your body becomes more efficient at utilizing stored body fat for energy. This will eventually cause a change in your body's set point for fat storage.

In other words, if you're eating a lot and your body is burning a lot of fat for energy, your overall levels of stored body fat are reduced. And since your daily diet provides plenty of energy on a regular basis, your body sees no reason to maintain high levels of body fat and your set point is therefore reduced.

For maximum results in terms of mass and cuts, bodybuilders need to do two kinds of workouts: bodybuilding workouts to build mass and aerobic workouts to burn fat. However, in the past bodybuilders have been cautious about doing *too much* aerobic or calorie-burning exercise in addition to their bodybuilding workouts for fear they would burn up muscle mass in the process. In most cases, bodybuilders would:

- Do additional aerobics only close to a contest (not for a long enough period to sufficiently develop the aerobic, fat-burning system)
- Do additional aerobic exercise while dieting, so the lack of caloric intake would result in all the negative metabolic responses described earlier (conserving of body fat, loss of muscle tissue, slowing down of the metabolism, etc.)
- Do additional aerobic activity along with overly long and too frequent bodybuilding workouts, resulting in an almost permanent state of overtraining

Bodybuilders also traditionally tend to increase sets and reps and decrease rest time in their workouts before a contest in an attempt to burn up additional fat. But this is a mistake. Bodybuilding is an anaerobic activity and doesn't work nearly as well as aerobic exercise when it comes to metabolizing fat. Bodybuilding workouts tend to use glycogen more than fat for fuel. Besides, all that high-rep pumping is not a particularly effective way to build and maintain muscle mass. To build muscle, the majority of your workouts should consist of relatively short, highly intense effort.

Ideal Approach

The ideal approach to bodybuilding involves:
- Using your bodybuilding workouts to build muscle rather than to burn excess calories, with enough heavy training that your highly hypertrophied muscle tissue doesn't shrink before a contest
- Doing a sufficient amount of aerobic exercise over a long enough period to burn excess fat, stimulate your metabolism, lower the fat content of your body, and reduce your overall fat set point

As far as diet is concerned, your goal should be to raise your caloric intake as high as possible to facilitate maximum muscle gain, while still being able to burn up excess energy using aerobic activity to avoid storing calories as body fat.

The result? You gain muscle and lose fat at the same time.

This system would certainly benefit bodybuilders with extremely slow metabolisms, like Mike Mentzer, for example. As good as Mentzer looked onstage, he had to reduce his calories to such an extreme to get cut for a show that it's doubtful we ever saw him at his full potential.

But this system also works for bodybuilders with metabolisms so fast that they get cut easily but have trouble eating enough to maximize their muscle gains. Individuals who try to diet too hard tend to develop insatiable appetites. However, those with naturally low set points, such as Mike Christian and Charles Glass, have run into the *opposite* problem. When they try to eat more they totally lose their appetites; they stop getting hungry at all. In fact, to gain weight they have to practically force-feed themselves because their bodies are attempting to maintain their set points and keep their body weight down by taking away their desire to eat.

For this type of bodybuilder, increasing caloric intake results in an increase in appetite. The competitor feels like eating more, so he or she consumes more calories and is able to gain a maximum amount of muscle mass as a result, but continues to burn fat efficiently so he or she doesn't store an undesirable amount of body fat.

The main benefit of aerobic activity, in this sense, is not so much to burn up a certain amount of calories in order to metabolize stored body fat. Rather, the benefit is to change the way the body metabolizes energy in general—to teach it to use body fat for energy on a more efficient basis to lower your set point and reduce your body-fat levels on a long-term basis.

Massive former Detroit cop Ron Love has won three IFBB pro events, including the Pro World Championship.

Of course, even though adding aerobic exercise to your program provides some immediate benefits, permanently changing your set point can take a great deal of time. But it's worth the effort, because changing your set point frees you from the clutches of the dieter's dilemma. You don't have to worry about getting hungry and putting back on all the lost weight. You won't have to close your eyes whenever you go past a pizza parlor. Since appetite is an instrument of set point maintenance, you won't want to overeat to any great extent, you won't have the cravings that plague most dieters, and, if you do binge occasionally, your body will simply burn off the excess calories as energy in order to maintain itself in a state of equilibrium.

However, it's important to emphasize that, if you're going to add aerobic, fat-consuming exercise to your program, you have to be certain not to overtrain when you do your bodybuilding workouts, and you must know what kind of aerobic exercise is of most benefit to bodybuilders, how much of it to do, and when to do it for maximum effect.

12
The Psychology of Mass and Power

"When you're in the gym training like a fanatic or at the dinner table eating scientifically to pack on gargantuan muscle mass, you're only halfway to your goal," states Lee Haney, who trained at Gold's Gym prior to his first Mr. Olympia victory and now owns a string of Lee Haney's Animal Kingdom Gyms. "Your mind must also be in gear, or all of the training and nutrition in the world won't get you anywhere.

"Without the right mental attitude over the years, today I might not be the man who has won eight consecutive Mr. Olympia titles between 1984 and 1991 and is gunning for more. Ten sounds like a nice, round figure to me at this point.

"Bodybuilding success is 50 percent training and 50 percent diet—with diet rising in importance to as much as 75 percent during a peaking cycle—but the mind is actually the rudder that steers the ship. If the rudder doesn't turn, the

Milos Sarcev knows every set counts as he concentrates intently prior to a heavy go at preacher curls for his biceps, particularly hoping to stress the lower insertions of the muscles down near the elbows.

ship keeps going straight, and it might end up like something similar to the Exxon *Valdez*, which ran aground up in Alaska a few years ago and dumped tens of thousands of tons of crude oil all over Alaska's formerly pristine aquatic environment.

"Correct mental programming is essential to success in gaining humongous muscle mass and becoming a champion. Your mental approach to bodybuilding first primes the pump and then keeps the water flowing.

"A champion bodybuilder's mind is like an organic computer that can be programmed to automatically carry out assigned tasks. It is possible to program your mind to allow you to gain muscle mass at an unprecedented rate of speed and to retain that mass while ripping up for an important competition. Surprisingly, it's rather easy to accomplish this mental programming."

Goal Setting

"In order to condition, or program, your mind to help you further your bodybuilding aspirations," continues Haney, "you should have a road map for your journey. Without a map, it's probable that you'll go down a lot of blind alleys and enter many cul-de-sacs en route to your goal. With a good map, however, you can immediately set yourself on a superhighway to success, getting to your destination in half of the time it takes normal bodybuilders who don't understand how to set goals.

"Your road map to success is the effective tool of goal setting. By setting up various goals in a systematic manner, you effectively add structure to your training and dietary efforts rather than aimlessly expending a lot of energy toward a single, clearly defined goal each year. The net result of this process is what all serious bodybuilders are after—faster and greater gains in muscle mass.

"The highest goal is the ultimate, which for me *was* to win Mr. Olympia at least eight times, thereby surpassing Arnold's record of seven, which I tied in 1990 in Chicago. I managed my eighth win at Orlando, Florida, in 1991. Now my upgraded ultimate goal is to win 10 Mr. Olympia titles!

"Normally your ultimate goal should be set early in your bodybuilding involvement and then maintained throughout your competitive career. In my case, I started out with the ultimate goal of winning a Mr. Olympia title, but then I was forced to upgrade the goal. Well, I can't actually say that I was *forced*, because I was overjoyed to find myself in a position requiring me to upgrade such a lofty initial ultimate goal.

"Your own ultimate goal should be broken down into a series of large, long-term goals. I set my long-term goals on a yearly basis and recommend that you do likewise. However, you can set your long-term goals at either longer or shorter temporal intervals. That's strictly up to you.

"My personal long-term goal each year is pretty logical—to win the next Mr. Olympia competition. Shortly after each Olympia I reset that goal. My own year runs from one Olympia each fall to the next, but most bodybuilders set their long-term goals from one January first to the next. This is totally arbitrary, however, and you can set your long-range goals at any point during the year that has significance to you, such as your birthday.

"Just as you break your ultimate goal down into smaller segments, you should subdivide each long-range goal into several short-term goals. Currently, my smaller goals each year are to progressively improve a weak body part prior to my next Olympia, to gradually increase general muscle mass and quality, and to better my overall stage presentation.

"Early in my bodybuilding career, I set the type of short-term goals you should consider utilizing in your quest for greater muscle mass. These were primarily training-poundage goals for basic exercises—to use an additional x number of pounds each month on a movement for a set number of reps done in strict form. As you know, there is a direct correlation between the amount of iron you pump in a particular exercise and the mass of the muscles that move that weight. When you're after greater muscle mass, it's logical that setting and achieving poundage goals will steadily increase your muscle mass.

"The key to success in goal setting is to work hard toward a goal, achieve it, and then shoot for a somewhat higher target the next time. You should visualize goals as stepping stones across a body of water to the opposite shore, which would represent competitive success. Take it one step at a time, and you'll inevitably get where you want to go."

Mental Priority

"Just as you use muscle-priority training to bring up a weak point so that it harmonizes perfectly with the rest of your physique," Lee Haney elaborates, "you must also give mental priority to any lagging muscle group. In the same way, you must use mental intensity to build greater muscle mass at an accelerated rate of speed. High mental intensity invariably fosters greater physical intensity, and you must have the union of mental and physical intensity if you wish to bring up your muscle mass as quickly as possible.

"As you gradually get in better touch with your mind, you'll discover that you can actually *will* a wide range of physiological responses to occur. For example, you'll be able to accelerate your pulse rate by thinking and feeling aggressive, or decelerate it by thinking and feeling calm. A lot of scientific types don't think this is possible, but Hindu fakirs have been doing much wilder things than the regulation of pulse rates for centuries, and they do it through strict mental control.

"If you put mental priority on developing quality muscle mass, you'll make gains. I'm no longer after huge muscle mass—who's bigger

The result of Sarcev's deep mental concentration—an almost unbeatable physique, despite the mental distractions of having his entire family in ethnically torn Yugoslavia.

than I am, anyway?—but I do place mental priority on lagging muscle groups, which everyone has at one time or another. I actually *will* the muscle to grow, and when I mentally force a lagging body part to grow, inevitably *it does grow*. But it won't grow unless I mentally prioritize it. You can do the same with your own weak points!"

Visualization

"To get really massive," says Lee Haney, "you have to *see* yourself as being really massive. This process is called *visualization*.

"Visualization is an exciting and effective method of programming your subconscious mind to assist it in bringing you bodybuilding

"Did I hear you right?" Lee Haney, one of the most massive competitive bodybuilders of all time, knows that there are no secrets to building all of that muscle bulk, save hard work, consistent attention to diet, and a sound mental approach.

success. Psychologists tell us that our conscious minds can be capricious and undependable, while the subconscious is logical, consistent, and dependable. You might as well have your subconscious mind working for you rather than against you.

"I personally work on visualization a lot, always when I'm certain I can be relaxed and free from distractions for at least 20 minutes at a time. That's essential for proper use of visualization, because you will need 15–20 minutes of totally uninterrupted time to do it correctly.

"Each year since I began winning the Mr. Olympia title in 1984, my business ventures have multiplied almost exponentially. You simply wouldn't believe the time demands on me to make decisions regarding various facets of my business empire these days. Business has become so distracting that I have been forced for the past couple of years to abandon my home base in Atlanta and for the final 10–12 weeks preceding an Olympia set up a training camp at some city far enough away that I can limit business to just one hour of calls in the late afternoon. How else could I do two or three iron-pumping sessions per day? At home I don't get 10 sets into a workout before someone tries to interrupt me with the most vital question of all time. For the same reason I can't train at home during the day, I have found it impossible to set aside 20 minutes for visualization at any point during the day.

"That's one reason why I recommend practicing visualization at night just before falling asleep. When you're in bed with the light off—perhaps also with the telephone turned off—you'll be as relaxed and free of distractions as possible. It's actually very positive if you fall asleep with your visualized image still imprinted on your mind.

"Once I'm relaxed, I begin to conjure up a vivid image of how huge and muscular I plan to look at my next competition. It's as if a movie projector is displaying the image on the backs of my eyelids. When I say that this is a vivid image, I mean that I can *see* each new ridge of muscle boldly delineated from the rest of my body. I can also see my entire physique in three-dimensional splendor—every cut, every vein, every hill, and every valley. I hold this image in my mind for 10–15 minutes.

"Don't jump to the conclusion that you'll be able to achieve as perfect a visualized image as I do the first time you go through the gate. It'll take time and plenty of practice to get good at visualization, but you have to stick with it in order to use it most efficiently. Looking back, I think it took me about 18 months to master the process."

Affirmations

"It's also essential that you constantly remind yourself what you plan to accomplish with your physique," Haney concludes. "For me this takes the form of a simple declarative sentence, what psychologists call an *affirmation*. A typical affirmation for you might be 'I will be huge!' Whatever your affirmation, you should repeat it to yourself throughout the day, every time you think about it, since this technique takes plenty of repetition.

"An oft-repeated affirmation gradually imprints itself on your subconscious mind, convincing you that it's going to happen. I've expressed my affirmations to myself so often each year that I'm always totally convinced that I'm going to win Mr. Olympia!"

Workout Concentration

The ability to fully concentrate on every rep of each set in your mass-building workout is invaluable to a serious bodybuilder. You'll see varying degrees of mental concentration in a large gym, but the best men and women seem to notice nothing around them when they're in the middle of a set. We've often seen some novice try to talk to a champion during a set without even denting the champ's ability to maintain concentration on the exercise he or she is performing.

Massive Mike Matarazzo, heavyweight and overall winner at the U.S. Championships in 1991, says this about concentration: "Good mental concentration during a set is something that ultimately just comes to a bodybuilder if he takes workouts seriously enough. But there are ways of speeding up the process. You should try them, because you won't make optimum progress toward a truly massive physique until you have a high level of mental concentration throughout each of your workouts.

"I'm talking to relative novices here, because most advanced bodybuilders have good levels of concentration. The first thing you have to know

Strapping up for a heavy set is a great time to put the final touches on preset mental concentration.

Francis Benfatto, Mohamed Benaziza, Andreas Munzer.

is what area or areas of your body a particular exercise should be affecting or, in other words, where you should be feeling it. The best way to do this is to read a good exercise description that tells you what the exercise stresses, then look up that muscle or muscle group on an anatomy chart if you don't already know where it is.

"Once you know which muscle you should be feeling, start to focus your mental attention on the working muscle as it slowly and powerfully contracts, then slowly extends as the weight returns to the starting point. If you can concentrate fully on the working muscle, you'll be able to feel it quite intensely as it goes through its paces in a particular bodybuilding movement.

"At first, you'll find that various stimuli in the gym—someone grunting out a heavy rep, for example—will distract you from your task. You might have concentrated for only one rep of dumbbell concentration curls before your concentration was broken. But as soon as you notice that it has broken—when you no longer feel your biceps straining against the dumbbell—force your mental attention right back on your biceps.

"Time after time you'll be distracted, but you'll soon get very good at forcing your attention back on the working muscle. Within a few weeks you will probably be able to maintain your mental concentration for a full set of these dumbbell concentration curls. Great! Now work for two straight sets and so forth until you don't find anything that will break your concentration for a full workout.

"I used dumbbell concentration curls as an example because isolation exercises make it easier to concentrate on the working muscle group—usually a single one—than basic compound movements that involve several muscle groups at one time. You'll gain the ability to concentrate fully on isolation movements first, then later on complicated basic exercises like bench presses and squats. It just takes some time and effort, and pretty soon you'll be concentrating like a champion!"

Hypnosis

Bodybuilders who find it difficult to concentrate, or virtually impossible to eliminate mental blocks that hold back training progress, should look into hypnosis as a means of improving workouts. In-person contact with a sports hypnotist is best, because hypnotists can tailor each hypnosis session to your exact needs. Their services usually cost in the range of $30–$50 per session.

Don't panic and think that a hypnotist will have you under some type of strange power, because you'll be perfectly alert and able to make your own decisions while under hypnosis. Rather than being some type of black magic, hypnosis is a modern psychological tool that helps you achieve pinpoint concentration and vault over hidden mental hang-ups blocking you from making gains in muscle mass.

You might be afraid of lifting particularly heavy poundages in your basic exercises, a requisite to getting big. The subconscious fear is usually that you'll suffer some type of training injury if you go as heavy as you should in each lift. The reality is that you won't get injured as long as you warm up completely, stay warm during your entire workout, and use optimum biomechanics in all of your workouts.

A hypnotist is trained to locate hang-ups like fear of going heavy in bench presses and squats. Once he locates these fears, he can steer you around the roadblock your subconscious mind has set up against going heavy. Sometimes a hypnotist will have to work with you several times to eliminate the more basic mental impediments to success and to help you achieve pinpoint mental concentration throughout each of your workouts. Believe us, the time and expense of sessions with a hypnotist are well worth it in the long run.

If you can't find a sports hypnotist in your

Note the intense concentration on the face of Joe Dawson during this set of precontest ab work. Joe made his pro debut at the highly competitive 1991 Mr. Olympia show.

Flex Wheeler in action, something that is frequently seen at Gold's in Venice. Something seen less often is Flex actually sitting around between sets talking with someone. He's a very serious trainer.

Jerry Rodgers.

area, Peter Siegel, who has worked with hundreds of athletes at Gold's in Venice has a series of tapes available which can help you sort of by remote control. Siegel has three series of tapes available, but the one most applicable to bodybuilders is *Series 1: The Absolute Personal Power/Training Intensity Series*. Siegel describes it thusly: "The intensity of your training effort has a direct bearing on muscular growth and increasing strength/power. This series leads to the steadily increasing ability to generate fierce power and intensity each rep of every set in *every workout*." Each series consists of five tapes, and you can obtain information on them by writing to Achievement Plus Institute, 444 Lincoln Blvd., Suite 308, Marina del Rey, CA 90291, or by calling (213) 399-1963.

Closing Note

Arnold Schwarzenegger, who is now a high-powered film star, trained at the original Gold's Gym on Pacific Avenue in Venice, California, for many years. He won six of his Mr. Olympia titles while pumping iron in that well-known little gym. Coauthor Bill Reynolds once asked Schwarzenegger for the secret to his success, just a few minutes after the giant Austrian had finished a chest workout.

"It's all in the mind," Schwarzenegger replied. "I'm the best bodybuilder in the sport because my mind is stronger and better disciplined than others'. I know what I want and I go after it.

"One of my mental secrets is that I always think big. Ever since I was a boy, I've had these fantastic visions of what I wanted to one day become. These were daydreams that just popped into my mind, not something I consciously planned. But I gradually grew to believe that I would definitely become the greatest bodybuilder in the sport.

"I also think big when it comes to visualizing my physique the way I want it to be. When I was working my biceps, I imagined them being as big as the Matterhorn. That got me over the problem of having a barrier to my arm measurement. Most bodybuilders start thinking about having an 18-inch arm measurement, and they never seem to achieve that level of development. It becomes a barrier for them. But when I think of my biceps as being as huge as a mountain in the Alps, there is no barrier!"

Dan Smith's massive rib cage makes this great side/chest pose come alive.

13
Rib-Cage Expansion

A minority of bodybuilding experts believe that a bodybuilder can use specific exercises to enlarge the volume of his or her rib cage. This concept was popular in the 1950s and 1960s but has fallen out of repute. Most modern-day bodybuilding experts think rib-cage expansion is complete hokum.

Coauthor Bill Reynolds attempted to enlarge his rib cage over the summer he was 16 years of age. He was rewarded with a six-inch increase in the circumference of his expanded chest measurement. Part of this was added latissimus dorsi and pectoral growth, but at least three inches of new chest size was actually increased rib-box size, so at least one of the four coauthors is a true believer in the process.

Rib-cage expansion is best attempted and most successfully accomplished between the ages of 14 and 19 when you are still growing in height. During this growth cycle, the cartilage that attaches your ribs to your sternum (breast bone) is pliable and can be stretched. But once adult height has been reached, this cartilage begins to harden and lose its resiliency, making it virtually impossible to stretch it any further.

With each small fraction that you can lengthen the cartilage between your ribs on each side and your sternum, your rib cage actually expands to a noticeable degree. If you could lengthen each rib cartilage by ½″ to ¾″ you would experience a true rib-box expansion of approximately four inches.

The rib cage is the foundation upon which your chest and back muscles lie; when the rib box is expanded, your torso appears noticeably thicker. It's to your advantage to expand your bony rib box to the limit, because only maximum chest expansion will yield optimum torso thickness when viewed from the front and particularly from the side. When your rib cage has been maximally expanded and you have thickened your pectorals and upper-back muscles, you'll appear very thick from the side when viewed in a contest lineup. This will give you a big jump ahead of all the razor-thin-torso types usually seen in even high-level competitions.

Rib-cage expansion also has health advantages. The type of high-rep squatting required in rib-box expansion programs will greatly increase your aerobic capacity and help turn your metabolism naturally anabolic. Plus, a roomy rib box will give your intrathoracic organs, such as the heart and lungs, more room to operate. It's somewhat like the case of a goldfish that only grows large enough to conform to his bowl; when you put the fish in a pond it will easily grow to two or three times its normal size once it has room to operate.

When specializing on rib-cage expansion, you should train the area three times per week on nonconsecutive days. We suggest giving this area

(and your legs, which are strongly involved in the expansion process) priority by training it first every week on Mondays. Therefore, it follows that you should again train for rib-box expansion on Wednesdays and Fridays.

You won't need to do specific quadriceps-buttocks work on rib-cage expansion days, because

Flavio Baccianini (Italy).

high-rep squats take care of these areas. But you'll need to work the balance of your body—calves, back, pectorals, delts, arms, and abdominals—intensely on a different training day. We suggest a Tuesday/Saturday regimen for these body parts, giving you a five-day split routine with emphasis on rib-cage expansion.

For extraneous body parts we recommend choosing one or two basic movements per muscle group: two for chest, back, and shoulders; one each for calves, abs, bis, tris, and forearms. On chest, back, shoulders, bis, and tris, do five sets of five reps (5 × 5) with moderately heavy weights to induce continued mass development. For calves, abs, and forearms, do 3–4 series of 20–30 repetitions each.

Let's move now to the key chest-expansion exercise—high-rep breathing squats. Start out with a bar set to your approximate body weight, even though that will be relatively light for you. Later, as your legs become more accustomed to the high reps, you can progressively add plates to your squat bar.

Shoulder the bar, grasping it out near the plates to hold it across your traps. Step back and set your feet about shoulder-width apart, with your heels on a 2 × 4-inch board and your toes angled slightly outward. Tense your back muscles and use this muscle tension to keep your torso upright as you perform each squat rep. You might find it useful also to pick a point on the gym wall at eye level on which to focus your eyes, since this helps keep your head up and your back straight.

For the first 10 reps of breathing squats, take three huge breaths, breathing out maximally and then in to the limit. Hold the third breath as you descend into a full squatting position, and exhale slowly as you rise. Repeat the movement without adding inhalations to your three-breath scheme for the first 10 repetitions.

For reps 11–20, take four huffing and puffing breaths between each repetition, again holding the last inhalation as you squat down. For the final five counts of your 25-rep set, take five full breaths between each set.

At the end of your set you will be panting and puffing like an old-style steam engine chugging up a long hill. Take advantage of this by supersetting 25 reps of breathing squats with 25 more reps of breathing pullovers to stretch your rib cage cartilage and allow your breathing to return to normal. Take as little rest as possible between exercises and leave only three to five minutes between supersets.

Breathing pullovers are performed lying on your back with a light barbell (25–35 pounds should be sufficient at first, regardless of your body weight) held in your hands. Take an overgrip on the bar with your hands set slightly wider than your shoulders. Your feet should be set flat on the gym floor to balance your body in position. Stiffen your arms and keep them locked straight throughout your set.

Starting with the bar held at straight-arm's length directly above your shoulder joints, allow it to descend to the rear in a semicircular arc down to as low a position as is comfortably possible to achieve. As you slowly lower the weight, inhale as deeply as possible and fill your lungs with air. Hold your breath as you slowly return the bar back along the same semicircular arc to the starting point, then exhale. Repeat the movement for the required number of repetitions.

As an alternative to barbell breathing pullovers, you can do dumbbell breathing pullovers, either holding a light dumbbell in each hand or a moderately weighted dumbbell in both hands as you do the movement. Occasionally, you might find that stiff-armed dumbbell flyes—in which the weights descend in semicircular arcs directly out to the sides rather than to the rear—will stretch your rib cage sufficiently to stretch the cartilage.

One superset of breathing squats and breathing pullovers will knock you on your butt if you aren't used to it. But as a beginning-level bodybuilder, you should work up to the beginning-level program. Brackets indicate supersetted exercises.

SAMPLE BREATHING-EXERCISE ROUTINES

Beginning Level

Exercise	Sets	Reps
{ Breathing Squats	3	25
{ Breathing Pullovers	3	25

Intermediate Level

Exercise	Sets	Reps
{ Breathing Squats	5	25
{ Breathing Pullovers	5	25

Advanced Level

Exercise	Sets	Reps
{ Breathing Squats	10	25
{ Breathing Pullovers	10	25

Andrian Batho, Tim Belknap, Steve Brisbois—the Killer Bees.

Ron Love (L) and Sonny Schmidt anxiously await the results of a close judges' decision at the 1991 San Jose Pro Invitational. Ron won, with Sonny second.

Renel Janvier, Thierry Pastel, Shawn Ray.

If you have worked up to either the intermediate or advanced level of rib-cage expansion work, you'll understand completely why you only do the breathing squats and breathing pullovers in one workout and the rest of your physique in another one. The supersets of breathing squats and breathing pullovers will feel like they are going to kill you, particularly when you have to repeat them for multiple supersets.

Three months on any of the preceding programs will yield noticeable results in rib-cage expansion. Three months is also about the maximum length of time that any bodybuilder can follow one of these routines before becoming borderline insane. If you're still young and have the potential to expand your rib cage, try spending every summer working as hard as possible on breathing squats and pullovers. The remainder of the year you can follow a more normal type of mass- and power-building program.

Don't worry if you feel dull pain in the ends of the cartilage that attaches your ribs to the sternum. You're not having a heart attack. This mild, dull pain is a sure sign that you are optimally stretching the area and your rib cage is gradually expanding.

While we have recommended this rib-expansion program to bodybuilders 19 years of age and under, don't despair if you're older. The program will still work for you, but more slowly. We've known bodybuilders in their thirties who have added two to four inches of expansion to their chests. If they can do it, so can you!

Flex Wheeler gets serious on a set of incline barbell presses with nearly 400 pounds on the bar!

14

The Greatest Bodybuilding Lies

Bodybuilding abounds with gurus who advise on every aspect of training, diet, and competitive mental approach, almost always for a substantial fee. You usually find these gurus hanging around gyms and contests from the local up to the international-pro level. Some even write books and articles with well-meaning—but highly inappropriate—advice in them.

Some of the more obvious falsehoods shouldn't be that difficult to pick up on, even if you're a novice trainee, but the rap of a few of the gurus is good enough to con even experienced bodybuilders. In this chapter we will dispel six of the most obvious dead-end roads you should avoid.

Superslow Reps

One writer who sells a lot of books champions superslow reps as the ultimate form of high-intensity training. He claims superslow reps will give a bodybuilder mass and powerful muscles in an incredibly short period of time. With this system each repetition should take 15 seconds to complete, raising each count in 10 seconds and lowering it in 5. Thus, an eight-rep set would take 120 seconds to complete.

No more than 12 sets of superslow reps should be performed each session for three weekly workouts. Follow the low-set program, and you'll soon look like Lee Haney, Shawn Ray, or Lee Labrada. From looking at the photos of champs illustrating these books (*none* of whom trains the way the author claims), you'd think there are hundreds of guys as good as these three, all of whom have been developed by superslow training. Unfortunately, these supermen exist only in the mind of the proponent of the superslow-rep training principle. What really builds muscle fastest and to the ultimate degree is a large range of training principles, not simply one "magic" one. For example, you should try training holistically.

Let's talk for a moment about holistic training. Some bodybuilders build huge, undetailed muscles by constantly lifting heavy poundages for low reps in almost exclusively basic exercises. Others develop smaller, highly detailed muscles by doing sets of high reps with relatively light poundages on a variety of exercises, but mainly isolation movements. There is a group in the middle who build middle-sized muscles with some degree of intramuscular detail doing exclusively medium reps with medium weights on a balanced program of basic movements and isolation exercises.

Holistic bodybuilding involves combining heavy, medium, and light sets—with comparable reps for each degree of weight change—but not necessarily all within the same workout for each muscle group. Over the course of one week you should handle all three types of weights when training holistically. If you stick to it, you'll have a much greater degree of muscle mass and detail a year from now than any bodybuilder who did superslow reps over the same period of time until he or she was blue in the face.

You can also add eclectic training to your holistic program. Eclectic training involves changing exercises constantly, doing every possible movement—and there are hundreds—for each body part. Long experience has shown serious bodybuilders that they achieve a more complete and detailed physique if they bomb

Parallel-bar dips work the lower and outer pecs.

Nimrod King (Canadian Overall Champion and winner of several IFBB pro titles) shows what a kneeling, twisting back shot should look like.

each muscle group from the widest possible number of angles (*eclectic* training) with a wide spectrum of weight-rep combinations on every movement (*holistic* training).

Superslow reps are just one more intensity technique you can try, but don't expect much from it. It's not a magic bullet that will make you into Arnold Schwarzenegger overnight!

Super-High-Intensity Training

Super-high-intensity training, often called *heavy-duty* training, has been pushed on the bodybuilding public for the past 25 years by Arthur Jones, who was hyping his revolutionary new Nautilus machines at the time. At least two competent writers have been pushing the concept ever since, sucking in gullible young bodybuilders with claims they'll be turned into supermen in a year on no more than 4–6 total sets per workout, three days a week.

After a minimum—and often nonexistent—warm-up, the trainees jump to the heaviest weight they can handle for 5–6 solid reps to momentary muscular failure, after which they are given 3–4 forced reps to push even further toward complete exhaustion, and often another 3–4 forced negative reps to completely obliterate the working muscle(s). And 2–3 more sets of this for each body part for a year or two is supposed

to turn someone into Hercules. Often—all too often—this type of training leads to arthritic joints and very little gain in muscle mass.

We don't have anything against doing low-set, heavy workouts. We just don't believe in sets so low that you are training delts, chest, and legs with only four all-out sets per workout for each of these complex muscle groups. Our thinking is more in line with that of Lee Labrada, IFBB World Grand Prix Champion and twice a second-place finisher in Mr. Olympia. While expressing admiration for Mike Mentzer's physique and Heavy Duty Training System, Labrada

Close-up, seated one-arm dumbbell concentration curls.

Few bodybuilders enjoy the sport as much as former full contact karate champ Flex Wheeler, who's a coming national champion and sure future IFBB pro bodybuilder.

Barbell reverse curls, as performed in an actual workout
by Tim Belknap at Gold's Gym in Venice.

keeps his total work load for each body part between 8–10 hard sets following warm-ups.

Labrada first warms up with one or two sets of a basic exercise, then jumps to his maximum weight for 8–10 reps. He rests about 60 seconds while changing the weight for his second set, which is 10 percent lighter, and goes again for 8–10 reps. Again he rests about a minute while reducing the weight a further 10 percent for 8–10 final reps. Doing three movements of three sets each like this would make up Labrada's full chest routine.

England's Dorian Yates (1991 victor at Night of the Champions and a runner-up at his first Mr. Olympia later that year) follows a program very similar to Labrada's but with slightly fewer total sets, say, 6–8 for most large muscle groups. But these 6–8 are only the hard, heavy, building sets, because Yates doesn't count warm-ups, which might add 30–40 percent to that figure.

Heavy-duty training does work well for a minority of bodybuilders, the ones with gigantic genetic gifts. Of course, they'd make good gains on virtually any type of bodybuilding system.

A final fallacy of high-intensity training is that relatively inexperienced trainees are able to take even one set to and past failure, let alone every set in a workout. We see beginners and other relatively inexperienced men and women attempting this type of program. *They* make minimal gains—if any—and usually end up with sore joints all over their bodies. That's why we don't turn cartwheels over high-intensity training for developing mass and strength.

You Have to Take Drugs

While drug usage in the sport has been cleaned up dramatically lately, bodybuilding still suffers from the stigma that "we have to take tissue-building drugs to look the way we do." Such an accusation simply isn't true because thousands and thousands of bodybuilders who are all training naturally look positively great. The 1990 Mr. Olympia competition was drug tested, and most of these huge male bodybuilders probably never looked better in any prior untested show.

During the early 1980s anyone who wanted to purchase steroids or androgens or even human growth hormone could openly buy supplies at almost any gym in America. Hundreds of physicians were writing prescriptions for the same drugs the black marketeers were purveying at somewhat higher prices in the gyms. It was absolute chemical heaven for bodybuilders. Even high-school boys were injecting steroids to look a little more buffed for the girls.

But in 1985 or 1986 the government began to crack down on underground steroid dealers, sending many of them on extended vacations in barred rooms. State medical boards came down on physicians who had become steroid-prescription mills; soon all of them were back practicing regular medicine, *if* they still had medical licenses.

Where there had once been a surplus of bodybuilding drugs, there was now a tremendous vacuum. Into that vacuum came unscrupulous forgers who sold salad oil as injectable steroids, God knows what as steroid tablets, and sugar water as growth hormone.

Some otherwise superhealthy athletes got very ill on the forgeries, and no one made gains on them, so an entire generation of bodybuilders has been forced to train naturally. They adapted by intensifying—while shortening—training sessions and paying much greater attention to nutrition. They soon had excellent physiques, even better bodies than most of the steroid monsters, because they didn't have the bloated tissues and terrible skin conditions of bodybuilders who depended heavily on chemicals. Natural bodybuilders proved beyond any shadow of a doubt that they don't need to take tissue-building drugs to look great and *feel* great at all times.

The age of natural bodybuilding is upon us, and it's one of the best things that has happened to the sport as a whole. No doubt you will be offered drugs by "friends" somewhere down the line. Do yourself a favor and turn them down. Stay natural, and you'll never regret it!

You Have to Have Awesome Potential

Ah, the god of potential raises its snakelike head again! To use a lack of potential as an excuse is one of the biggest cop-outs in bodybuilding for athletes who don't have the gumption to train hard and consistently enough to build great physiques.

One basic fact of nature is that God gives some bodybuilders much better genetic potential for the sport than others. All this means is that a man or woman will have to work longer, harder, and more intelligently—plus be strictly attentive to nutritional practices—to reach the same ultimate level as a more gifted bodybuilder. The gifted athlete will arrive at a competitive level much more quickly than a less gifted counterpart, and sometimes the gifted bodybuilder will be able to push his or her level of physical excellence higher than others'.

Over our many collective years in the sport, we have seen men and women with very poor genetic gifts for bodybuilding still reach the top of the sport: Larry Scott is often pointed to as an example. He was not tall (only about 5'8"), was very skinny when he began pumping iron (120 pounds body weight), his bony shoulder girdle was actually narrower than his pelvic structure, and he had to move heaven on earth to put on only a single ounce of new muscle mass.

Scott persevered. He trained very hard, regularly, and scientifically, and gradually he added muscle to his skinny frame. It was a grinding process, but every ounce he added was pure muscle, because his speedy metabolism wouldn't allow a vestige of fat to cling to any area of his body. The point is that Scott could *see* each tiny gain, which redoubled his enthusiasm and efforts.

To broaden his shoulders and achieve a V-shaped torso, the Great Scott found innovative deltoid, chest, and latissimus dorsi exercises and training techniques that brought these areas up to an unprecedented level. Scott's arms responded well and ultimately became the envy of international bodybuilding. With systematic, superhard training his legs and calves also improved until they were in proportion with his upper body.

Larry Scott began to take titles—Mr. California and Mr. Pacific Coast—at a shredded 175–80 pounds. He then began experimenting with food supplements, particularly milk and egg protein powder (with his speedy BMR, he could mix it with cream and still maintain his cuts), huge quantities of B-complex vitamins, and liver extract capsules. His muscular body weight kept gradually climbing, and in 1963 he was up to 190 pounds when he won his Mr. America title. In 1965 he almost broke the 200-pound barrier, weighing 198 as he won the IFBB Mr. Universe title.

After the Universe victory, Scott was ready for retirement, but Joe Weider decided to run his first Mr. Olympia competition in the fall of 1965. The Olympia was open to all former Mr. Universe and Mr. World winners, so Scott had something new to shoot for. By contest time he weighed a solid 207 and was crowned the first Mr. Olympia. A year later Scott's contest muscular body weight had reached an all-time high of 212 pounds to win him another Olympia. Certifiably the greatest bodybuilder of his era, Larry Scott—the man with no potential—retired, married, raised a family, and still looks great in his fifties!

Scott's lesson is to ignore your physical limitations and get to work achieving your goals. If you leave no stone unturned and you're willing to put in the required time and energy, there's no such thing as genetic deficiencies in bodybuilding!

One facet of genetic potential that is seldom discussed—despite the fact that it is of vital importance—is intelligence. Most psychologists will argue that intelligence is not a genetic trait but develops as a result of your being in a good environment for intellectual attainment. You *do* have to be lucky enough to grow up in an enriched environment, and you'll need some education, too, because a knowledgeable bodybuilder has a big head start on his less informed counterparts.

Bodybuilding has become very scientific and technical, and you need the smarts to understand such diverse topics as anatomy, kinesiology, exercise physiology, biomechanics, biochemistry, dance, acting, and finance. What type of genetic potential do you now feel you have for bodybuilding?

It's Easy

Bodybuilding is definitely not an easy sport to excel at. In fact, it's probably the toughest sport in the world. We certainly train as hard and as often as any other athletes—both in terms of intensity and total workout load—and we often have to do so on a severely calorie-restricted diet!

Top bodybuilders put out tremendous amounts of energy in every workout, and it is genuinely painful to train as hard as you must in order to become a successful competitive bodybuilder. We're not talking about injury pain—although minor, chronic injuries are a fact of life in almost any sport, and certainly in bodybuilding—but the deep pain in oxygen-starved, fatigue-toxin-washed muscles.

Bodybuilders frequently talk about the "pain barrier" in training. This is the point at which mortals feel so much fatigue pain in their muscles that they are forced to put the bar down and terminate the set for a rest. True bodybuilders ignore this pain effectively enough to be able to crash past the pain barrier for 2–3 reps mere mortals never experience. That is why the muscles of a serious bodybuilder are so much more impressive than those of a bodybuilding dilettante.

Gold's in Venice annually attracts hordes of the world's best, this time Francis Benfatto, born in Algeria and nominally living in France. He's giving the works to a set of leg extensions here.

Bodybuilders become so goal-driven that they willingly sacrifice parties, films, high-cal meals, and many other pleasures pencilneck geeks enjoy. They are self-sacrificing in order to improve their own already great physiques, but they will still have time to spot you for a heavy set of benches if your training partner is missing.

No, bodybuilding is not easy. But there is an old saying that the finest piece of steel is the one which has passed through the hottest flame during its manufacture. All bodybuilders are men and women of steel!

Belknap again, this time maxing out his triceps with an all-out set of pulley pushdowns.

It Can Be Done Quickly

In competitive bodybuilding there have been legendary fast-gainers such as Arnold Schwarzenegger, who won his first Mr. Universe title after only five years of training. But for most of us success at bodybuilding just doesn't happen so fast. There are many documented cases of bodybuilders laboring in the gym for 15–20 years before winning a runner-up trophy, let alone an actual title.

The median length of training for amateur national champions these days is about eight years for men and six for women. But these superdedicated individuals watch their diets with microscopic precision, never miss a workout, and *always* put out the maximum at every training session, regardless of how tired or raunchy they happen to feel prior to the workout. They constantly study all of the new training and nutrition literature published in the sport so they can stay a step ahead of the competition. In short, they are very dedicated individuals, and they're winners because they *are* so dedicated.

Winning bodybuilders are also patient people, because they fully understand how long it takes to develop a quality physique. When you personally come to that same conclusion—that it'll take time to get where you want to go—you have to make a decision. Do you want to be a serious competitive bodybuilder, or do you want to just keep training recreationally? There's no shame in being a recreational iron pumper, and it always leaves you with the option of becoming serious somewhere else down the road.

If you're serious now, make the commitment to become and to stay totally dedicated. Be dedicated for a sufficiently long period of time and you'll become a champion by any definition currently acceptable. You'll be on top of the world!

Renel Janvier, Vince Taylor, J. J. Marsh.

15
Special Problems

Inevitably, specialized problems still confront bodybuilders craving new degrees of muscle mass and physical power, problems that haven't been fully explained in prior chapters. These special problems include the following:

- Stretch marks and how to cure them
- Finding stylish clothing for huge bodies in regular stores
- What to wear in the gym
- Following the safety rules
- Warming up properly
- Long-term injury prevention, cure, and rehabilitation
- Managing time during busy days so a set hour to start and a set length of time to train are always available
- Managing the expense of gym dues, extra food bills, concentrated food supplement bills, and travel/lodging expenses when attending competitions
- Factors of special interest to women, such as strength ratios compared to those of men, menstrual problems, and pregnancy

As you can see, this final instructional chapter is a catchall of problems that don't fit in an orderly fashion into better-defined chapters. You can be assured that we have answers to all of the questions generated by these special problems.

Stretch Marks

Stretch marks are tears in the skin which heal to form scars somewhat lighter in pigmentation than the surrounding undamaged skin. They are common among bodybuilding men and somewhat less common among women. Stretch marks are rampant among bodybuilders who try to gain weight too quickly, as is often the case with the classic approach to weight gain. Even a few bodybuilders who have gained more slowly have stretch marks over their forearms and calves, places where these scars are seldom seen.

Women bodybuilders sometimes fare even worse than their male counterparts. They not only can get the common type of stretch mark found in the armpit, where the pectoral-deltoid tie-in is, but many become pregnant, and the rapid expansion of their abdomens during pregnancy causes stretch marks all over the abdominal wall.

When the tissues of a muscle or fatty mass expand too quickly for the skin to accommodate

Flex Wheeler again fries his upper chest, this time with incline dumbbell presses using massive weights.

it, the skin actually does tear, usually in one of the lower levels of the skin where most of the pigmentation (melanin) is stored. It's easiest to visualize your skin as several layers of cloth laid one on top of the other. When the threads making up the cloth are weak in one layer, that layer of cloth can tear.

The skin fibers weaken and tear due to a diet lacking in various amino acids, vitamins, and minerals, but particularly the mineral zinc. If you are simply careful to supplement your diet with daily doses of zinc, you'll have little fear of collecting stretch marks. Zinc is vital for making the skin elastic and therefore less prone to tears.

If you follow a diet high in vitamins A, B_6, C, E, and F, combined with zinc, you should completely eliminate any danger of incurring stretch marks. It's still a good plan to avoid pigging out during the off-season. Instead, make your gains in muscle mass slowly, and with those gains in pure muscle tissue rather than in fat.

If you do start to see a stretch mark forming, increase your zinc intake immediately and rub vitamin-E oil over the tear and surrounding tissues. This can stop a baby stretch mark in its tracks.

One great anti-stretch-mark preparation with plenty of zinc in it is VitaDerm, which is being sold by Sintek labs in Florida. Their toll-free number for information and order placement is 1 (800) 356-5758.

Finding Stylish Clothing

Whenever you've seen Arnold Schwarzenegger, Lou Ferrigno, and Shawn Ray on television talk shows, they were undoubtedly wearing immaculately tailored clothing. They've earned the right and the bucks to go to the best tailors. Most of us average gym rats don't have the jingle and are forced to buy off the rack.

If you like double knits and are willing to shop in the tall and fat stores, you can find excellent fits, and stylish ones at that, at normal prices. I'm talking in terms of business and evening wear here, but you can also find casual clothing like blue jeans and polo shirts, which will look great on you throughout an informal day.

Women have a lot less difficulty in finding stylish clothing off the rack than men, as can easily be seen at any high-level competition as in-shape women strut their stuff in awesome outfits. Men are much more exaggerated in terms of limb girths, so they have more trouble than women in finding decent clothing off the rack.

With baggies in style in the gym, it doesn't matter how big you get in the off-season—there'll always be a bottom and top that will fit you, and probably even be color coordinated. Keep gym clothes clean and no restaurant worth going into for lunch will kick you out, and no mall shop will eject you and your credit cards for being dressed in bad taste.

Gym Wear

Let's start from the ground and work upward. Start with your choice of color, style, and cut of sweat-absorbing socks, worn under sturdy shoes with a solid arch support and a good tread. In the past we've recommended purchasing running shoes for use during heavy training in the gym. But that was prior to the recent advent of cross-training shoes constructed specifically for weight workouts, aerobics sessions, *and* running.

All sporting-goods stores, shoe departments in large department stores, and shops specializing in athletic footwear will have cross-training shoes available in a broad array of styles and color combinations. Don't be shocked when you have to pay something in the range of $100, because cross-training shoes are a tad more expensive than running shoes and a lot more costly than normal sneakers. However, they are quite durable and well worth the expense.

Training shoes need a good tread that won't slip off a toe block when you're doing heavy, specialized calf exercises. Ordinary sneaks and boating-dock shoes are a couple of types of footwear that don't meet this requirement. If your shoe treads don't stay on the calf block under a heavy load, you can easily sprain an ankle or strain an Achilles tendon; both injuries will set you back weeks on your calf-training schedule and can also limit the type of leg exercises you can perform in a workout.

A strong arch support is essential to keep the heavy loads inherent in mass and power training from causing compression injuries to the arches of your feet. We still occasionally see bodybuilders doing heavy squats or deadlifts either barefooted or in rubber flip-flop sandals, and we cringe every time we see it. You'll be much better off if you do your heavy lifting in sturdy shoes with solid arch supports.

Many bodybuilders wear orthotics inside their shoes for more specialized foot support. A podiatrist can fit you with orthotics to balance out foot irregularities and either reduce or eliminate many chronic back, knee, and hip problems.

Again, these appliances can be expensive, but they are indispensable to many bodybuilders. You should at least consider ponying up the cost of a podiatric exam to determine if you need orthotics—you might not need them, but then again, you might.

Minimum lower-body wear is a pair of shorts, which can be quite functional in warm weather

Selwyn Cottrell (England).

Flex Wheeler sets up for barbell bent-over rows.

but insufficient when it's cold in the gym. More often than not, we see men wearing baggies (overly large pants with a drawstring, frequently worn as casual street wear in California). Women are quite comfortable at Gold's in Venice wearing tights and a G-string *if* they have the anatomy for it. Women in off-season shape are often too heavy for such brief attire; these women also will be seen in baggies, but in brighter colors.

Tops can be an area where personal style comes into play. If you're really buffed—male or female—show it off with a tank top (the women's versions are lacy and sexier than the guys' tops). A step down is a tight Gold's Gym T-shirt; another step down is a tight Gold's sweatshirt, preferably with the sleeves cut off and the neckline ripped out. This is worn over a tank top, because a bodybuilder's traps can look good at any body weight. There are baggy tops for bodybuilders in deep off-season shape.

Hats or headbands are optional, and both are frequently worn at Gold's in Venice. They are not only a style statement but also functional, because both hats and headbands keep sweat from rolling down into your eyes.

Wrist sweatbands come in handy for brushing random rivulets of perspiration off your face. You can carry around a small hand towel for the same purpose. Many bodybuilders tote around a larger towel for use over sweaty vinyl bench tops. It's not much fun to lie in someone else's puddles.

Most bodybuilders these days wear protective gloves to keep their hands from becoming too rough. Normally these gloves are leather in the palm and inside finger areas, with heavy, airy nylon covering the backs of the hands and fingers. Gloves come in a range of colors and sizes, and we suggest trying on several pairs to be sure of correct fit.

Where can you find good gym gear? There are more than 100 licensed Gold's Gyms in the United States and Canada, and most of them have pro shops in which you can purchase quality gym clothing and other equipment, even posing suits and the current issues of various bodybuilding magazines.

You can also buy gym gear via mail-order ads in large bodybuilding magazines such as *Flex*. J. J. Marsh, Mike Christian, Andreas Cahling, and Tonya Knight are just four of the top bodybuilders who have personal clothing lines. There are many nonbodybuilders selling similar clothing and equipment.

Supportive Gear

Every serious bodybuilder needs a weight-lifting belt. Belts come in heavy leather or in the newer composite fabrics such as those manufactured by Valleo. Gym pro shops and sporting-goods stores are good sources of belts, or you can mail order them. Wear your belt whenever you are squatting, doing heavy back work, and lifting heavy poundages overhead. The belt will protect your midsection and lower back from injury.

Neoprene-rubber bands can be purchased for use around the waist, if you have a sore lower back, or around your knee or elbow, if one of these joints is chronically sore. The rubber provides only minimal support to an injured joint, but it keeps therapeutic moist heat around the joint as you work out.

Finally, there are fabric wraps for use around knees, elbows, or wrists. Wrapped tightly, they provide plenty of support, but they should be used *only* to protect an old injury. Both neoprene and fabric wraps can be purchased at pro shops and sporting-goods stores and through mail-order ads in various magazines.

Safety Factors

"Bodybuilding is normally a very safe form of exercise," asserts Albert Beckles, who won the IFBB Niagra Falls Pro Grand Prix in 1991 at the age of 61. "It's safe despite its high intensity level and the huge weights you can use, but the following safety rules should be carefully observed."

- Warm up thoroughly and stay warm throughout your workout by wearing sufficient clothing and starting your next set within two minutes after your last one.
- Always perform all of your exercises in perfect form, particularly when using heavy weights.
- Use a spotter whenever you do bench presses, squats, or other heavy bodybuilding exercises.
- Try to avoid working out in an overly crowded gym so you won't have to rest for an excessively long period of time while waiting for an occupied piece of equipment.
- Try to avoid training when you are mentally distracted.
- Learn as much as possible about bodybuilding, because the better informed you are, the better you'll be able to avoid potential injuries.
- Observe good housekeeping practices at the gym. Pick up loose equipment and place it in the racks or the other designated storage areas.
- Always use collars on all barbells to prevent weights from sliding off, which may cause the bar to whip violently up or down.
- Wear a weight-lifting belt whenever you do overhead presses, squats, or heavy back work. (We can't emphasize this point excessively.)
- Always try to work out in a gym that has qualified instructors.

Warm-Ups

According to Anja Langer, second place at the 1988 Ms. Olympia and a frequent visitor at Gold's in Venice, "If every bodybuilder warmed up properly, was careful to keep warm throughout each workout, and maintained proper form at all times, training injuries could be cut almost to zero. But too many athletes avoid warming up and use atrocious form in their movements, and they end up incurring injury after injury.

"It's easiest to notice the traumatic injuries, such as pulled or torn muscles, dislocated joints, strained backs, and broken bones. But just as serious in the long run are the microtraumatic injuries to joints that gradually accumulate over a period of years until a bodybuilder will suffer constantly from sore joints that restrict range of

Mike DeVitis (France).

Bob Cicherillo—seated pulley rows—start.

motion and limit use of maximum weights in exercises.

"A proper warm-up actually increases the core temperature of your body, making you break a light sweat and increasing your rate of respiration. It warms up the joints and starts the flow of synovial fluid that lubricates the joints under heavy stress. It also makes the muscles more pliable and resistant to heavy stress, such as that incurred in a hard workout.

"Surprisingly, a good warm-up also improves motor coordination, helping to prevent the chance that you might fall over backward with one of your standing barbell presses halfway up to straight-arm's length.

"A good warm-up should consist of aerobic activity, light-to-moderate-intensity stretching, gymnastics exercises, and also some light, high-

rep sets on the first basic exercise you intend to do for a particular body part. In the gym where I train in Stuttgart, I often see many of the bigger male bodybuilders doing just the last part of this warm-up. They'll jump on a bench, do two or three light sets of bench presses, then skip upward to as heavy a weight as they can handle on this movement for six to eight reps. Little wonder they incur so many injuries.

"Up until the middle 1980s most experts recommended starting a warm-up with stretching, but research has demonstrated that stretching a cold muscle can actually cause small tears in the tissues. Therefore, it's best to first do several minutes of some type of aerobic activity to increase the body's core temperature prior to initiating the stretching portion of your warm-up.

"Jogging in place and skipping rope are the

Bob Cicherillo—seated pulley rows—finish.

easiest aerobic activities to practice indoors, because they require a minimum of both space and equipment. I'd suggest about five minutes of either, starting out slowly and gradually working up the intensity and tempo until you are really cooking for the final minute or so.

"If you are lucky enough to work out in a large gym, you will have a wide variety of aerobic equipment available to you. Some of the best equipment are stationary bikes (which come in standard upright models as well as recumbent machines where you pedal while lying on your back), stair climbers, Versa-climbers, and tread-

mills. Five minutes or so on any of these machines can really get your heart jump-started and your blood flowing.

"Next, stretch each major muscle group for at least 30–60 seconds per stretch. For warm-ups, I don't believe in the type of stretching in which a partner forces you farther into the stretched position than you are capable of assuming on your own. Rather, I prefer to ease slowly into the stretched position until I begin to feel some small degree of pain. Then I hold that position motionless for 30–60 seconds.

"I'm sure you already know many stretching

movements you can use. If you don't know any, the best book on the subject is called, appropriately enough, *Stretching*. The reference guide was written by Bob Anderson.

"You should be getting really well warmed up by this point, so you should move immediately into calisthenic exercises, choosing at least one for each major muscle group and doing 20–30 repetitions. Following is a good list that you can use."

- Jumping jacks
- Push-ups
- Alternate toe touches (in standing position)
- Deep knee bends
- Sit-ups
- Standing side bends
- Freehand calf raises

"Before beginning to train each body part, you should also do a short warm-up with weights," Langer continues. "Let's take the chest, for example, assuming that you are starting out with bench presses and plan to use 225 pounds for your first true workout set. I'd suggest doing three progressively heavier warm-up sets before hitting the 225. For example, try doing 15 reps with 135 pounds, 12 counts with 175, and 10 reps with 205 before starting your first set with 225 pounds. In this way, your joints and working muscles will have grown gradually accustomed to the increased stress of weight work when compared to aerobics, stretching, and gymnastics exercises.

"The final key to a good warm-up is to keep the pace of your workout sufficiently fast enough that your body stays warm until the end of your session. This means that you can't take time out to talk with a friend for a few minutes here and there, and it implies that you shouldn't rest excessively long between sets. After more than 90 seconds between sets, you're courting cooldown and disaster."

Injuries—Prevention, Cure, and Rehabilitation

"Injuries are the bane of any bodybuilder's existence," says Lee Labrada, the winner of many IFBB Pro Grand Prix titles and twice runner-up in the Mr. Olympia competition. "While the bodybuilder works like a dog to improve his physique, the injury demon sets up roadblocks to competitive success. Whenever you incur an in-

jury, it will take two or three times as long as the duration of the injury itself to reach peak training intensity again. It should be obvious that injury prevention should be high on your list of bodybuilding priorities.

"I've been lucky enough to suffer only a couple of very minor injuries, so I've been able to keep gaining muscle mass at a steady—albeit non-spectacular—rate of speed. As a result, I was able to become a solid pro bodybuilder and place as high as second in the Mr. Olympia while equally talented, but more injury-prone, bodybuilders never made it out of the amateur ranks."

Injury Prevention

Two factors must be kept consistent if you wish to avoid progress-stalling training injuries:

- Always warm up thoroughly prior to every heavy training session, and be sure to stay warm during your workout by maintaining a relatively fast pace between sets.
- Always use perfect form in all of your exercises, particularly the heavy basic movements but also the lighter isolation exercises.

Correct Form

"I can tell you quite a bit about exercise form," Labrada continues. "There is a correct biomechanical position that should be assumed and maintained during each exercise. Correct descriptions of all popular bodybuilding movements can be found in various muscle magazines and in books devoted to the sport. Adopt the correct positions and move only those joints and limbs that should be mobile during the exercise.

"It's essential to move the weight over the complete range of motion described for it, and it should be moved relatively slowly to prevent momentum from taking over part of the lifting process. Never jerk, bounce, or heave a weight in the bottom position of an exercise, since this can cause tiny microscopic tears in the muscles and connective tissues. Often the long accumulation of such microtraumas is what gives an experienced bodybuilder sore joints.

"Everywhere I go on seminar/exhibition tours, however, I see bodybuilders bouncing heavy barbells off their chests while doing bench presses. How much do you want to bet that these men and women will be complaining of shoulder and elbow pain 10 years from now?

"Make all of the movements slow, smooth, precise, and full, moving only those parts of the body that are supposed to accomplish the exercise, and you'll probably never end up with an injury problem of any consequence. Think seriously about avoiding ego poundages on some of the basic movements. Such low-rep sets do nothing for bodybuilders, nor power lifters either. Keep your reps above five per set with good form, and all of your muscles should explode into huge size."

Injury Treatment

"Occasionally, it will be impossible to avoid a serious bodybuilding injury such as a dislocated joint, seriously torn muscle, or broken bone," Labrada goes on. "In such a case, you should immediately consult a sports-medicine physician or an orthopedist whom you trust. Serious bodybuilding injuries should *never* be self-treated, because doing so can often make them more serious and hold back your workouts for an even longer period of time than if you'd immediately consulted a good physician.

"Less serious injuries *can* be home-treated. Minor joint pain, minor muscle pulls, minor back injuries, and so forth fall into this category. If you treat these problems forthrightly and correctly, you should be back training at peak intensity within three or four weeks after incurring the original injury.

"The main problem with minor joint and muscle injuries is the swelling that inevitably accompanies them. Swelling is one of the body's natural defense mechanisms when an injury occurs, in that it helps to immobilize the injured area. But as long as an area is swollen, it won't heal. The actual healing process only begins once the swelling has gone down.

"To keep swelling under control—and thus speed healing—athletic trainers use a method called *RICE*, an acronym in which each letter stands for a key process in treating the injury:

R = *R*est
I = *I*ce
C = *C*ompression
E = *E*levation

"Obviously, every injured area should be rested until it is healed, so the first active measure you should take is to apply ice to the injured area. The easiest way to do this is to wrap ice cubes and/or ice chips in a towel, then form the towel over the anatomical area, lightly crushing ice together so a fit is achieved in which no air pockets are present between the skin and the towel with the ice in it.

"The most common pattern of icing is to place the towel on the injured area 15 minutes out of every hour, resting the intervening 45 minutes before a second icing. Keep this pattern up every waking hour for the first 24–36 hours after the injury has taken place.

"When the towel is first put on your skin, it will be a bit painful—have you ever plunged your hand into ice-cold water? But your skin will very quickly become numb as a result of the cold, and the joint will gradually cool off until it's almost the same temperature as the ice. I think if you polled injured bodybuilders and other athletes, they'd tell you that the icing component is their least favorite part of the RICE method of injury treatment.

"As an aside on injury-site icing, you should also consider icing chronically sore joints immediately after a workout for 15–20 minutes. This will help prevent accumulations of histamines, which can cause continued soreness in the joint. If you're icing an area consistently, one of the most convenient methods is to prefreeze paper cups full of ice with tongue depressors in the middle of them to serve as handles. Then you can hold on to the handle and rub the ice vigorously over the affected joint. Every top guy I know who uses this method on his sore joints swears by it.

"Compression is the third component of the RICE injury-treatment method. This simply involves tightly wrapping the injured area with an elastic bandage between icings. The compression provided by a tight bandage does much to reduce swelling in the injured area. But keep in mind that the bandage should be loosened for a couple of minutes each 15–20 minutes, or you'll end up with some very strange blood circulatory patterns. This is the same type of idea as loosening a tourniquet in a first-aid situation.

"Elevation is the final component of the RICE injury-treatment technique. It simply involves keeping the injured ankle, knee, elbow, or whatever elevated on a pillow so it's above the level of the rest of your body. Liquid runs downhill, so it's difficult for an area to become swollen if it's held higher than the main source (the torso) of blood and other bodily fluids.

"If you religiously follow RICE for a couple of days, you'll find that swelling should be minimal. In many cases the injured area won't swell up at all. That means it's ready to be rehabilitated, so you can get back into the gym and train the area both hard and heavy as soon as possible."

Injury Rehab

Labrada points out, "Rehabilitation should start out each post-injury workout session by warming up the injured area, either by using a hot-water bottle—if it's covered with a damp towel it'll conduct heat into the injury site much more efficiently—or sitting in a Jacuzzi or whirlpool. Ten to 15 minutes of heating should be plenty.

"Once the area is warmed up thoroughly, begin to lightly stretch the injured section using the widest variety of flexibility exercises at your

Flex Wheeler—presses behind the neck, near the start.

command. Use pain as your guide. Whenever you begin to feel pain in a stretch, back off a bit, and don't return to that amplitude of stretch until a day or two later.

"After three or four days of warming up first and then thoroughly stretching the injured area, you can begin to use light poundages and high reps—try something in the range of 20–30 per set—on basic exercises that affect the area. Again, use pain as your guide, and back off immediately if any single repetition causes any pain at the injury site. Then, a couple of days later, you can try the same weight again, with chances being good that it won't cause a single twinge of pain.

"Gradually build up to the amount of weight used in each exercise affecting the formerly injured area. Within two or three weeks you should be right where you were before the incident. Pay attention to all of the injury-prevention rules, and you'll probably never incur a similar injury again. Then you'll know you're on the path toward a championship physique at the fastest rate of speed humanly possible."

Time Management

"I have a doctor's appointment and six hours of homework, so I won't be able to train today." How many times have you heard this or similar excuses for avoiding a workout—a workout, we might add, that your competition isn't going to miss?

On the other side of the coin, we know top bodybuilders who fit more into one 24-hour day than most mortals could handle in 48 hours. Mike Christian, who won two IFBB Pro titles before moving over to the WBF, trains twice per day for a total of four hours in the gym, manages his Mike Christian's Everywhere clothing business for at least another eight hours daily, and still finds time for his family and friends before falling into a deep sleep for eight hours each night. He has maintained this killer schedule day in and day out since he founded his business in 1987.

How does Mike Christian do it? It's simply a matter of setting up a basic time schedule each day and sticking to it. This is what we call time management, and we'll give you some tips for fitting everything into your day.

First, write down your main priorities for each day. Here are a few choices:

- Workout(s)
- Mealtimes
- Work
- School and homework
- Social commitments
- Family commitments
- Rest and relaxation
- Sleep

See? We've already conned you into writing things down. It should come as little surprise that the secret to efficient time management is writing everything down.

Once you have your priorities detailed, map out a trial schedule for one day. Meal and sleep times should be obvious. Jot in a set time each day for your workout, and then try to fit everything else into the written schedule.

Give your provisional schedule a trial for a few days, fine-tuning it so everything fits together like the gears of an expensive Swiss Rolex watch. But don't make your schedule too rigid, because occasionally you'll have to jam in that dentist appointment you've been avoiding.

Only one facet of your daily schedule should be rigidly set if you're a serious iron pumper—that time of the day when you do your workout. This is particularly true if you have a training partner you have to see at a precise time. Also, it's been noted by exercise scientists that your body will reach an energy peak at a set time of the day if you consistently train at the same time each day.

Now that you know how to manage your time, you can only blame yourself if you miss a scheduled training session. No excuses now: get into the gym and pump some iron!

Expense Factors

We're not going to kid you about the cost of high-level bodybuilding. Anyway you cut the cheesecake, bodybuilding costs money that you wouldn't have to spend if you chose to remain a pencilneck. You have to fork over gym dues (at least until you've achieved some degree of fame in the sport), money for extra food and supplements, bucks for travel expenses to competitions, money for special clothing, posing suits, and custom music tapes at contest time, and so on, ad infinitum.

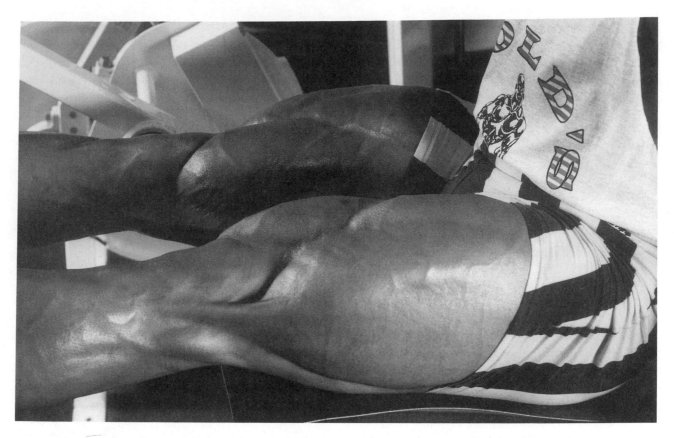

Close-up of Frank Hillebrand's quads under tight tension during a set of leg extensions.

It can really add up. For example, we know many bodybuilders who spend $800–$1,000 per month on supplements alone. If you happen to eschew the natural route to physique excellence supported by Gold's Gym, your drug expenses can be astronomical. In a bylined article in a July 1991 issue of *Sports Illustrated*, Lyle Alzado confessed that he spent $20,000–$30,000 per year on steroids and $4,000 per 16-week cycle on growth hormone. Alzado, a frequent habitué of Gold's in Venice, was an all-pro football player, *not* a bodybuilder. We certainly do *not* advocate drug use like this—and Alzado contended in his article that his drug usage resulted in an inoperable brain tumor—but it's undoubtedly true that many pro and high-level amateur bodybuilders are spending the same type of money, if not actually more.

The pot of gold at the end of the rainbow for most young bodybuilders is the amount of money some pros make. The painful truth is that less than 1 percent of all competitive bodybuild-

ers ever make the pro ranks, and even then a bodybuilder isn't guaranteed of making a living from the sport. Most pros have to look outside the sport—say, to a regular job—in order to support themselves.

One way around the expense of high-level bodybuilding, once you've made a name for yourself, is to find a sponsor to help defray your expenses. Sponsors range from gym owners to health-food concern owners to private individuals who have extra cash on hand. It can take some digging, but most good bodybuilders can eventually come up with sponsors to defray at least some of the cost of preparing for and entering competitions.

If you don't have a sponsor, the healthiest way to look at bodybuilding is as a moderately expensive—but eminently health-promoting—hobby. It costs money, but it repays you in so many tangible and intangible ways. You look great, feel great, and function at a much higher physical and mental level than John or Jane Q.

Nimrod King (Canada).

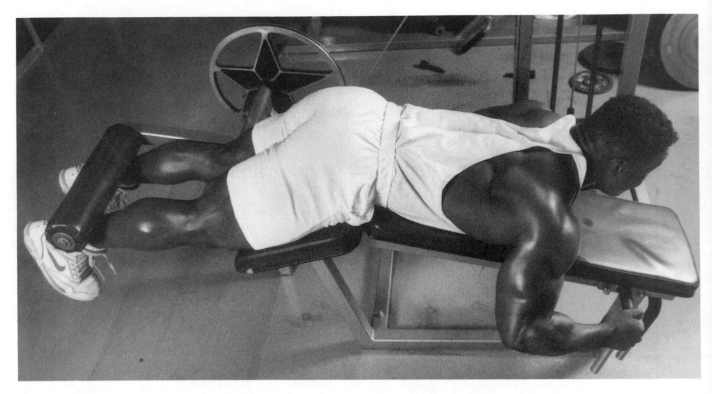

Lying leg curls.

Public. Besides all that, once you have iron fever, you'll pump iron until you die anyway, and damn the expense!

Male Versus Female Strength

God didn't exactly create men and women equally when it came to relative strength levels. Generally speaking, the male sex hormone testosterone helps men out, making them stronger pound for pound than women. But there are many exceptions to this rule—at a Gold's Gym you'll often see a very strong woman who can completely embarass a weaker man of the same body weight, *if* the guy is foolish enough to make an issue of it.

Visualize male and female strength levels as two plastic rulers. Place them lengthwise flat on a table, edge to edge, with the long sides touching. Let's mark the top one "men" and the bottom one "women," and we'll say that the *weak* end is to the left with the *strong* end to the right. Now if you slide the top ruler to the right until about two inches of it still overlaps the lower one, you'll have a visual representation of male versus female strength levels.

Most of the women are at the weak end, and they grow weaker and weaker the closer they approach it. Similarly, most of the men are at the strong end, and they grow stronger and stronger the closer they approach it. But look also at that two-inch overlap of the two rulers. It shows that some of the naturally stronger women are definitely more powerful than a few of the naturally weaker men.

This is why you can occasionally see a woman like multiple Ms. Olympia runner-up Bev Francis (who, incidentally, has won five power-lifting World Championships) bench press 330 and squat 500 for reps at a body weight of 175 pounds, while a larger number of male 175-pounders can't come close to equaling these poundages. Or you can see 150-pound Debby McKnight (an overall NPC U.S.A. Champion and successful IFBB pro bodybuilder) knock out 8-10 reps with 80-pound dumbbells on incline presses when only a few men of the same weight could equal her strength levels.

Obviously, length of training experience has a lot to do with how strong a man or a woman is. So does style of training, since individuals who shoot specifically for increased mass and power—as is advocated in this book—will always be stronger than pump artists who go in for high-set/high-rep workouts with lighter weights. Fundamentally, however, it boils down to the testosterone issue: men are stronger on an average because their bodies produce far more test than women's bodies do.

There are also some inequities from body part to body part if you compare a man and woman of equal weight and strength levels. Generally speaking, women are proportionately much stronger in the legs than upper bodies, while the strength of men tends to be more balanced between the two areas. Again, there are many exceptions to this rule. We've seen Lisa Elliott Kolakowski (winner of the first Gold's Classic Bodybuilding Championships) do sets of 8–10 reps in dumbbell side laterals with 45-pounders at a body weight of only 130. How many 130-pound men could equal this feat, which Lisa did *every* time she trained delts? Certainly not many!

As you can see, the strength of males versus females can be a complex issue. But in general, remember that men will be stronger overall than women of equal body weight. And women tend to have disproportionately strong lower-body muscles.

Female Factors

Since the authors of this book are all men, we turned to eminently qualified Lynne Pirie, a Phoenix, Arizona, sports-medicine physician who won the Heavyweight U.S. Championships and placed as high as third in the Women's Pro World Championships during her competitive career. We sought data on uniquely female factors in bodybuilding. Lynne is quite articulate and well-informed, and we are fortunate that she candidly discussed each factor in layperson's terms that anyone can understand.

"As a physician and former competitive bodybuilder, I have been quite interested in a variety of specifically female factors in bodybuilding and weight training," Dr. Pirie told us. "Among these factors are birth control and competitive bodybuilding, menstruation and amenorrhea, pregnancy and childbirth, menopause, and anorexia nervosa and bulimia."

Birth Control

"Many sexually active women bodybuilders are on birth-control pills," Dr. Pirie noted, "but because of their estrogen and progesterone con-

tent these pills can cause significant water retention. This is particularly true before the menstrual cycle begins, and it can be a problem for many women bodybuilders. A woman doesn't know if the extra weight is body fat or retained water, and it's very hard to peak for a competition under such circumstances.

"Few women understand that progesterone has a protein-catabolic effect. In other words, it breaks down muscle tissue, the exact opposite effect desired by a bodybuilder. The progesterone in oral contraceptives contraindicates the use of birth-control pills by any serious woman bodybuilder.

"There also are other facts that contraindicate the use of birth-control pills, and these are evident in a woman's medical history. One of these is the possibility of blood clotting. If you are dehydrating—and many women bodybuilders use a diuretic to bring out the maximum degree of muscular definition—you are going to increase thromboembolytic potential, that is, you will increase your body's potential to form blood clots.

"Blood clots are most likely to be very small, but they can occasionally be large as well. Small clots can damage various organs, such as the spleen, liver, kidneys, or any organ through which blood flows. Larger clots can cause strokes by blocking blood flow to part of the brain.

"If a woman is taking birth-control pills and using anabolic steroids to increase muscle mass, she can do herself great damage. I don't know of any actual research that has been aimed specifically at this problem, but I can tell you that such a practice throws the whole endocrine system out of balance. It changes your entire hormonal environment. If you have a dormant tumor in your body and it responds to the new environment, it could grow with disastrous consequences. Steroids can also destroy your entire neural-hormonal axis, which can affect every organ system in your body. In short, it's much worse to take steroids under any circumstances.

"What birth-control method should a sexually active woman bodybuilder use? The use of an IUD was once considered quite safe, but with an IUD there is always a danger of perforation of the uterus or of the body's outright rejection of the device. An IUD is made of metal and is foreign to the human body, so if the uterus doesn't want one, it'll try to reject it.

"Sometimes IUDs have actually gone through the wall of the uterus, and if the perforation is serious enough, it can force a hysterectomy. If a woman has never had children, that's a very high price to pay.

"I personally recommend the use of a diaphragm. It's a minor inconvenience at times, but it only takes a couple of minutes to insert one. Correctly used, a diaphragm is an effective birth-control device."

Menstruation and Amenorrhea

"There appears to be an optimum level of exercise that assists menstruation and relieves menstrual complications but still does not interfere with menstrual function," Dr. Pirie continues. "The menstrual cramps younger women often experience can definitely be eased by exercise, but excessive exercise can affect menstrual function.

"There are certain anti-inflammatory products, such as wine and tryptophan, that can relieve menstrual cramping to a small degree. Overall, however, exercise does a better job of relieving cramps.

"Bodybuilding, track, gymnastics, and other sports that require a low body weight and involve a high degree of stress can cause amenorrhea, or a cessation of menses. This is probably due to a very quick weight loss and/or general stress.

"Delayed menses are relatively common among girls who are serious bodybuilders, dancers, gymnasts, or runners or who participate in other strenuous sports and must maintain a low degree of body fat. There appears to be a height-weight ratio that must be achieved before such a young woman will menstruate.

"There is considerable speculation on whether or not an amenorrheic woman ovulates, but there is no scientific evidence to support either stand. Therefore, it would be foolish to assume that amenorrhea is an effective birth-control system. Without relying on other forms of birth control, you could become pregnant.

"All of the investigations I have done on amenorrhea indicate that the condition is not dangerous. The menses simply seem to resume as soon as a woman's body weight goes back up to a 'normal' level.

"Unfortunately, many gynecologists are not experienced in treating amenorrhea, and they immediately prescribe hormonal therapy to induce menses. Such a procedure is both expensive and unnecessary. To resume your menses, simply gain body weight and perhaps reduce your physical activity level."

Pregnancy and Childbirth

"If a woman bodybuilder has been training regularly prior to becoming pregnant, she can profitably continue to work out," Dr. Pirie reports. "It's not a good idea, however, for an out-of-shape woman to commence hard training once she discovers she's pregnant. A pregnant woman shouldn't be doing anything physically that she's not used to. And it's important to avoid overtraining, which can cause anoxia—a deficiency of oxygen—to the fetus.

"Many women athletes have continued to train fairly vigorously up to and through the seventh and eighth months of their pregnancies. The better a woman's musculature, the better control she can have over her own delivery. This also takes into consideration such athletic-related abilities as self-control, self-discipline, and the ability to control pain. A woman who is in very good physical condition can push down harder and deliver more quickly. There's a lot of pain associated with childbirth, and a woman who is used to training in pain can handle it better.

"Nutritionally, a woman bodybuilder should make the same changes in her diet that any other pregnant woman should make, including an increased uptake of folic acid and other vitamins. A pregnant woman bodybuilder should not be dieting—or training—for a contest. This should be obvious, but it must be said nonetheless, considering the competitive nature of most bodybuilders.

"After giving birth, all women are concerned with regaining their prepregnancy appearance and physical condition. Any woman who remained in excellent physical condition during her pregnancy will have a full and rapid recovery following childbirth. As a footnote, numerous champion women bodybuilders have had children and yet regained such superb condition that they have been consistent winners in bodybuilding competition."

Bev Francis, Pro World Champion in both power lifting and
bodybuilding, gives it to a set of stiff-armed pulldowns.

Bev again, in bottom position of medium-grip front lat machine pulldowns.

Menopause

Dr. Pirie reveals, "There has been little research on the relationship between exercise and menopause, and none on the relationship between bodybuilding and menopause. I can only give you an informed opinion on it.

"Menopause is a time of general deterioration of the body as a consequence of the natural aging process. The effects of bodybuilding are in the reverse direction, that is, bodybuilding promotes tissue growth rather than atrophy. Thus, regular bodybuilding and weight training will probably help minimize the negative effects of menopause."

Anorexia Nervosa and Bulimia

"Anorexia nervosa, a mental/physical disorder that affects primarily women—and more women from the upper middle class than from any other socioeconomic group—has gained considerable publicity in recent years," Dr. Pirie states. "It is characterized by prolonged fasting or subsistence on a bare minimum of calories, as well as by frequent endurance-type exercise, all aimed at making an anorexic 'fashionably thin.' As the disorder becomes progressively more serious, it can be life threatening.

"Anorexia nervosa is often difficult for a family member to identify, because anorexics become very devious about disguising their symptoms. They will even begin to pad their clothing to hide the fact that they are losing weight.

"While I personally know of no anorexic women bodybuilders, the requirements of the sport—strict dieting and copious exercise—can lead to anorexia nervosa. If a woman becomes anorexic, it's not something that should be handled by a friend in the gym or even by the family general practitioner. In my opinion, anorexia nervosa is a psychiatric emergency that should be treated only by a psychiatrist specifically experienced in handling the disorder. An anorexic should also be hospitalized in many cases.

"Bulimia is a related disease that also should be treated psychiatrically. Bulimics will gorge themselves with food and then purge themselves with a finger down the throat. As with anorexia nervosa, this is a potentially serious disorder that could occur to women in competitive bodybuilding, as well as in a variety of other sports."

Vicki Sims—one-arm dumbbell bent-over rows—finish.

Glossary

Abdominals: The muscles of the midsection: *rectus abdominis*, *obliques* (external, internal, and transverse), and *intercostals*. The abdominals help flex the torso forward and from side to side, twist the torso in relation to the hips, depress the rib cage, and stabilize the midsection during squats, deadlifts, and overhead lifts.

Abduction: Movement of the straight legs, accomplished by contraction of muscles at the sides of the hips, from a position in which they are pressed together to one in which they are as far apart as possible.

Adduction: Movement of the straight legs, accomplished by contraction of the leg adductor muscles (the *sartorius*, primarily), from a fully abducted position back to one in which the legs are again pressed together.

Advanced Trainee: A man or woman with at least one year of steady, systematic resistance training under his or her belt.

Aerobic Exercise: Prolonged, moderate-intensity work that uses up oxygen at or below the level at which your cardiorespiratory system can replenish oxygen in the working muscles. *Aerobic* literally means *with oxygen*, and it is the only type of exercise that burns body fat to meet its energy needs. Bodybuilders engage in aerobic workouts to develop additional heart/lung fitness, as well as to burn off excess body fat to achieve peak contest muscularity. Common aerobic activities include running, cycling, stair climbing, swimming, dancing, and walking. Depending on how vigorously you play them, most racket sports can also be aerobic exercise.

AMDR: An abbreviation for the Adult Minimum Daily Requirement of certain nutrients as established by the United States Food and Drug Administration (FDA).

Anabolic Drugs: Also called *anabolic steroids*, these are artificial male hormones that aid in nitrogen retention and thereby add to a male bodybuilder's muscle mass and strength. Some women also use anabolic drugs to improve mass and strength. These drugs are not without hazardous side effects, however, and possession of anabolics is a felony in most states. Steroids are available in some gyms via the black market, but it is very dangerous to use such unknown and probably forged substances to increase muscle mass.

Anaerobic Exercise: Exercise of much higher intensity than aerobic work, which uses up oxygen more quickly than the body can replenish it in the working muscles. Anaerobic exercise eventually builds up a significant oxygen debt that forces an athlete to terminate the exercise session rather quickly. Anaerobic exercise (the kind of exercise to which bodybuilding training belongs) burns up glycogen (muscle sugar) to supply its energy needs. Fast sprinting is a typical anaerobic form of exercise.

Androgenic Drugs: Androgenics are drugs that simulate the effects of the male hormone testosterone in the human body. Androgens do build a degree of strength and muscle mass, but they also stimulate secondary sex characteristics such as increased body hair, a deepened voice, and high levels of aggression. Indeed, many bodybuilders and power lifters take androgens to stimulate aggressiveness in the gym, resulting in more productive strength workouts.

Antagonistic Muscle: One with the polar-opposite function of a primary muscle. As examples, the leg biceps are antagonistic to the quadriceps, the triceps antagonistic to the biceps, and forearm flexors antagonistic to the forearm extensors. Antagonistic muscle groups are frequently supersetted in a high-intensity workout.

ATP: Adenosine triphosphate, a substance that breaks down into ADP (adenosine diphosphate) within a working muscle, thereby yielding one phosphate radical to provide energy for muscle contraction.

Balance: A term referring to an even relationship of body proportions in a man's or woman's physique. Perfectly balanced physical proportions are a much-sought-after trait among competitive bodybuilders.

Bar: The steel shaft that forms the basic part of a barbell or dumbbell. These bars are normally about one inch thick, and they are often encased in a revolving metal sleeve.

Barbell: Normally measuring between four and six feet in length, a barbell is the most basic piece of equipment used in weight training and bodybuilding. Indeed, you can train every major skeletal muscle group in your body using only a barbell. There are two major types of exercise barbells in common use: adjustable sets (in which you can easily add or subtract plates by removing a detachable outside collar held in place on each side by a set screw) and fixed

barbells (in which the plates are either welded or bolted permanently in place). Fixed weights are arranged in a variety of poundages on long racks in commercial bodybuilding gyms, the weight for each one painted or etched on the barbell plates. Fixed weights relieve you of the problem of changing weights on your barbell for each new exercise. While fixed barbells and dumbbells are normally found in large commercial gyms, adjustable sets are more frequently used in home gyms.

Basic Exercise: A bodybuilding exercise which stresses the largest muscle groups of your body (e.g., the thighs, back, and/or chest), often in combination with smaller muscles. You will be able to use comparatively heavier weights in basic exercises in order to build great muscle mass and physical power. Typical basic movements include squats, bench presses, and barbell bent-over rows. (See *Isolation Exercise.*)

Beginning Trainee: A man or woman with less than six months of bodybuilding experience.

Benches: A wide variety of exercise benches are available for use in doing barbell and dumbbell exercises either lying or seated. The most common type of bench, a flat exercise bench, can be used for chest, shoulder, and arm movements. Incline and decline benches (which are set at angles between 30–45 degrees) also allow movements for the chest, shoulders, and arms. Adjustable benches are available for home-gym use. They can be adjusted to flat, decline, and incline angles.

Biomechanics: The scientific study of body positions, or form, in sport. In bodybuilding, biomechanics studies body form when exercising with weights. When you have good biomechanics in a bodybuilding exercise, you will be safely placing maximum beneficial stress on your working muscles.

Blood Pressure: The pressure exerted against the inner blood-vessel walls during heart contractions (called *systolic* blood pressure) and heart relaxation (called *diastolic* blood pressure). Normal blood pressure is 120/80 in the systolic/diastolic ratio.

BMR: Your basal metabolic rate, or the speed at which your resting body burns calories to provide for its basic survival needs. You can elevate your BMR and more easily achieve lean

Flex Wheeler—parallel-bar dips, weighted—midpoint.

body mass through consistent exercise, and particularly through aerobic workouts.

Bodybuilding: A type of weight training applied in conjunction with sound nutritional practices to alter the shape or form of one's body. In the context of this book, bodybuilding is a competitive sport nationally and internationally in both amateur and professional categories for men, women, and mixed pairs. However, a majority of individuals use bodybuilding methods merely to lose excess body fat or to build up a too-thin part of the body.

Body-Fat Percentage: The total percentage of fat weight in a bodybuilder's physique. Male bodybuilders frequently compete with body-fat percentages under 5 percent, women with percentages under 8 percent.

Burn: A beneficial burning sensation in a muscle you are training. This burn is caused by a rapid buildup of fatigue toxins in the muscle and is a good indication that you are optimally working a muscle group. The best bodybuilders consistently forge past the pain barrier erected by muscle burn and consequently build very massive, highly defined muscles.

Burns: A training technique used to push a set past the normal failure point and thereby to stimulate a muscle to greater hypertrophy. Burns consist of short, quick, bouncy reps 4–6 inches in range of motion. Most bodybuilders do 8–12 burns at the end of a set that has already been taken to failure. They generate terrific burn in the muscles, hence the name of this technique.

CAFBB: Canadian Amateur Federation of Bodybuilders. The CAFBB is the sports federation responsible in Canada for administering amateur bodybuilding for men, women, and mixed pairs. The CAFBB is one of more than 120 national bodybuilding federations affiliated internationally with the IFBB.

Calorie: The amount of energy necessary to raise one liter of water one degree Celsius. A bodybuilder's maintenance level of calories can be calculated relatively easily, then either a caloric deficit (to lose body fat) or caloric surplus (to gain weight) can be initiated. Tables of caloric content of most foods are widely available.

Canthaxin: A food-coloring dye approved by the FDA and sold in capsule form to change the color of a bodybuilder's skin to something between yellow and true tan.

Cardiorespiratory Fitness: Physical fitness of the heart, circulatory system, and lungs indicative of good aerobic fitness.

Cheating: A method of pushing a muscle to keep it working far past the point at which it would normally fail to continue contracting due to excessive fatigue buildup. In cheating you will use a self-administered body swing, jerk, or otherwise poor form once you have reached the failure point to take some of the pressure off the muscles and allow them to continue a set for two or three reps past failure.

Chinning Bar: A horizontal bar attached high on the wall or gym ceiling on which you can do chins, hanging leg raises, and other movements for your upper body. A chinning bar is analogous to the high bar male gymnasts use in competitions.

Cholesterol: A type of fat manufactured within the body but more often ingested from fatty animal-source foods like beef, pork, eggs, and milk products. Over the long term cholesterol can clog arteries and other blood vessels, leading to stroke or heart attack.

Circuit Training: A special form of bodybuilding through which you can simultaneously increase aerobic conditioning, muscle mass, and strength. In circuit training you will plan a series of 10–20 exercises in a circuit around the gym. The exercises chosen should stress all parts of the body. These movements are performed with an absolute minimum of rest between exercises. At the end of a circuit a rest interval of 2–5 minutes is taken before going through the circuit again. Three to five circuits would constitute a circuit-training program.

Clean: The movement of raising a barbell or two dumbbells from the floor to your shoulders in one smooth motion to prepare for an overhead lift. To properly execute a clean movement you must use the coordinated strength of your legs, back, shoulders, and arms.

Collar: The clamp used to hold plates securely in place on a barbell or dumbbell bar. The cylindrical metal clamps are held in place on the bar by means of a set screw threaded through the collar and tightened securely against the bar.

Renel Janvier.

More frequently called *Mixed Pairs Competition*, this event is rapidly gaining international popularity with the bodybuilding community and general public and is held in both amateur and professional world championships.

Cut Up (*or* Cut): A term used to denote a bodybuilder who has an extremely high degree of muscular definition due to a low degree of body fat.

Definition: The absence of fat over clearly delineated muscle masses. Definition is often referred to as *muscularity*, and a highly defined bodybuilder has so little body fat that very fine grooves of muscularity called *striations* will be clearly visible over each major muscle group.

Density: Muscle hardness, which is also related to muscular definition. A bodybuilder can be well-defined and still have excess fat within each major muscle complex. But when he has muscle density, even this intramuscular fat has been eliminated. A combination of muscle mass and muscle density is highly prized among all competitive bodybuilders.

Dipping Bars: Parallel bars set high enough above the floor to allow you to do dips between them, leg raises for your abdominals, and a variety of other exercises. Some gyms have dipping bars that are angled inward at one end; these can be used when changing your grip width on dips.

Diuretics: Sometimes called *water pills*, these are drugs and herbal preparations that remove excess water from a bodybuilder's system just prior to a show, thereby revealing greater muscular detail. Harsh chemical diuretics can be quite harmful to your health, particularly if they are used on a chronic basis. Two of the side effects of excessive chemical diuretic use are muscle cramps and heart arrhythmia (irregular heartbeat).

Double-Split-System Training: Doing two weight workouts per day. Double-split training is a further refinement of the split-system routine, which results in even shorter and higher intensity workouts. The double-split is used only by the most advanced competitors. A handful even use a triple-split, doing three workouts each day for a short period of time prior to a competition.

Dumbbell: For all intents and purposes, a dumbbell is a short-handled barbell (usually

Inside collars keep the plates from sliding inward and injuring your hands, while outside collars keep plates from sliding off the barbell in the middle of an exercise.

Couples' Competition: A relatively new form of bodybuilding competition in which man-woman teams compete against others with particularly appealing posing routines featuring adagio and other dance movements and lifts.

10–12 inches in length) intended primarily for use with one in each hand. Dumbbells are especially valuable when training the arms and shoulders but can be used to build up almost any muscles.

Endurance: Stamina, or the ability to continue voluntary muscle contractions for a sustained period of time.

Ergogenesis: From the Latin *ergo* ("to work") and *genesis* ("a beginning"). Ergogenesis is the use of work-producing aids—mainly nutritional in nature, but also new techniques or mechanical aids—that help produce higher-intensity work and/or improve the appearance of the physique.

Estrogen: The primary female sex hormone.

Exercise: Each individual movement (e.g., a seated pulley row, barbell curl, or seated calf raise) that you perform in your bodybuilding workouts.

EZ-Curl Bar: A special type of barbell used in many arm exercises, but particularly for standing EZ-bar curls wherein it removes from your wrists strain that might be present when doing the movement with a straight bar. An EZ-curl bar is also occasionally called a *cambered curling bar*. Albert Beckles, one of the sport's most successful professionals, whimsically calls this piece of equipment a *wiggly bar* because of its shape.

Failure: That point in an exercise at which you have so fully fatigued the working muscles that they can no longer complete an additional repetition of a movement with strict biomechanics. You should always take your postwarm-up sets at least to the point of momentary muscular failure, and frequently past that point.

Fast-Twitch Muscle Fibers: White muscle fibers which contract quickly and powerfully, but not with great endurance. Fast-twitch fibers are developed by heavy, low-rep, explosive weight training.

FDA: United States Food and Drug Administration.

Flexibility: A suppleness of joints, muscle masses, and connective tissues which lets you move your limbs over an exaggerated range of motion. A valuable quality in bodybuilding training, it promotes optimum physical development. Flexibility can only be attained through systematic stretching training, which should

form a cornerstone of your overall bodybuilding philosophy.

Forced Reps: A frequently used method of extending a set past the point of failure to induce greater gains in muscle mass and quality. A training partner pulls upward on the bar just enough for you to grind out two or three reps past the failure threshold.

Form: Simply another word to indicate the biomechanics used during the performance of any bodybuilding or weight-training movement. Perfect form involves moving only the muscles specified in an exercise description, while moving the weight over the fullest possible range of motion.

Free Weights: Barbells, dumbbells, and related equipment. Serious bodybuilders use a combination of free weights and such exercise machines as those manufactured by Nautilus and Universal Gyms, but they primarily use free weights in their workouts.

Giant Sets: Series of 4–6 exercises done with little or no rest between movements and a rest interval of 2–3 minutes between giant sets. You can perform giant sets for either two antagonistic muscle groups or a single body part.

Glycogen: Blood sugar stored in the muscles, liver, and—to a lesser extent—the bloodstream. Glycogen helps fuel muscle contractions.

Holistic Workouts: Sessions in which a broad spectrum of weight-rep combinations, ranging from heavy/low-rep work to light/high-rep training, is followed.

Hyperplasia: The theoretical ability of a single muscle fiber to split into two fibers.

Hypertrophy: The scientific term denoting an increase in muscle mass and an improvement in relative muscular strength. Hypertrophy is induced by placing an "overload" on the working muscles with various training techniques during a bodybuilding workout.

IFBB: The International Federation of Bodybuilders, the gigantic sports federation founded in 1946 by Joe and Ben Weider. With more than 130 member nations, the IFBB proves that bodybuilding is one of the most popular of all sports on the international level. Through its member national federations, the IFBB oversees competitions in each nation. It directly administers amateur and professional competitions for men, women, and mixed pairs internationally.

Instinctive Training: Using subtle biofeedback signals to guide your choice of training routines and dietary regimens. Instinctive training ability can take months or years to master; once learned, it saves time that would be wasted going down blind alleys.

Intensity: The relative degree of effort you put into each set of every exercise in a bodybuilding workout. The more intensity you place on a working muscle, the more quickly it will increase in hypertrophy. The most basic methods of increasing intensity are to use heavier weights in good form on each exercise, do more reps with a set weight, or perform a consistent number of sets and reps with a particular weight in a movement, but progressively reducing the length of rest intervals between sets.

Intermediate Trainee: One with 6–12 months of training.

Isolation Exercise: In contrast to a basic exercise, an isolation movement stresses a single muscle group (or sometimes just part of a single muscle) in relative isolation from the remainder of the body. Isolation exercises are good for shaping and defining various muscle groups. For your thighs, squats would be a typical basic movement, while leg extensions would be the equivalent isolation exercise.

Judging Rounds: In the universally accepted and applied IFBB system of judging, bodybuilders are evaluated in three distinctly different rounds of judging, plus a final posedown round for only the top five competitors after the first three rounds have been adjudicated. In Round One, groups of competitors are viewed semirelaxed from the front, both sides, and back; in Round Two they are viewed in groups and individually in seven well-defined compulsory poses (for women there are five compulsories); and in Round Three they perform their own uniquely personal free-posing routines to their own choice of music. Overall, this use of three rounds of judging and a posedown round results in a very fair choice of the final winners of a bodybuilding championship.

Juice: A slang term for anabolic steroids, e.g., being "on the juice."

Layoff: Most intelligent bodybuilders take a one- or two-week layoff from bodybuilding training from time to time, during which they totally avoid the gym. A layoff after a period of intense precompetition training is particularly beneficial as a means of allowing the body to completely rest, recuperate, and heal any minor training injuries that might have cropped up during the peaking cycle.

Lean Body Mass: That part of the body including the muscles, bones, and connective tissue which remains when all body fat has been eliminated from a physique.

Lifting Belt: A leather belt 4–6 inches wide at the back that is fastened tightly around your waist when you do squats, heavy back work, and overhead pressing movements. A lifting belt enhances stability in your midsection, preventing lower-back and abdominal injuries. Recently, some manufacturers have been constructing serviceable belts from nylon fabric with Velcro fasteners.

Mass: The relative size of each muscle group, or of the entire physique. As long as you also have a high degree of muscularity and good balance of physical proportions, muscle mass is a highly prized quality among competitive bodybuilders.

Mixed Pairs Competition: *See* Couples' Competition.

Muscle Contraction: Any one of five types of movement caused by muscular work. *Isometric* contraction is intense muscle work done in a stationary position. *Concentric* contraction is a shortening of the muscle against resistance, as opposed to *eccentric* contraction, in which a muscle lengthens while resisting against downward pressure of a weight. *Isotonic* contraction is muscle movement against a consistent degree of resistance, while *isokinetic* contraction is muscle movement at a set rate of speed.

Muscularity: An alternative term for *definition* or *cuts.*

Myofibril: An individual muscle fiber formed by muscle cells being attached end to end.

Nautilus: A brand of exercise machine in common use in large gyms.

Negatives: The downward half of a repetition, referred to scientifically as *eccentric contraction.* By placing resistance on the negative half of a movement, you can induce a high degree of muscle hypertrophy.

NPC: The National Physique Committee, Inc., which administers men's and women's amateur bodybuilding competitions in the United States. The NPC National Champions in each weight class are annually sent abroad to compete in the IFBB World Championships.

Nutrition: The applied science of eating to foster greater health, fitness, and muscular gains. Through correct application of nutritional practices you can selectively add muscle mass to your physique or totally strip away all body fat, revealing the hard-earned muscles lying beneath your skin.

Nutritionalysis: A registered trademark for a computer-assisted program tailoring specific nutritional programs to uniquely individual bodybuilders. Nutritionalysis was originated by competitive bodybuilder Neal Spruce and is widely available at Gold's Gyms worldwide.

Olympian: A term reserved for use when referring only to a bodybuilder who has competed in the Mr. Olympia or Ms. Olympia competitions.

Olympic Barbell: A special type of barbell used in weight-lifting and power-lifting competitions, but also used by bodybuilders in heavy basic exercises such as squats, bench presses, barbell bent-over rows, standing barbell curls, standing barbell presses, and deadlifts. An Olympic barbell sans collars weighs 45 pounds (20 kilograms, or 44 pounds, internationally); each collar weighs five pounds (2½ kilograms, or 5½ pounds, internationally).

Olympic Lifting: The type of weight lifting contested at the Olympic Games every four years, as well as at national and international competitions each year. Two lifts (the snatch and the clean-and-jerk) are contested in a wide variety of weight classes.

Overload: The amount of weight that you force a muscle to use that is over and above its normal strength ability. Applying an overload to a muscle forces it to increase in hypertrophy.

Overtraining: Chronically exceeding the body's recovery ability by doing too lengthy and/or too frequent workouts. Chronic overtraining can lead to injuries, infectious illness,

Bev Francis in finish position of close-grip front lat machine pulldowns.

and worse: a cessation or even regression in gains of muscle mass, tone, and strength.

Peak: The absolute zenith of competitive condition achieved by a bodybuilder. To peak out optimally for a bodybuilding show, you must intelligently combine bodybuilding training, aerobic workouts, diet, mental conditioning, tanning, and a large number of other preparatory factors.

PHA: The abbreviation for *peripheral heart action*, a system of circuit training in which short 4–6 exercise circuits are performed in order to stimulate cardiorespiratory conditioning and further physical development.

Plates: The flat discs placed on the ends of barbell and dumbbell bars to increase the weight of the apparatus. Although some plates are made from vinyl-covered concrete, the best and most durable plates are manufactured from metal.

Pose: Each individual stance that a bodybuilder does onstage in order to highlight his or her muscular development.

Posedown: A fourth round of judging conducted at the evening show in which the top five or six competitors are compared in their own choices of poses for a few final, vital placing points.

Posing Routine: The well-choreographed series of individual poses a bodybuilder presents to his or her choice of music in the public presentation (Round Three) of the NPC/IFBB judging system. In this posing routine the competitor can choose individual poses, as opposed to the required poses done in the mandatory round at the prejudging, and thereby camouflaging weak points and emphasizing particularly well-developed areas.

Poundage: The amount of weight that you use in an exercise, whether that weight is on a barbell, dumbbell, or exercise machine.

Power: In bodybuilding and power lifting, this is strength, or the ability to use very heavy poundages on all basic movements. In a sports context, power is the ability to move heavy weights explosively.

Power Lifting: A second form of competitive weight lifting (not contested at the Olympics, however) featuring three lifts: the squat, the bench press, and the deadlift. Power lifting is contested both nationally and internationally in a wide variety of weight classes for both men and women.

Preexhaustion: A technique used primarily on torso-muscle groups (chest, back, shoulders) which makes the weaker arm muscles temporarily stronger than normal, so basic exercises like bench presses, lat machine pulldowns, and standing barbell presses can be pushed far past the point at which a bodybuilder would normally fail to continue a set. Preex involves supersetting an isolation exercise for a particular torso muscle (e.g., flat-bench flyes for pecs) with a basic movement (e.g., bench presses) for the same muscle.

Prejudging: Judging of the first two rounds of the IFBB judging system during a morning or afternoon session separate from the evening public presentation at which Round Three is judged.

Progression: The act of gradually adding to the amount of resistance that you use in each exercise. Without consistent progression in your workouts, you won't overload your muscles sufficiently to promote optimum increases in hypertrophy.

Pump: The tight, blood-congested feeling in a muscle after it has been intensely trained. Muscle pump is caused by a rapid influx of blood into the muscles to remove fatigue toxins and replace supplies of fuel and oxygen. A good muscle pump indicates that you have optimally worked a muscle group.

Pump Set: A high-rep set (usually in the range of 15–20 repetitions) of a basic exercise which is done after a peak weight has been handled in that movement. Usually a pump set is the last one done on a particular basic movement. A pump set is also sometimes called a *down set*.

Pyramiding: A strength- and mass-building system in which the weight is increased 10–15 percent and the reps are successively decreased each set on a basic exercise until a peak weight is reached. In a full pyramid the weights are then progressively dropped and reps increased in a mirror of the first half of the pyramid. Normally bodybuilders and those interested in strength development do only a half pyramid, plus perhaps a high-rep pump set after the peak weight has been reached.

Quality Training: A type of workout used just prior to a competition in which the lengths of rest intervals between sets are progressively reduced to increase overall training intensity and to help further define the physique.

Recovery Cycle: The process between workouts during which the body flushes out fatigue toxins, restores muscle glycogen, repairs itself, and increases in hypertrophy. The length of this cycle varies from as few as 2 days to as many as 7–9 to complete. Recovery is enhanced by sufficient sleep and rest and attention to proper bodybuilding nutrition.

Repetition (or Rep): Each individual count of an exercise that is performed. Series of repetitions called *sets* are performed on each exercise in your training program.

Resistance: The actual amount of weight you are using in any exercise.

Rest Interval: The brief pause lasting 30–90 seconds between sets that allows your body to partially recuperate prior to initiating the succeeding set.

Ripped: The same as *cut up*.

Routine: Also called a *training schedule* or *program*, a routine is the total list of exercises, sets, reps, and sometimes weights used in one training session. Often a routine is either presented in written form for someone to follow or is written down in a training diary as it is completed.

Set: A grouping of repetitions (usually in the range of 6–15) followed by a rest interval and usually another set. Three to five sets of each exercise are usually performed before moving on to another movement.

Sleeve: The hollow metal tube that fits over the bar on most exercise barbell and dumbbell sets. This sleeve makes it easier for the bar to rotate in your hands as you perform an exercise.

Slow-Twitch Muscle Fibers: Red muscle fibers that contract slowly, weakly, and continually for long periods of time. Slow-twitch fibers are developed by light, high-rep weight workouts.

Split Routine: A program in which the body is divided into segments and trained more than three times per week, as most beginners do. The most basic split routine is done four days per week (e.g., Monday/Thursday for half of the body and Tuesday/Friday for the other half). Progressively more intense split routines are performed five days per week, six days per week in which the body is divided into three sections (each worked twice a week), and six days per week in which each half of the body is trained three times in the week. The most popular type of split routine at the present time involves dividing the body into three parts which are done

over three consecutive days, followed by a rest day and a repeat of the routine on day five. This is called a three-on/one-off split.

Spotters: Training partners who stand by to act as safety helpers when you perform such heavy exercises as squats, bench presses, and incline presses. If you get stuck under the weight or begin to lose control of it, spotters can rescue you and prevent needless injuries. Spotters can also assist you in performing forced reps if your program calls for them.

Steroids: Prescription drugs that mimic male hormones, but without most of the androgenic side effects of actual testosterone. Many bodybuilders use these dangerous drugs to help increase muscle mass and strength, even though possession of them is now a felony in most states.

Sticking Point: A stalling of bodybuilding progress. Also that point in a movement at which you fail to continue the upward momentum of the bar.

Straps: Heavy fabric webbing used to reinforce a bodybuilder's grip on the bar. Usually these straps have a loop at one end which is passed around the wrist and a loose end which is wrapped around the bar and then grasped in the hand. As long as you maintain your grip on the strap/bar, your grip will be very secure regardless of the weight being used.

Stretching: A type of exercise program in which you assume exaggerated postures that stretch muscles, joints, and connective tissues, hold these positions for several seconds, and then relax and repeat the postures. Regular stretching exercise promotes body flexibility and reduces the chance of injuries while training with heavy iron.

Stretch Marks: Tiny tears in a bodybuilder's skin caused by poor diet and too rapid increases in body weight. If you notice stretch marks forming on your own body (usually around your pectoral-deltoid tie-ins), rub vitamin-E cream over them two or three times per day, and try cutting back on your body weight by reducing body-fat levels. It's much better to add pure muscle mass than excess fat when attempting to gain body weight.

Striations: The tiny grooves of muscle across major muscle groups in a highly defined bodybuilder. If you have muscle striations even when

Ron Love reaps the rewards of victory!

completely relaxed, you know you're in optimum competitive condition.

Stripping Method: A term coined by Arnold Schwarzenegger to denote descending sets, a technique in which weight is progressively reduced during an extended set. This is also sometimes called *going down the rack*, particularly when dumbbells are being used. In a usual descending set, you start with a heavy weight for about 6–8 reps to failure, immediately use a somewhat lighter poundage for 5–6 more repetitions, and finally use an even lighter weight for a last, excruciatingly difficult 4–5 reps.

Supersets: Series of two exercises performed with no rest between movements and a normal rest interval between supersets. Supersets increase training intensity by reducing the average length of rest interval between sets.

Supplements: Concentrated vitamins, minerals, and proteins used by bodybuilders to improve the overall quality of their diets. Many bodybuilders believe that food supplements help promote quality muscle growth.

Symmetry: The shape or general outline of a person's body, as when seen in silhouette. If you have good symmetry, you will have relatively wide shoulders, flaring lats, a small waist-hip structure, and generally small joints.

Testosterone: The male hormone primarily responsible for the maintenance of muscle mass and strength induced by heavy training. Testosterone is secondarily responsible for developing such secondary male sex characteristics as a deep voice, body and facial hair, and male pattern baldness.

Trisets: A series of three exercises performed with no rest between movements and a normal rest interval between trisets. Trisets increase training intensity by reducing the average length of rest interval between sets. As such, trisets are markedly more intense than supersets.

Vascularity: A prominence of veins and arteries over the muscles and beneath the skin of a well-defined bodybuilder. Vascularity can be enhanced by properly carbing up prior to appearance onstage at a competition.

Volume Training: The use of very high numbers of sets for each body part. The high volume of a workout necessitates the use of lighter-than-normal weights in each exercise, but it does build muscle in some individuals.

Warm-Up: 10- to 15-minute session of light calisthenics, aerobic activity, and stretching taken prior to handling heavy bodybuilding training movements. A good warm-up helps prevent injuries and actually allows you to get more out of your training than if you went into a workout totally cold.

WBF: The World Bodybuilding Federation, founded in 1990 to offer competition for bodybuilders not interested in the IFBB system.

Weight: The same as *poundage* or *resistance*.

Weight Class: In order for bodybuilders to compete against men or women of similar size, the IFBB has instituted weight divisions for all amateur competitions. The normal men's weight classes are under 70 kilograms (154 pounds), under 80 kilos (175 pounds), under 90 kilos (198 pounds), and over 90 kilograms. In a minority of competitions, particularly in the Far East, one additional class, under 65 kilos (143 pounds), is also contested. Women compete in three weight classes: under 114 pounds, under 123 pounds, and over 123.

Weight Lifting: The competitive form of weight training in which each athlete attempts to lift as much as he or she can in well-defined exercises. Olympic lifting and power lifting are the two types of weight-lifting competition.

Weight Training: An umbrella term used to categorize all acts of using resistance training. Weight training can be used to improve the body, to rehabilitate injuries, to improve sports conditioning, or as a competitive activity in terms of bodybuilding and weight lifting.

Workout: A bodybuilding or weight-training session.

Wraps: Neoprene rubber or elasticized fabric used to wrap an injured or weakened joint, such as a knee, elbow, or wrist. Rubber wraps usually are tubular and are slipped over the joint, where they keep heat in the area and provide a bit of support. Fabric wraps are normally long bandages wrapped in spirals over the injured/weakened joint, where they hold in little heat but provide maximum support. The combination of rubber and fabric wraps is sometimes used in situations a bit more extreme than those requiring either one or the other type of wrap.

Index